The Jossey-Bass Nonprofit and Public Management Series also includes:

Evaluation

An Integrated Framework for Understanding, Guiding, and Improving Policies and Programs

Melvin M. Mark
Gary T. Henry
George Julnes

JOSSEY-BASS
A Wiley Company
San Francisco

Jossey-Bass books and products are available through most bookstores. To contact Jossey-Bass directly, call (888) 378-2537, fax to (800) 605-2665, or visit our website at www.josseybass.com.

Substantial discounts on bulk quantities of Jossey-Bass books are available to corporations, professional associations, and other organizations. For details and discount information, contact the special sales department at Jossey-Bass.

 Manufactured in the United States of America on Lyons Falls Turin Book. This paper is acid-free and 100 percent totally chlorine-free.

Library of Congress Cataloging-in-Publication Data

Mark, Melvin M.
    Evaluation : an integrated framework for understanding, guiding, and improving policies and programs / Melvin M. Mark, Gary T. Henry, George Julnes. — 1st ed.
        p. cm. — (The Jossey-Bass nonprofit and public management series)
      Includes bibliographical references and index.
      ISBN 0-7879-4802-0 (acid-free paper)
    1. Policy sciences. 2. Evaluation research (Social action programs)
3. Social policy—Evaluation. I. Henry, Gary T. II. Julnes, George,
date. III. Title. IV. Series.
      H97 .M373 2000
      361.6'1'0684—dc21
                                                                  00-010232

FIRST EDITION
HB Printing   10 9 8 7 6 5 4 3 2

Contents

Preface

The evaluation of social policies and programs has become commonplace in most modern democracies. Public officials and the public too learn about policies and programs—how they are implemented, what their intended and unintended effects are, and for whom and under what circumstances they work best—largely from evaluations. Evaluation is also a growth enterprise in the private sector. Virtually every day, evaluators add to the list of books, reports, journal articles, Web pages, briefings, and newspaper articles that describe how well social policies and programs work.

This book presents a theory of evaluation as assisted sensemaking. This approach holds that the primary role of evaluation is to enhance and supplement the natural sensemaking efforts of democratic actors as they seek social betterment. In other words, evaluation consists of a set of activities developed to help correct, support, and extend the way that people, individually and collectively, naturally make sense of policies and programs implemented to meet human needs. Evaluation aids sensemaking by providing systematic information about such things as the outcomes or valued effects of a social program, the causes of program success or failure, and the degree to which policy directives are being followed.

In this book, we discuss how evaluators should go about providing the assisted sensemaking that can support the ultimate goal of social betterment. We consider in detail the practice of evaluation, presenting a framework of evaluation purposes, inquiry modes, and methods of assisted sensemaking. We also survey a wide range of evaluation methods and critique their potential contribution to sensemaking. We emphasize the planning of evaluations. In large part this involves considering the factors that should influence an evaluator's choice of evaluation purposes, inquiry modes, and methods in varying circumstances. We also address selected political and philosophical issues that are related to the practice of evaluation. Our primary focus throughout is the evaluation of social programs and policies in the public sector, broadly defined, although we also address evaluation of private sector programs and policies.

In the course of this book, we present a comprehensive theory of program and policy evaluation. This theory respects and integrates the practices that have served evaluators well in the past. We believe that aspects of it will seem familiar to many evaluators. At the same time, this theory breaks new ground by assembling best practices in a novel way and makes new contributions to the ways that evaluators and others can think about, plan, and carry out evaluations. We hope that this theory will help evaluators to better understand, plan, and conduct evaluations; sponsors to better determine their evaluation needs; and consumers of evaluation to better interpret and understand what evaluation findings do and do not mean.

We have two general, interlinked goals in presenting this theory of evaluation as assisted sensemaking. The first goal is to provide a sensible way to think about evaluation and its role. Such thinking requires reasonable answers to a set of questions: What is the objective of evaluation? How does the practice of evaluation relate to everyday judgments? How does it relate to other institutions, such as legislatures and agencies that deliver services? In the current intellectual climate, how does one justify claims based on evaluation evidence? And finally, is it possible for today's evaluators to pass beyond the remnants of the paradigm wars and a rising Tower of Babel, where evaluators of different traditions tend to talk past, rather than to, one another?

We make the case that social betterment is the ultimate objective of evaluation. We argue that in the public sector, evaluation has a distinct role in assisting the sensemaking of those in democratically established institutions and of the public. (In the private sector, evaluation's analogous role is to provide information to key decision makers and other socially legitimated actors). We present a perspective, grounded in commonsense realist philosophy, that we hope offers both some justification for making claims based on evaluation evidence and a way to get beyond the paradigm wars. Taken together, the theory's framework and language may help evaluators of different persuasions to talk with each other and discuss how evaluation can be improved.

Our second general goal is to help evaluators and others think through the most important decisions that must be made in planning an evaluation. Again, this requires answers to a specific set of questions: Should evaluations always focus on the merit and worth of a program or policy, or should other evaluation purposes sometimes come to the fore? If, in a given instance, it is legitimate to pursue more than one purpose, how should an evaluator decide which combination of purposes to pursue? How should the evaluator choose the evaluation methods? Whose values are represented in an evaluation, and how are these values to be ascertained?

We contend that, although assessing merit and worth is an especially important purpose of evaluation, in many cases other purposes will contribute more to social betterment. To aid in the choice of evaluation purposes in practice, we lay out the function that each evaluation purpose can serve in the long and complex path toward social betterment. We further specify which contexts imply priority to which evaluation purposes. We discuss guidelines for deciding which type of inquiry should be conducted given the evaluation purpose and the decision context. And we discuss in some detail how to systematically study values (including the values of those directly affected by the program or policy and of those who have important roles in democratic societies) and how to incorporate these values in planing evaluations and interpreting their results.

Overview of the Contents

The first part of this book (Chapters One through Four) examines evaluation practice and its potential role in the service of social betterment. Chapter One briefly defines program and policy evaluation and presents a thumbnail sketch of the theory of evaluation that is developed more fully in subsequent chapters. Chapter Two discusses the concept of social betterment and identifies some of its implications for evaluation practice. It also addresses the importance of values inquiry. Chapter Three describes four evaluation purposes and the general function that each serves in relation to social betterment. Chapter Four addresses inquiry modes, which are groupings of methods, and examines the way in which choices about methods should follow from the specific evaluation purpose and from the attributes of the decision context.

The second section (Chapters Five and Six) expands the previous discussion of linkages between evaluation practice and social betterment and also presents a form of realism that has important implications for these linkages. In Chapter Five, we consider complex combinations of evaluation purposes, and the associated inquiry modes, because the complexities of democratic systems (and of private sector organizations) commonly require evaluations that address multiple purposes. Chapter Six focuses on the philosophy of realism, which both grounds and extends the framework for evaluation planning presented in the preceding chapters.

The third section of the book (Chapters Seven through Ten) reviews and critically examines the four key inquiry methods that evaluators have at their disposal—description, classification, causal analysis, and values inquiry—with one chapter devoted to each. Finally, the Conclusion reviews and synthesizes some of the lessons of the assisted sensemaking approach to evaluation.

The evaluation theory presented in this volume is designed to help members of the evaluation community and others to hold a sensible view of evaluation and its role and to be better able to work their way through the key decisions that must be made in planning an evaluation. Evaluation is already an active field, institutionalized in contemporary political and social processes and contributing to people's understanding of and decision making about social policies and programs. The most effective evaluators already intuitively follow the lion's share of the prescriptions we offer for evaluation as assisted sensemaking, even in the current absence of an explicit guiding theory. However, we believe evaluation will contribute more to social betterment if more evaluators follow the practices described in this book and if more evaluators share a guiding theory such as the one we offer here. As Cook (1997) said in calling for "more and better evaluation theory" (p. 43): "without active theoretical debates about core issues in evaluation that transcend method, the field may not grow, even if it does not atrophy" (p. 47). We are optimistic that evaluation can move forward. And we hope that the present work will help it do so.

July 2000

Melvin M. Mark
State College, Pennsylvania

Gary T. Henry
Atlanta, Georgia

George Julnes
Logan, Utah

To our parents—
Mildred M. Mark
Otis D. Henry and Marcella Tyler Henry
Marilyn Julnes

The Authors

Melvin M. Mark is professor of psychology and senior scientist at the Institute for Policy Research and Evaluation at Pennsylvania State University, where he has received the Liberal Arts Alumni Society Outstanding Teaching Award. He received his Ph.D. degree in social psychology at Northwestern University. His current interests include the theory and methodology of program and policy evaluation and the application of social psychological theory and research (especially work on affective regulation and goals) to prevention programs. He is the coeditor of *Evaluation Studies Review Annual* (vol. 3) (with Thomas D. Cook and others, 1978), *Social Science and Social Policy* (with R. Lance Shotland, 1985), *Multiple Methods in Program Evaluation* (with R. Lance Shotland, 1987), *Realist Evaluation: An Emerging Theory in Support of Practice* (with Gary T. Henry and George Julnes, 1998), and coauthor of a forthcoming book on quasi-experimentation (with Charles S. Reichardt). He is also editor of the *American Journal of Evaluation*.

Gary T. Henry directs the Applied Research Center at Georgia State University and serves as professor of political science, public administration and urban policy studies, and educational policy studies. He also directs the Georgia Council for School Performance. After completing his bachelor's and master's degrees in political science at the University of Kentucky, he received his Ph.D. degree at the University of Wisconsin from an interdisciplinary social science program housed in the UW Graduate School. Henry has also frequently served as a faculty member for the National Conference of State Legislators and the Evaluators' Institute.

Prior to joining the faculty at Georgia State University, he served in the Department of Public Administration and Institute of Statistics at Virginia Commonwealth University. His other professional positions have included Deputy Superintendent of Education for Policy Analysis, Research, and Information Systems in Virginia, Deputy Secretary of Education in the governor's cabinet in Virginia, and Chief Methodologist for Virginia's Joint Legislative Audit and Review Commission.

In 1998, Henry received the Outstanding Evaluation of the Year award for his work conducted on behalf of the Council for School Performance. In 1994, he was appointed associate editor of New Directions for Evaluation and subsequently became co-editor in chief (along with Jennifer Greene). His books include *Practical Sampling* (1990) and *Graphing Data* (1995). He is the editor of *Creating Effective Graphs: Solutions for a Variety of Evaluation Data* (1997), and *Realist Evaluation: An Emerging Theory in Support of Practice* (with George Julnes and Melvin M. Mark, 1998). His current research interests include the effects of preschool programs and merit-based financial aid, performance measurement systems, evaluation theory, and the effects of education policy on teachers, schools, and students.

George Julnes is assistant professor of psychology in the Research and Evaluation Methodology Program at Utah State University. He received his Ph.D. degree in clinical psychology at the University of Hawaii at Manoa and subsequent master's degrees in public policy and business administration at the University of Michigan. He is currently completing a policy evaluation of welfare reform and has been engaged in other evaluations of public and nonprofit programs to provide services to at-risk individuals and families. His theoretical interests in evaluation theory and methods are reflected in his articles for such journals as *Evaluation Review*, the *American Journal of Evaluation*, and *Evaluation*. More specifically, his efforts to develop the view of evaluation as assisted sensemaking can be found in his chapters written with Melvin Mark and Gary Henry in *Realist Evaluation: An Emerging Theory in Support of Practice* (1998).

PART ONE

Social Betterment
Through Evaluation

1

Introducing a Framework for Evaluation

Evaluation assists sensemaking about policies and programs through the conduct of systematic inquiry that describes and explains the policies' and programs' operations, effects, justifications, and social implications. The ultimate goal of evaluation is social betterment, to which evaluation can contribute by assisting democratic institutions to better select, oversee, improve, and make sense of social programs and policies.

The preceding definition encompasses a broad view of the field of policy and program evaluation. Like the definitions espoused by Patton (1997), Rossi and Freeman (1993), and Weiss (1998), it describes evaluation as an enterprise including many alternative approaches and activities. According to this view, evaluation can take place at any stage in the life cycle of a program, from before a social problem has even been identified as such to long after a program has been put in place. It can address any of a wide range of issues, including the needs of a potential program's target population, the way a program is implemented, and a program's effects. This definition also justifies a range of methods of inquiry. In short, we view evaluation as a big tent that can encompass different approaches, a variety of methods, and diverse short-term purposes.

There is an alternative and narrower view of evaluation that defines evaluation as the determination of merit and worth (for example, Scriven, 1993), a definition that corresponds to only one of the four purposes of evaluation that we describe. We prefer an evaluation theory that does not attempt to define important parts of current practice out of the field but instead helps evaluators make thoughtful decisions about when to emphasize one evaluation purpose and when to emphasize another. The following discussion, a preview of the remainder of the book, describes what such a theory looks like in general terms.

In this chapter we introduce several broad concepts that link together to make up the evaluation theory presented in this book. We begin with the concept of sensemaking, which provides a perspective that permeates the other pieces of our approach to evaluation. Next we discuss the concept of social betterment, the piece of the theory that motivates the rest. We then briefly overview a conceptual framework for describing and guiding evaluation practice. This framework consists of evaluation purposes, inquiry modes, and methods from which evaluators may choose in planning an evaluation. Finally, we introduce the realist philosophy that undergirds much of our theory of evaluation.

Sensemaking

Sensemaking is a natural process that each person engages in daily (Weick, 1979, 1995). We humans have evolved (or, if you prefer, were created with) an impressive set of *natural sensemaking* capabilities. These capabilities allow us to observe regularities, to develop accounts about why these regularities occur, and to undertake behaviors designed to capitalize on what we have learned. This process of sensemaking can itself be viewed through an evolutionary metaphor. We can think of people developing explanatory accounts that are then winnowed out by the selection mechanism of subsequent observations (Campbell, 1974b, 1977).

Natural and Assisted Sensemaking

Natural sensemaking enables people to maneuver successfully in the world. Natural sensemaking has important limits, however. For example, people's expectations and desires can influence their interpretations of events. As Francis Bacon put it in *Novum Organum* in 1620: "what a man would like to be true, that he more readily believes." This tendency can lead supporters of a program to see success even when it is not present. Another shortcoming of natural sensemaking is that people are often willing to adopt an explanatory account if it is plausible, even if there is inadequate evidence of its accuracy (Fiske & Taylor, 1991; Weick, 1995). For example, when people see that a troubled youth exhibits improved behavior after participating in an intervention program, they may attribute the improvement to the program without asking how much improvement might have occurred spontaneously or for reasons other than the program. Entire research areas, such as the psychological literature on biases in judgment, focus on these and other limits of natural sensemaking (see, for example, Kahneman, Slovic, & Tversky, 1982). Although scholars often focus on the psychological and organizational processes that limit natural sensemaking (Weick, 1995), other limits are purely pragmatic. In the case of program and policy evaluation, the individuals interested in a program often cannot, for example, observe all program sites or see what happens to clients years after they have left the program. In short, as impressive as natural sensemaking is, its limits are considerable.

Because of the limits and imperfections of natural sensemaking, people have created technologies that help extend, support, and improve their natural abilities to make sense of the world around them. Historical examples of *assisted sensemaking* abound. For example, eyeglasses have been created to assist natural vision. Number systems and mathematics have been developed to assist people's natural abilities to quantify (see Wynn, 1992, for evidence of basic counting even in infants). Similarly, we argue, the field of evaluation has been developed to assist, support, and extend natural human abilities to observe, understand, and make judgments about policies and programs.

Representational and Valuative Aspects of Sensemaking

Natural sensemaking has at least two components: representational and valuative. The *representational component* refers to individuals' efforts to know and understand—to represent—what is going on in the world around them. Natural representations, in general, are formed inductively through sense perceptions, as filtered through existing cognitive frameworks. People observe events, categorize, and make causal judgments. They observe patterns, develop hypotheses, and move back and forth between evidence and explanations to create representations of their world. The *valuative component* of sensemaking refers to human tendencies to make judgments about what is better and what is worse. People have their own subjective experiences, and they have empathy for others. They like some things more than others, they make moral judgments, they weigh values, and they even consider what might be best for the common good. Even though the representational and valuative components are usually intertwined in people's sensemaking about policies and programs, it can nevertheless be helpful to keep each distinctly in mind when planning evaluations.

Evaluators have developed techniques (and borrowed them from other fields) to assist both the representational and the valuative component of sensemaking. With respect to representation, evaluators use a variety of methods to describe, to classify, and to investigate causal relations. With respect to valuation, evaluators stimulate deliberations, conduct focus groups and surveys about values, and engage in critical analysis of the values embodied in the services delivered by program staff and in evaluations themselves. Both representational sensemaking and valuative sensemaking are vital parts of evaluations. Past approaches to evaluation have often emphasized one or the other. One of the advantages of a theory of evaluation as assisted sensemaking is that it offers the promise of properly balancing and integrating the two.

In sum, the idea of sensemaking has important implications for the way people think about and practice evaluation. It should be a reminder that, without any special urging, the people who establish, administer, or are affected by policies and programs engage in natural sensemaking about them. It should also be a reminder that natural sensemaking capabilities are limited and that these limits create the need for systematic evaluation. If evaluation findings are to make much of a difference, evaluators need to respect and be sensitive to natural sensemaking, including its representational and valuative components.

The concept of sensemaking provides a general perspective through which to view evaluation and its relationship to evaluation users. This perspective highlights both the similarities and the differences between evaluators' systematic inquiry on the one hand and the natural sensemaking of those who are involved in and care about policies and programs on the other. However, the concept of sensemaking does not by itself explain *why* the practice of evaluation exists, why it is worthwhile to assist natural sensemaking about policies and programs. For that, we turn to another of the major components of the theory of evaluation as assisted sensemaking: social betterment.

Social Betterment

The *raison d'être* of evaluation, we argue, is to contribute indirectly to social betterment by providing assisted sensemaking to the democratic institutions that are directly charged with defining and seeking that betterment. By *social betterment*, we mean the reduction or prevention of social problems, the improvement of social conditions, and the alleviation of human suffering. A belief in social betterment (or something like it) seems to us necessary for the enterprise of evaluation. Without it, there is no plausible, defensible justification for doing policy and program evaluation— or even for having social policies and programs in the first place (Covert, 1995; Henry & Julnes, 1998).

Our model of social betterment, detailed in Chapter Two, contends that the primary reason social policies and programs exist is to lead to social betterment. Of course, in the real world of politics and organizational dynamics, additional motives exist for policies and programs. Programs and policies may be supported, for instance, for symbolic reasons or to serve the special interests of some group. Similarly, the decision to evaluate may be motivated by concerns other than social betterment, such as the desire to delay action. Nevertheless, we believe that it is appropriate to view social policies and programs as being produced by democratic institutions that *over the long haul,* strive to respond to those social conditions that have come to be collectively defined as social problems.

Whereas democratic institutions directly act to alleviate social problems, evaluation's contribution is indirect and mediated. It contributes to social betterment by supplying information that can be used in democratic deliberations and administrative actions. In other words, evaluation can assist democratic institutions and agents to better select, oversee, improve, and make sense of social programs and policies.

The Parties to Evaluation

Our conception of social betterment takes a broad view of democratic institutions. First, our view of how to serve democracy involves multiple, embedded levels. That is, the process of considering the qualities and trade-offs that will define the common good takes place at multiple levels including the individual, the family, and the community. Thus the public is an important player. Second, democratic institutions include both representative and administrative components, such as the legislatures that fund programs and the agencies that actually carry them out. *Democratic institutions,* as we use the term, include street-level program staff as well as legislators and high-level executives. Third, in addition to formal democratic institutions, we include such other institutions as not-for-profit agencies, foundations, interest groups, and the media that take part in the public dialogue about what should be done and how. These organizations, though not listed in the Constitution, commonly play a major role in democratic processes. In addition, although our primary focus is on these democratic institutions, most aspects of our approach can be translated fairly directly into the private sector, as we shall briefly discuss. There are, in short, many audiences who can and should benefit from the assisted sensemaking of evaluation.

The Focus of the Theory

Evaluation, in principle, has a broad scope. One can evaluate any-thing—including evaluation—as Scriven (1993), Shadish, Cook, and Leviton (1991), and others have pointed out. For example, people can evaluate the books they read, the cars they drive, and the employees they supervise. Scriven (1993) alliteratively identi-fied the "Big Six" P's that can be evaluated: programs, policies, products, personnel, performance, and proposals. Scriven (1980, 1991, 1993) contends that the reasoning underlying evaluation transcends the object of evaluation. This leads him to describe eval-uation as a *trans-discipline*, that is, as an endeavor that, like statis-tics, cuts across other areas of scholarship and practice (Scriven, 1993). We agree that at a fundamental level, the *logic* of evaluation is the same regardless of what is being evaluated. However, a theory of evaluation practice does not involve fundamental logic alone. Evaluation theory is also about why evaluation is carried out, for whom, and how. Context matters. Because Scriven's Six P's are markedly different types of things, because they operate in markedly different contexts, there are differences in the important details of how and why and for whom they are evaluated.

We therefore restrict our focus here to the evaluation of social programs and policies. We address both social programs and social policies because they generally share similar contexts. They usually share a common goal, social betterment, and a common source, democratic institutions. Thus they also share a common ra-tionale about why, how, and for whom evaluation should be done. Not surprisingly, then, similar approaches to evaluation apply to both social programs and social policies (Mohr, 1995; Weiss, 1998).

Indeed, the distinction between them is often fuzzy (Mark & Henry, 1998), suggesting that it might be artificial or even futile to try to distinguish the two for the purpose of evaluation practice.

Yet another reason why we focus on both social policies and social programs is related to the current state of evaluation practice. Professional evaluators who focus on programs typically also are concerned with policies and vice versa. They systematically evaluate other types of things far less often, if ever. Instead, there are distinct groups of professionals who focus on evaluating personnel (for example, industrial psychologists and human resource specialists), products (evaluators for *Consumer Reports*), performance (theater critics and personnel and educational psychologists), and proposals (National Science Foundation review panels).

Thus, in the remainder of this book, the term *evaluation* refers to *social program and policy evaluation*.

The Driving Force Behind Evaluation Choices

Social betterment, we argue, is what evaluators should strive for. It is evaluation's long-term goal, and the success of an evaluation should be defined as the extent to which it indirectly aids social betterment by assisting sensemaking within democratic institutions. This goal of social betterment should therefore drive the major decisions about how to do an evaluation. This is an important though perhaps subtle shift from most ways of defining the success of evaluation and from most views of what should drive decisions in evaluation.

There are several established traditions that offer guidance in planning evaluations and defining success. For instance, one tradition, associated with Donald Campbell (1969b) and his colleagues, directs evaluators to employ causal analysis, in the form of an experiment or the closest feasible approximation, presumably for the purpose of assessing the merit and worth of social programs. Because of the strong identification of evaluation with a specific, restricted set of methods for causal analysis, this approach has been labeled, often critically, as a *method-driven* approach to evaluation (for example, Chen & Rossi, 1983). Success in this tradition has often been defined, at least implicitly, in terms of the rigor of methods used. Another, more recent tradition has been labeled *theory driven* by its advocates (for example, Chen, 1990, Chen & Rossi, 1983). According to this approach, evaluators should begin by identifying a program theory, that is, a model of the mechanisms that link program activities and outcomes, and then use this program theory as a guide to evaluation design. Success in this tradition may be judged by the quality of the theoretical model constructed and the adequacy with which the model is tested. Yet another tradition is *utilization focused* (Patton, 1997). In this approach the evaluator identifies the intended users and uses of an evaluation and then selects inquiry methods to match those uses. Success in this tradition is explicitly defined by whether the intended utilization takes place. A more recent approach, falling in the area of participatory evaluation (Whitmore, 1998), may be labeled *empowerment driven*. Although some critics claim that it is unclear who is supposed to be empowered to do what (Sechrest, 1997), it appears that the goal of this approach is to empower those involved in the program to evaluate it themselves (for example, Fetterman, Kaftarian, & Wandersman, 1996). Success in this tradition accordingly would be defined as the extent to which program staff or clients or both take up the task of systematic evaluation (Schnoes, Murphey-Berman, & Chambers, 2000).

Each of these traditions has influenced some evaluators' decisions about evaluation designs. Each provides a way of defining success. And we believe that advocates of each approach believe that its use will contribute to social betterment in one way or another. However, we also believe that these existing traditions provide guidance that is either overly restricted (specifying a method such as using an experiment, for example) or fails to be sufficiently sensitive to context to support democratic institutions in their strivings for social betterment. Evaluation success should not be defined solely in terms of method, theory, direct utilization, or staff or client empowerment. Different methods can be appropriate in different contexts. Theories need not always be detailed and tested. The search for direct utilization can sometimes lead evaluators away from the most important questions. A division of labor is often justified, with evaluation specialists rather than program staff or clients doing the work of an evaluation, while staff go about the other business of providing services.

The alternative we present might be called *betterment-driven* evaluation. That is, decisions about an evaluation and the definition of its success should be driven by an analysis of the potential contribution that the evaluation can make, in the particular circumstances, to the democratic processes that define and seek social betterment. Simply specifying social betterment as the purpose for evaluation provides inadequate guidance for planning, however, because many types of evaluation may in certain circumstances support this overall goal. To translate the general goal of social betterment into the specific details of an actual evaluation, one must have a way of characterizing some of the key decisions in evaluation planning.

Framework for Practice

Another important element of the theory of evaluation as assisted sensemaking is a framework intended to capture critical aspects of evaluation practice. This framework is designed to help guide evaluation planning by facilitating the translation of a general interest in social betterment into the details of evaluation design. The framework distinguishes between evaluation purposes (reasons for doing an evaluation) and inquiry modes (families of research methods).

Evaluation *purposes* offer reasons for doing evaluation that are more specific than the ultimate reason of social betterment. We distinguish four general and relatively common evaluation purposes. They are summarized in the following box (and discussed in more detail in Chapter Three). Each of these purposes has unique ways of triggering the process of social betterment. One of the major tasks of evaluation planning should be the thoughtful selection of the evaluation purpose or mix of purposes most likely to contribute to social betterment in a given case.

Four Purposes of Evaluation

1. **Assessment of merit and worth:** the development of warranted judgments, at the individual and societal level, of the value of a policy or program

2. **Program and organizational improvement:** the effort to use information to directly modify and enhance program operations

3. **Oversight and compliance:** the assessment of the extent to which a program follows the directives of statutes, regulations, rules, mandated standards or any other formal expectations

4. **Knowledge development:** the discovery or testing of general theories, propositions, and hypotheses in the context of policies and programs

---

The selection of evaluation purpose(s) should be based on an informed judgment of which purpose or set of purposes will best support democratic institutions and processes in the pursuit of betterment in a specific case. As we shall see, the choice of evaluation purpose should depend largely on contextual factors, such as whether the program in question has plausible competitors. Among the four purposes for evaluation, the assessment of merit and worth has a unique standing as a means of supporting social betterment through democratic processes. Assessments of merit and worth inform the public and their representatives about the value of the policies and programs that have been selected or are being considered as instruments to realize social betterment. Assessments of merit and worth thus assist sensemaking and reasoned deliberations about which course of action is best. However, assessments of merit and worth are most likely to be useful when a democracy or an organization faces a major fork in the road, and this does not occur every day. In other circumstances, evaluations with other purposes may better serve social betterment. For instance, evaluations that emphasize program improvement may enhance the operation of a previously chosen program. Evaluations that emphasize oversight and compliance can contribute by ensuring that formal expectations (for example, rules and regulations) are met as policies and programs are carried out. Knowledge development may in the long run inform deliberations and lead to improved policies and programs, though the path is likely to be indirect and tenuous. In short, there are multiple possible paths to social betterment, and one of the chief objectives of this book is to suggest good ways to work through the process of reaching a reasoned choice of one or more evaluation purposes in a specific case.

After choosing an evaluation purpose, the evaluator, perhaps in collaboration with others, must consider the type of inquiry methods to use. The second level in our practice framework enables evaluators to organize and select specific *inquiry modes* that fall under the representational or valuative sides of assisted sensemaking. Inquiry modes consist of broad families, or clusters, of methods for systematic inquiry in evaluation. Each mode is a functional grouping that supports a different aspect of natural sensemaking. We have identified four inquiry modes, outlined in the following box, that include most of the methods evaluators use.

Numerous specific *methods* fall within each of these four inquiry modes, and each mode includes methods on both sides of the traditional quantitative-qualitative divide. Although all the specific methods have limitations and are fallible, each mode has evolved as a collection of the assisted sensemaking methods that can aid people in compensating for the shortcomings of natural sensemaking. As we shall see, the choice of inquiry mode (and of specific methods) should depend in large part on the purpose of an evaluation as well as on other factors such as the level of certainty required

---

Four Inquiry Modes for Evaluation Practice

---

1. **Description:** methods used to measure events or experiences, such as client characteristics, services delivered, resources, or client's standing on potential outcome variables

2. **Classification:** methods used for grouping and for investigating the underlying structures of things, such as the development or application of a taxonomy of program subtypes

3. **Causal analysis:** methods used to explore and test causal relationships (between program services and client functioning, for example) or to study the mechanisms through which effects occur

4. **Values inquiry:** methods used to model natural valuation processes, assess existing values, or dissect value positions using formal or critical analysis

---

for any decisions about the program. The final component of our theory of evaluation, realism, also has implications for the choice of inquiry modes.

Realist Philosophy of Science

The final part of the theory of evaluation as assisted sensemaking is a synthesis of the work of several contemporary realist philosophers. In particular we draw largely from philosophical work known as *commonsense realism* (Putnam, 1987, 1990). Realism presumes the existence of an external world in which events and experiences are triggered by underlying (and often unobservable) mechanisms and structures (Bhaskar, 1975). Commonsense realism also gives standing to everyday experiences. It is antiformalist in the sense of not expecting logical, formal solutions to vexing problems such as the nature of truth. And it places a priority on practice and the lessons drawn from practice.

The realist foundation of our evaluation theory offers several advantages. First, it justifies the general concept of sensemaking. One can make sense only if "something is out there to be registered and sensed accurately" (Weick, 1995, p. 55). Another noteworthy benefit of the realist position is that it offers a satisfactory way to get beyond the *paradigm wars* that have consumed so much attention in the last decade. In evaluation, the two opposing views in this conflict have commonly been labeled in terms of their predominant methodological approaches. Thus, the paradigm wars have also been called the qualitative-quantitative debate. As realists, we see no meaningful epistemological difference between qualitative and quantitative methods. Instead we see both as assisted sensemaking techniques that have specific benefits and limitations. And as commonsense realists, we believe that although there is a world out there to be made sense of, the specific constructions and construals that individuals make are critical and need to be considered. Given the attention the paradigm debate has received (see, for example, Reichardt & Rallis, 1994), and the energy it has siphoned away from the substance and practice of doing evaluation (House, 1994), the possibility of a reasonable long-term resolution of the paradigm wars is important.

Realism can also help guide and support some important aspects of evaluation practice (as detailed in Chapter Six). For example, the four inquiry modes parallel key concepts in realist views of the nature of the world. As this example suggests, in the theory of evaluation as assisted sensemaking, the philosophy of commonsense realism has practical implications.

Conclusion

Evaluation assists sensemaking about policies and programs through systematic inquiry that describes and explains the policies' and programs' operations, effects, justifications, and social implications. A sound theory of evaluation as assisted sensemaking includes several components: an account of sensemaking; a model of evaluation practice as it has evolved; a grounding in realism that can both provide some foundation and help synthesize and guide practice; and an overarching rationale for evaluation. The ultimate rationale, or goal, of evaluation is social betterment. Evaluation contributes to this goal by assisting democratic institutions to better select, oversee, improve, and make sense of social programs and policies. Social betterment is the wellspring of evaluation, the fundamental motivation for the field.

2

**Understanding Social
Betterment and the Role
of Values in Evaluation**

Informal evaluations of social programs and policies have almost certainly occurred since the first social policies and programs were developed. Those who designed the programs and policies and those affected by them presumably made evaluative judgments about them. People naturally take note of the outcome of their own and others' attempts to manipulate the environment in order to solve problems (Campbell, 1974b; Heider, 1944).

Even systematic forms of evaluation have a long history, according to Wortman (1983), who points to systematic personnel evaluation in China over four thousand years ago. Most chroniclers of evaluation start with a considerably more recent focus, however. Although program evaluation has important intellectual predecessors, such as the work of Tyler (1935) in education, and although one might identify alternative histories of evaluation for different disciplines and policy areas, most histories of evaluation identify the 1960s and the expanding Great Society as the cradle (Shadish, Cook, & Leviton, 1991), or at least the first major growth spurt (Rossi & Freeman, 1993), of modern program evaluation. That period in the United States witnessed an explosion of social policies and social programs. New programs were created, and old ones infused with funds. And evaluation was mandated or authorized for many of these programs (Boruch & Cordray, 1980; Shadish, Cook, & Leviton, 1991). Along with this emphasis on evaluation, there developed groups of individuals who called themselves evaluators (along with other individuals who, even though they labored under different titles, also did the work of evaluation). With this growth of evaluation and of a labor pool of evaluators, came writings and theories specifying how evaluation should be done.

Over time, evaluation has emerged as a specialty area, as a concentrated field of professional and scholarly focus (Shadish, Cook, & Leviton, 1991). There are specialized journals, conferences, and associations. The professional associations have developed standards for practice (Joint Committee on Standards for Educational Evaluation, 1994; Shadish, Newman, Scheirer, & Wye, 1995) and debated such topics as professional credentialization (for example, Altschuld, 1999; Worthen, 1999). And the members of this field carry out a wide array of activities with the ultimate goal of social betterment.

The endeavor of program and policy evaluation has never been a homogeneous one. Several different approaches have emerged, some long lived and others quickly passing fads (Mark, Henry, & Julnes, 1999). Consistent across all the various approaches, we presume, is the belief of the adherents that their approach to evaluation will contribute in some fashion to social betterment. It is hard to imagine anyone laboring in the field of evaluation who does not think in terms of making the world a better place through his or her work (Covert, 1995).

In this chapter we examine the idea of social betterment, what it is and what it is not. In our view, evaluation should be motivated by the goal of providing information that women and men as administrators, as legislators, and as citizens in a democracy can use to better make sense of the objectives, operations, and effects of social policies and programs. Social betterment, rather than the more popular and pervasive goal of utilization, should motivate evaluation. In this chapter we also review the lengthy path from individual need to collective action to social betterment. We also identify, based on that review, guideposts that evaluators might use in designing an evaluation, including program goals, client needs, and stakeholder inputs. We conclude that systematic values inquiry is probably the best available guidepost for many of the decisions that must be made in an evaluation. The view of social betterment presented in this chapter also has other important implications for evaluation practice, most notably for the selection of evaluation purpose (as discussed in Chapter Three).

Social Betterment as the Ultimate Goal of Evaluation

This society holds many widely shared ideals. For example, most people agree that children should receive a good education. Of course, not all ideals are widely shared, as illustrated by continuing debate in such topics as abortion and sex education. But even when there seems to be a consensus that something such as a good education is part of the *common good,* it is another matter to define the common good in more specific terms and to agree on how to try to achieve it. Consider some of the questions that arise in defining what constitutes a good education for our children. How important are self-esteem enhancement, morals training, and social skills development relative to math and reading? What are the acceptable standards for reading? Do the same standards really apply to children in wealthy suburban school districts and children in poverty-stricken central city school districts? Should education be supplied for the children of illegal immigrants? Even when some consensus is obtained about issues such as these, additional questions typically arise over how to achieve what people desire. For example, there is consensus that teaching reading is part of a good education, but should reading be taught by phonics or by whole language methods? Does an early emphasis on correct spelling enhance or hinder the development of reading skills?

In short, substantial questions arise regarding the ends and the means of social policies and programs. Evaluation can contribute to social efforts to answer these questions by providing information that assists sensemaking about what makes up the common good and about how successful a particular course of action is in getting there. By addressing the ends and means of social interventions, evaluation contributes to the attempts to define and realize social goals, to meet human needs, to promote social betterment. That is, evaluation has been institutionalized as a sensemaking support for efforts in modern democracies to define and strive for social betterment.

Social Betterment Versus Utilization

Evaluators' desire to make the world a better place through their work has led to a considerable interest in the use of evaluation results, or *utilization,* as it is commonly referred to in the literature. This focus is not surprising: when evaluation results are not used, it might seem apparent that they are not making the world a better place. But even direct use does not guarantee betterment. Nor does the absence of direct use imply that an evaluation was a failure.

Utilization has been a long-standing concern and perhaps the greatest source of frustration among professional evaluators (Shulha & Cousins, 1997). The literature on utilization appeared to emerge, at least in part, as evaluators recognized that evaluation results did not automatically translate into immediate decisions about keeping, ending, or revising policies and programs (see, for example, Patton et al., 1977; Weiss, 1977a, 1997b; Weiss & Bucuvalas, 1980). Stakeholder-based evaluation approaches have been proposed as the route to greater direct utilization, with Patton's "intended use by intended users" (1997) serving as the motto for a league of evaluators. An often repeated view says that stakeholders are more likely to use evaluation information if they have bought into the evaluation early on, had a chance to influence the values embedded in it, and have thereby conferred legitimacy and credibility on the results (Weiss, 1983).

Despite such long-standing advice, concerns persist about utilization (Shulha & Cousins, 1997). Some evaluation theorists have called for better developed theories to guide evaluation to higher levels of use (Weiss, 1997a, 1997b). In contrast, others encourage evaluators to make conclusions about merit and worth and let the results be used if, and as, others choose (Scriven, 1993). Our view of evaluation as sensemaking in service of social betterment offers an alternative to both. In effect, it denies that direct utilization should be a criterion for judging the worth of evaluation and that the evaluator's responsibility is to judge merit and worth and be done with it.

One past response to the apparent low level of direct, instrumental evaluation use has been to broaden the definition of use. Even in the absence of direct use, evaluation results often appeared to help shape people's assumptions, beliefs, and expectations, and these in turn appeared to influence subsequent decisions about programs and policies, sometimes distant in time and place from the original evaluation. Such indirect, conceptual uses of evaluation are often called *enlightenment* (Weiss, 1997a, 1997b).

We hope to reshape the diffuse notion of enlightenment use, replacing it with a focus on the role of evaluation in supporting the deliberations, decisions, and actions carried out through democratic institutions. From this perspective, instrumental use of evaluation findings is not intrinsically positive because it may imply that these findings have a special status, above the other considerations that influence democratic decision making. To inform reasoned deliberations and the actions that follow is a noble and ambitious aspiration for evaluation; further than that evaluators should not aim.

Although the goal of social betterment can be seen as a more specific variety of the goal of enlightenment, its greater specificity carries some important implications for evaluation practitioners and for scholars of utilization. Utilization should not be construed so diffusely that it is thought to have occurred if anyone thinks in any way differently as a result of the evaluation. Instead, an evaluation should be judged by (1) how well the evaluator determines what information can best serve social betterment in the context, (2) what quality of information is obtained, and (3) how well the findings are disseminated to relevant democratic institutions, program personnel, and the public.

Social Betterment, Not "Progress"

With its commitment to social betterment, the field of evaluation might seem to be caught up in the idea that social conditions *will* improve. In fact, earlier views of evaluation have been criticized in part for assuming that decision makers are rational and that given rational decision making, progress is inevitable (see, for example, Cronbach, 1982). As one of the critics of social progress has summed it up, "The fact of change is unquestioned, but has there been *progress?*" (Lanier, [1930] 1991, p. 125).

In the Western tradition, social progress is commonly seen as a continual, linear development of human potential, usually linked to discovering and applying "universal truths" from the natural, physical, and social sciences (Ginsberg, 1973). This concept of social progress has been called into question by such developments as economic convulsions after the onset of industrialism, the construction and use of the atomic bomb, and disparities that persist within and between societies in material well-being. Prominent critics of social progress have laid to waste the notion of continual, linear, universal development. Conservatives such as Lanier ([1930] 1991) romanticize the past and focus on the losses wrought by change. Christian philosophers such as Reinhold Niebuhr (1952) emphasize the limits to change, the shallowness of material improvements, and the persistence of inequalities. Marxists and neo-Marxists focus on the role of the myth of social progress in the maintenance of class-based societies (Habermas, 1975). Postmodernists, drawing on the Frankfort School, have argued that unequal social patterns persist long after the originating social conditions (such as slavery or discrimination against women) have been officially halted, maintaining the preexisting power relationships (Jay, 1973). In short, critics of the concept of progress focus on the implicit assumption that progress is inevitable, uniform, and linear and on the complexities that arise once it is acknowledged that different people may have different ideas as to what progress entails.

Although these criticisms have led us to shun the myth of continual social progress, we have not shied away from a "non-utopian view of social betterment" (Putnam, 1987). This latter perspective holds that although certainly not inevitable, social betterment—the reduction of social problems and the increased meeting of human needs—is possible. This view is influenced by the apparent positive changes in Western Europe and the United States in the past two centuries, such as "increases in wealth and population, . . . the growth of democratic institutions, universal education, . . . the abolition of slavery and reform of criminal law, the emancipation of women" (Ginsberg, 1973, p. 636). Again, this is not to say that progress is inevitable or uniform. There have been enough policy failures, such as the deinstitutionalization of the mentally ill without adequate community-based support services, to disabuse any thoughtful observer of that notion. It is, again, to say that betterment is possible.

Indeed, without the possibility of social betterment, evaluation would be at worst an empty exercise, at best a fulfillment of curiosity. That the possibility of social betterment exists is both a personal motivation for evaluators and a critical part of the rationale for the field.

The Path to Social Betterment

If, then, the ultimate goal for evaluation as a form of assisted sense-making is to contribute to social betterment by informing deliberations in democratically established institutions, we must consider how some problems come to fall within the purview of government institutions, what is done about them, and how evaluation influences the democratic determination of problems and the solutions that are pursued. Table 2.1 summarizes the movement from human needs to social problems to social policies and programs to social betterment.

TABLE 2.1. The Path from Human Needs to Social Betterment.

Stages in Development	Institutional Roles	Potential Roles Policy for Evaluation Findings
Identification of human needs	Entrepreneurs advocate social conditions as unmet needs.	Findings provide an empirical check on claims about conditions identified as human needs.
Recognition of social problem	Media, legislature, or executive place the problem on the policy agenda.	Findings document the problem, lend credibility.
Adoption of social policy	Social action, usually by the legislature, legitimizes the problem.	Findings inform the selection process.
Implementation of policy or program	Agencies carry out the policy, with additional direction from elected or appointed officials.	Findings document agency operations and guide improvement.
Oversight, review, and reconsideration	Problems, goals, policies, and operations are subject to examination and reexamination.	Findings used to oversee implementation, show unforeseen by-products, estimate effects, explain impacts, and inform opinions about betterment.

From Human Needs to Social Problems

Achieving social betterment is the *raison d'être* for social policies and programs. One way to assess whether or not a particular course of action leads to social betterment is by determining whether it meets human needs better than its alternatives (Scriven, 1993). But not all troublesome conditions, not all perceived needs, are construed as social problems. Needs change into recognized social problems as they find a place on the agenda of democratic institutions. When a need receives a certain threshold of attention in society through the media, the policy community, the activities of foundations, or political campaigns, it comes to be defined as a social problem (Hilgartner & Bosk, 1988; Glazer, 1994; Kingdon, 1995; Mark & Henry, 1998). In other words, what are defined as social problems are those unmet human needs that achieve standing on the public agenda through discussion in democratic institutions.

The list of social problems that compete for attention on the public agenda expands in part as matters that were considered private concerns for individuals or families come to be seen as social responsibilities. Habermas (1996a) has described the process of converting "private matters" to public actions as "a long road until the controversial contributions on such issues— contributions that depend on competing interpretations of self and the world, or on different 'visions of the good life'—adequately articulate the needs of those affected" (p. 314). Child abuse (Nelson, 1984), public smoking, and drunk driving (Glazer, 1994) are all examples of once private concerns that have become public agenda items.

Whereas some needs are private concerns when first brought forward by the advocates who push for their adoption as social problems, others have substantial histories in the public arena. Many needs are manifest in long-standing social problems such as poverty and hunger or are by-products of social changes, such as the homelessness that resulted from deinstitutionalization of the mentally ill. Alternatively, social problems sometimes come to be identified when research findings, such as Wright's study of the medical problems of the homeless (1987, 1991), receive attention by the media, policy entrepreneurs, foundation boards, and others who influence the public agenda (Kingdon, 1995; Mintrom, 1997). But it is not only information that fuels the movement from need to social problem. Values matter too, and—as we discuss later in the chapter—democratic institutions play a central role in adjudicating the values conflicts that arise in defining social problems in modern democracies.

From Social Problems to Social Policies and Programs

In societies with democratic governments, social policies and programs arise in response to social problems. Of course, policies are occasionally developed primarily for their symbolic effect, without real intent to address a social problem (Edelman, 1964). And some critical theorists cynically argue that all policies and programs are directed not toward social betterment but toward keeping social order while maintaining unequal power distributions. Although it is important to consider this position, which can sometimes be illuminating, we do not see a place for it as a foundational assumption of evaluation. Working with this premise, evaluators would be singers who knew but one song, belting out the same tune about inequality and power distributions in every evaluation. We find it more reasonable, as well as more accurate, to presume that although self-interest and other motivations have a role, most social policies and programs arise *at least in part* from democratic institutions' attempts to address social problems.

Assuming that some social problem has been identified, democratic institutions and processes move toward social betterment in a variety of ways, including

- Choosing to initiate new policies or programs (as in the case of legislation mandating gender equity in collegiate sports) (Office of Civil Rights, 1991)

- Trying out a new policy or program in a demonstration project before considering universal implementation (as illustrated by a series of demonstration projects for the homeless mentally ill; Rog, 1999)

- Using subunits (for example, states are subunits relative to the federal government) as *laboratories of democracy*, perhaps with one state implementing novel programs that might be considered by other states (as in the case of boot camps for juvenile offenders; Austin, Jones, & Boylard, 1993) or by the federal government (as in the case of the HOPE scholarships; Henry & Bugler, 1998)

- Changing the way an ongoing policy or program is implemented, either universally (as illustrated by revisions to basic compensatory education programs in primary schools; Trochim, 1982) or more locally (as occurred when the federal government gave waivers to selected states so they could try out variations in welfare programs; Gueron, 1997)

- Allowing program managers and staff the latitude to seek better ways of implementing a program (as happens in the implementation of many if not most educational interventions; McLaughlin, 1985)

- Verifying that a program or policy is being carried out responsibly (as in the case of congressional requests for a study of the implementation of the earned income credit; U.S. General Accounting Office, 1997)

In these and in other ways, democratic institutions move from recognizing social problems to offering programs and policies that address them.

In addition, citizens in democracies have a special role in guiding the direction of social policy (Page & Shapiro, 1992). Their values and preferences act as direct constraints on the votes of the elected deliberative bodies that produce social policies and programs (Fishkin, 1995; Stimson, 1998). Although a spate of research shows the impact of mass opinion on public policy actions (Monroe, 1998; Page & Shapiro, 1992; Stimson, 1998), citizens as a whole have rarely been considered directly relevant to evaluation and have only occasionally been identified as *stakeholders* (Henry, 1996b; Henry & Julnes, 1998). We address the inclusion of the views of the citizenry and other groups in more detail in the context of values inquiry.

From Programs and Policies to Social Betterment

In principle, social policies can be judged by the extent to which they reduce or prevent social problems. When social problems are reduced or prevented or, moving further back along the path laid out in Table 2.1, when human needs are met, social betterment is the result. But with a panoply of conflicting values, with the emergence of needs over time, and with an absence of formal theories to adequately guide the selection of evaluation criteria (House, 1994; House & Howe, 1999), how are people to know when betterment has occurred?

Again, democratic processes historically are the mechanism by which this determination is made. Deliberation, based on discussions among the public, in the media, and in representative bodies, is the principal mechanism for democratic determinations of worth. At the core of the issue of worth is whether the policy or program has produced a net positive in terms of betterment. These deliberations may be influenced by evaluation information, but they are not controlled by it. In short, democratic institutions and processes lurch toward social betterment, albeit in fallible, faltering, tentative ways.

The Role of Democratic Processes and Institutions

Democracy, through its processes and institutions, arbitrates value choices that are too complex to be formally derived (Henry & Julnes, 1998). Each of the steps in the path from individual needs to social betterment involves value choices that are arbitrated by democratic institutions. For example, when claims are made that some condition constitutes a human need requiring public rather than private remedies, the need is legitimated as a social problem when the claims result in deliberation and action by democratic institutions (Estlund, 1997).

To understand the role of democratic processes and institutions in the pathway to social betterment, evaluators should have at least a basic understanding of the nature of democracies. Theories of democracy are of two basic types. The first type views "the political process as a struggle for power among competing interests rather than a search for the common good" (Bohman & Rehg, 1997, p. x). These theories see the threat of civil unrest and violence as the reason both for majorities to give rights to minorities and for minorities to abide even by decisions they feel are wrong (see Dahl, [1956] 1973, on James Madison). Although these theories may be useful to evaluators in understanding the ways that conflicting views are resolved in democracies, evaluators will benefit even more from considering the implications of the second type of theory. Rather than characterizing democracy as the art of placing appropriate checks and balances on the competition between interested groups, this group of theories gives more credence to consensus and reason in democratic decision making.

Recently, the second type of theory, known as normative theories of deliberative democracy, has been concerned with republican ideas of participation and "mediated forms of public reason among citizens with diverse moral doctrines" (Bohman & Rehg, 1997, p. xiii). According to these theories, autonomous individuals form their idea of the common good based on their own moral outlook and self-interests (Putnam, 1990; Habermas, 1996a, pp. 289–321). These theories also assume that individuals have equal access to and no constraints on participating in deliberations about the conception of the common good and how to achieve it. Of course, such stringent criteria are not fully met in practice, but they serve as ideal yardsticks against which to measure democracies. We believe that deliberative theories of democracy hold important implications for evaluation practice even when the actual democracy is imperfect relative to the standards of normative theorists and even when many decisions are made by representatives of the citizenry rather than through direct deliberation.

Another necessary part of the deliberative process, according to normative theorists, is that after an issue has been deliberated and decided based on majority rule, it can subsequently be reconsidered if the minority's arguments become more convincing (Cohen, 1997). In addition, visions of the good life can change, as can the actual facts regarding a social condition. In all these cases, methods for corrective actions must be sanctioned and institutionalized.

The democratic theories that underlie our approach to social betterment emphasize the importance of taking a broad view of the participants in democratic processes. In addition to governmental entities, advocacy organizations and foundations have a variety of important roles in this framework, as does the public. Advocacy organizations often press for public consideration of some human need as a social problem. They also advance new ideas of the common good and champion new social programs. Foundations likewise have multiple means for influencing the identification of human needs, pressing these needs onto the policy agenda, and bringing particular solutions to the fore. In some cases they provide substantial resources for demonstration projects and evaluations that cause legislative bodies and the media to consider novel social programs. In these and other ways, foundations and advocates play important roles in democratic processes and are well within the scope of our model of social betterment and of the evaluation approach offered here. Deliberative theories of democracy can also remind evaluators that the public, broadly defined, is a key player in sensemaking about social betterment, thus helping evaluators avoid the trap of serving only those in official government posts (House, 1980, 1993).

In review then, the path to social betterment begins with the individual determination of a human need. Not all needs come to be construed as social problems, however. Needs are screened by institutions, such as legislatures and the media (Fishkin, 1995), and this process is influenced by policy entrepreneurs, advocates, and even evaluations. Once a need has been recognized as a social problem, it is framed, and either a potential solution is attached, in the form of a social policy or program, or the problem may recede from view. Although evaluation findings can influence any of the steps in the pathway from needs to social betterment (see Table 2.1), most evaluation activities begin when policies and programs are adopted.

Normative theorists have addressed the sensemaking that goes on in democracy's search for social betterment. For example, Hurley (1989) argues that democratic institutions are more likely than other arrangements to lead to "the truth about what should be done." And she also argues that democracy "is a way of realizing as well as discovering what ought to be the case" (p. 349). That is, democratic institutions provide a forum and a means for the collective struggle to make sense about ends (Which conditions are human needs requiring collective action?) and about means (Which policies and programs are best at reducing or preventing the problems?).

The institutions that aid sensemaking in democratic societies—and here we include evaluation—have been shown to serve a powerful role in debunking incorrect assumptions and opinions (Hurley, 1989). In fact, this sensemaking characteristic, with an openness to multiple iterations between explanatory accounts and evidence, is one of the distinct benefits of democracy. Evaluation delivers a potentially potent message that can help those in democratic institutions and the public make better sense about policies and programs. The actual potency of evaluation is determined by the attention its findings receive in other democratic institutions, including agencies, legislatures, and the press.

The Role of Values

As we have discussed, a complex road leads from individual needs to social betterment. To maximize evaluation's contribution to social betterment, evaluators need to design their studies in light of this complex pathway. In the next chapter, we discuss how considerations related to social betterment should drive the selection of an evaluation's purpose (which in turn affects the choice of inquiry methods). But there are also a number of more specific questions that must be answered in designing an evaluation. For example, in an evaluation designed to assess the relative impact of two alternative programs, evaluators and others need to decide what possible outcomes to measure. More generally, unless evaluators know the details of what social betterment is, how can they appraise whether some policy or program has moved the society toward betterment? Historically, evaluators dealt with this challenge through several approaches—most of them lacking.

Goals as the Guide

Many early evaluators sought to avoid the difficulty of defining social betterment with a sleight of hand. They professed, at least implicitly, what has since come to be called a *value-free* approach to evaluation (House, 1995; Shadish, Cook, & Leviton, 1991). Explicit program goals were converted to measurable objectives, these were tested, and then the program's performance was compared to the objectives. In this approach the evaluator's role was thought to be simply to test fact-based claims that originated in statements about program or policy goals; the complex issue of which outcomes should be selected for evaluation and why—that is, of what social betterment consists of—was left to others. The only language evaluators had to speak was the language of measurable objectives. By sidestepping this issue, early evaluators implicitly preempted debate on any additional effects or side effects that might bear on the worth of the program.

This value-free approach is, of course, sorely wanting. The issues addressed through any social program are not necessarily well represented by the needs mentioned explicitly or implicitly in the associated policy statements. In polycentric liberal democracies, policies are the product of compromises and partial consensus across conflicting and common interests, values, and objectives (Bohman & Rehg, 1997). The push and pull of competing interests can vest any single policy with numerous objectives that could be used to assess performance. Moreover, deliberative bodies often agree on a course of action without agreeing on underlying beliefs about the social problem. In legislating programs aimed at disadvantaged children, for instance, liberals may hope to avoid social conditions that they believe cause dysfunctions, whereas conservatives may want to increase individual responsibility and to "break the cycle" of welfare. Even when people define the root cause of a social problem differently, based on their different deep-seated ideological beliefs about human nature (Etzioni, 1995), deliberative bodies such as legislatures often come to sufficient agreement on a course of action to be followed. In the face of these disparate objectives, however, official policy statements are not likely to provide an adequate map of the issues that evaluation should explore.

In addition, policy proponents' public justifications for the policy may differ from their underlying private values. For example, publicly funded school vouchers, which are offered as a way of improving education, especially for disadvantaged students, are sometimes alleged to have other, less public spirited intentions. Certain objectives may be left out of formal policy statements to reduce controversy, whereas others may be assumed but unstated. Still others may be omitted due to limits on current understanding about how the program works. In addition, democratic institutions themselves, both political and administrative, also have their own needs, such as self-preservation, that can affect policy statements (Habermas, 1997). In some cases advocates may have acquired political support for a program by overselling what it might reasonably accomplish. In cases in which support is initially strong, program documents may set the sights low to increase the likelihood that the program will be found to be a success. Thus, for a variety of reasons, formal statements do not constitute the final word on needs, program goals, or values. Consequently, the old value-free approach to evaluation based on these statements does not well serve the cause of sensemaking for social betterment.

Relativism: Denying All Guides

For some evaluators the lack of formally derived definitions of goals, needs, or social betterment has spurred a move to relativism (Henry

& Julnes, 1998; Schwandt, 1997). Relativism renders the choice of values arbitrary because any claim about a program's goals is seen as being as worthwhile as the next. In principle, relativism opens the evaluator to discovery, allowing him or her to consider any possible outcome of the program, whether presented in formal policy statements or not. In principle, relativism also allows the evaluator to take the role of negotiator, facilitating discussion among those with different views. In practice, it appears, the relativistic stance inflates the role of the evaluator because he or she must arbitrarily select one group's values over others or somehow blend the values of several groups (Shadish, Cook, & Leviton, 1991).

More important, relativism is deeply unsatisfactory when the goal is social betterment. As a prominent commonsense realist has stated, "It is because there are real human needs, and not merely desires, that it makes sense to distinguish between better and worse values, and, for that matter, between better and worse knives" (Putnam, 1987, p. 79). The point is that everyday sensemaking is based on normative judgments. In contrast, relativism denies that some outcomes reflect real human needs whereas others do not. Relativism denies that some values are better than others. Although such denial may be a useful (though artificial) stance for a mediator, we believe it is unsatisfactory for an evaluator. Relativism cannot guide—indeed, cannot justify—efforts to assess merit and worth or to improve programs.

Of course, rejecting relativism does not answer the question of how evaluators should define betterment in the absence of some formal system. One approach, advocated by some influential evaluators, is to focus on needs.

Needs as the Guide

If human needs are the starting point of the path to social betterment, it might then seem that humans needs would also provide the criteria by which social betterment could be defined and programs could be evaluated. Michael Scriven has led the argument that needs should guide evaluation (for example, Scriven, 1991, 1993; also see Fournier, 1995). Although seemingly logical, this approach faces three significant problems: the difficulty of identifying and defining human needs, the reality that needs and values emerge over time, and the difficulty of assigning priorities among the panoply of needs that may be relevant to a given program or policy.

Let's consider each of these three problems, beginning with the difficulty of defining and selecting human needs. A need is typically defined as a gap between two states. For McKillip (1998), a need is the difference between the actual state of affairs for some group and the expectations people have about how things should be. But expectations are malleable and subjective. When needs are defined as the gap between current outcomes and expectations (or an ideal state), it may be impossible to differentiate the "real human needs" to which Putnam refers from mere wants. And something is amiss if an approach to evaluation cannot distinguish between a child's expressed need for a pony and his or her real need for food and shelter.

In an attempt to make the definition of needs more objective, some have tried to restrict the gaps to those involving either physical needs (Ramsey, 1992) or the maintenance of human functioning (Scriven & Roth, 1978). For example, Scriven (1993) says, "Needs are not the gap between the status quo and an ideal state but rather the gap between nothing and what is required to stave off malfunction" (p. 29). In principle, this definition of need allows one to separate needs from mere wants or subjective preferences. But this approach too is inadequate. Certainly, many real human needs, including food, shelter, and clothing, do have a biological base related to survival. Such *minimal* needs, if relevant to a program's activities, should not be ignored in evaluation. But as a society, we frequently accept definitions of the common good that go well beyond physical needs for survival, minimal functioning, or the avoidance of malfunction. We even welcome them into our basic covenants of democracy. For example, liberty for all, established in the equal protection clause of the Fourteenth Amendment, is probably not justified under a minimalist conception of needs. But as

Rawls (1997, p. 113) has stated, the Fourteenth Amendment is a necessary change to the original language of the Constitution and is based on the ideals of the Declaration of Independence ("life, liberty and the pursuit of happiness"). This nonmaterial and nonminimalist view of needs is not unique to the United States; consider, for example, the trilogy of "liberty, fraternity, and equality" that connects social policies in France to higher order public values (Habermas, 1996a).

In light of such aspirations, evaluators who defined needs in terms of the avoidance of malfunction would aim too low. Democracies should, for example, be able to support programs for talented youths in which the objective is to enhance positive functioning rather than avoid malfunction. Similarly, democracies should be able to make judgments that they want to prevent spousal or child abuse, or increase work satisfaction because these things are seen as good in themselves, whether the evidence suggests that they are or are not related to people's ongoing level of functioning. Although it would be tidy to restrict need to the gap between absolutely nothing and the physical necessities for survival, and thus to sidestep the role of values in determining needs, it does not correspond to the way democracies work. This is not how people make sense of needs and of the common good. Finally, a malfunction-based definition of need may simply mask the difficulties of operationalizing need, by hiding the fact that the term *malfunction* is also malleable. And who in a democracy is authorized to define and set the threshold for malfunction? Certainly not evaluators!

A second complexity is that perceived needs emerge over time—as societies evolve, people define additional outcomes as valued, as part of the common good, and as appropriate for social intervention. Needs emerge as people learn more. They emerge as a function of affluence (Yankelovich, 1994), which changes expectations and perceived possibilities. Unanticipated benefits or negative side effects or both can emerge once a program is operating, as has been the case for day-care and preschool programs. Although early evaluations focused on children's cognitive skills, it became

clear over time that policymakers and the public were also interested in the social outcomes, such as staying on grade and avoiding
assignment to special education (Barnett, 1995; Zigler & Muenchow, 1992). Research also began to show that cognitive skills were
not the only means by which the other valued outcomes were triggered (Entwhisle, 1995). As Dewey (1966) noted, needs are malleable and plastic, not fixed by some objective standard; they are in
some sense socially constructed. Putnam (1987) similarly indicates
that "human needs . . . do not preexist, that humanity is constantly
redesigning itself, and that we *create* needs" (p. 79). Because needs
are not fixed and instead emerge, it may be futile to expect that
needs will provide some preexisting, formal foundation for judgments about social betterment.

A third problem is that a focus on needs does not give evaluators a ready way to establish priorities across outcomes and criteria.
Which is the more important need that preschool might meet—
increases in traditional academic aptitudes, enhanced social development, reductions in special education assignments, or decreases
in the rate at which children are held back in grade? The outcomes
of interest may be in some sense incompatible with each other.
Needs themselves may sometimes be in conflict, as happened in a
support program for pregnant teens that met some of their material
needs but increased other needs by leading the teens' own mothers
to feel less responsible (Julnes, 1995). Focusing on needs does not
tell evaluators faced with a multitude of potential outcomes how
these outcomes should be enumerated, sorted out, and reduced to a
tractable number for an evaluation.

All these difficulties lead to a conundrum: if needs are at least
partially socially constructed, changing, and in conflict, then how
can betterment be established and pursued?

Stakeholder Input as the Guide

Many evaluators have tried to avoid this conundrum by incorpo-
rating the views of others in operationalizing social betterment. For

the most part, this has occurred under the rubric of stakeholder-based evaluation. In one of the earliest discussions of this approach, Bryk (1983) defined stakeholders as "the people whose lives are affected by the program under evaluation and the people whose decisions will affect the future of the program," stating that this approach "strengthens [stakeholders'] voice in determining the kind of evaluation that is conducted" (p. 1).

Stakeholder-based evaluation evolved in the main out of concern that evaluation results were not being used (Weiss, 1983). It was presumed that if stakeholders provided key input on values at the front end of an evaluation, they would take more "pride of ownership," the results would gain credibility and authority, and utilization would increase (Weiss, 1983). The desire was to give standing to those stakeholders who were influential in decision making (see Patton, 1997; Wholey, 1994) or to those who had previously had no voice in the formal policymaking processes (see House, 1995). Today the general notion that stakeholders should have a voice in evaluation is commonplace, but that belief has not resolved a host of questions. In a recent distillation of good evaluation practices prepared for the U.S. Centers for Disease Control and Prevention (CDCP), for example, the first step in the proposed evaluation framework was "involve stakeholders" (Toal, 1998). Still, the CDCP workgroup also felt the need to ask: "What is a stakeholder? . . . When should we involve a stakeholder? . . . How inclusive should we be? . . . Why should we involve stakeholders? . . . How should we involve stakeholders? . . . When should we involve stakeholders?" (Toal, 1998, pp. 12–15).

Despite such questions, stakeholder involvement is both appropriate and valuable, helping evaluators clarify multiple and overlapping values regarding programs and policies. Still, stakeholder approaches are limited. First, they typically do not differentiate mere stakeholder preferences from stronger needs or values—or even tell evaluators whether, why, or when such differentiation is important. Second, the nature of stakeholder involvement is often unclear, as indicated in the questions raised by the CDC workgroup.

Put differently, methods of stakeholder analysis have not been well articulated. Third, when the "usual suspects" are rounded up for stakeholder analysis, the broader public is usually omitted (Henry, 1996b; Henry & Julnes, 1998), yet the public plays a very important role in normative theories of democracy (Habermas, 1996a; Hurley, 1989) and effectively sets the direction for many changes in public policy over time (Monroe, 1998; Page & Shapiro, 1992; Stimson, 1998). Because social policies and programs are products of democratic governments, the public should have an important place in articulating the vision of social betterment used to guide evaluation.

By clarifying stakeholders' values about programs and policies, stakeholder involvement does assist evaluators to identify evaluation criteria. But there are also other methods that can strengthen the link between evaluation and betterment. These methods fall under the general rubric of values inquiry.

Values Inquiry as the Guide

Values inquiry refers to attempts to identify the values relevant to social programs and policies and to infuse them into evaluations. To better understand the rationale for values inquiry, consider again the concept of needs. As noted earlier, needs lie at the beginning of the path to social betterment. They are a gap in or a violation of an expectation as perceived by some individual or set of individuals. But needs, as we prefer to define them, are not the result of the violation of just *any* expectation. One might expect doctors to wear white or desks to have four legs or preschool boys to have shorter hair on average than preschool girls, but if these or similar expectations are violated, the result is not a need. Instead, needs are violations of expectations that are *based on values*. On one hand the expectation that doctors wear white or that boys have shorter hair than girls is not related to any deeply held value but is simply based on convention. On the other hand the nonminimal needs such as emotional development that have emerged for day-care and preschool programs are related to many people's deeply held values. Thus *the identification of needs occurs through a lens of values*.

By bringing values into the definition of needs, evaluators can better deal with the fact that needs emerge over time and that they can exceed some minimum required to avoid malfunction. Needs emerge as values change. Needs can exceed minimums when they reflect shared values. Bringing values into the picture also helps evaluators to sort out criteria when there are too many to examine, and to make sense of a program that meets one perceived need but creates another. When there are too many criteria to examine them all, the most important are the most highly valued. When a program meets one need but creates another, its judged worth depends in large part on the relative importance of the values associated with each need. In short, sensemaking about needs and about social betterment must be seen in relation to values.

What then are values? Values are beliefs, normative beliefs, that is, deeply held beliefs about how things should be. Although values may be deeply held and relatively enduring, values must also be subject to reason and changeable if democracies are to work and betterment is to occur (Richardson, 1997). Commonsense realists tell us that deciding issues as a function of values is a natural, everyday activity (Putnam, 1990). People go to work in the morning and back home to family at the end of the day largely because of values. Some parents choose not to go to work outside the home when their children are young. In the context of evaluating social programs and policies, the relevant values are beliefs about what society's responsibilities are and how government should act. For some people, for example, the belief that government should provide individuals with a decent standard of living after their retirement is a strongly held value.

Although it may be difficult to make the distinction in practice, in principle values can be differentiated from preferences, which are mere reflections of taste. Some people, for instance, like coffee better than tea. Earlier scholars expected values to differ from preferences by reflecting consistent systems of beliefs or by being ideologically constrained. However, this does not appear to be the case, at least for the public at large (Bishop, Tuchfarber, & Oldendick, 1986; Converse, 1964, 1971). Still, the normative component of values may be useful in differentiating values from preferences. Those who prefer coffee to tea rarely feel strongly that others *should* feel the same way or that government programs are *better* if they lead others also to prefer coffee. In addition, individuals may express their preferences strategically rather than revealing their real preferences. They may also be unaware of all available choices due to lack of forethought. These and related limits on preferences may generally be less severe for values (Elster, 1997).

Methods. As described earlier, stakeholder involvement is an important approach to evaluation, but one that is not without problems (Greene, 1988; Henry & Julnes, 1998; Henry, Dickey, & Areson, 1991; Mark & Shotland, 1985). One of these problems is that the public is usually neglected, even though the public is a stakeholder for any publicly funded program and even though the public effectively sets the direction for many changes in public policy over time. Values inquiry can open to the public a role in providing input. One way to do this (described further in Chapter Ten) is to carry out a survey in which members of public, like members of other more specialized stakeholder groups, report their priorities and values regarding a policy or program.

In addition to such methods as public opinion surveys and focus groups, formal theories can be employed to expose assumptions about values. Such formal theories are inadequate to guide social policy decisions or to set evaluation criteria, but they do provide a means for critiquing the values that have been (or have failed to be) operationalized in a program or policy (or an evaluation) (House, 1995). Yet another approach to values inquiry is to simulate the deliberative democratic process (House & Howe, 1999), gathering representatives of various stakeholder groups and the public for discussion in a variant on focus groups. These specific individual methods of values inquiry can also be used together. For example, the findings from set of surveys about values might be part of the input for a deliberative simulation. (The specific methods of values inquiry are discussed further in Chapter Ten.)

The methods of values inquiry generally focus on the values specific to a particular policy or program. The relatively common general values that typically apply across most programs and policies—values such as equality, justice, and fairness—also must be considered. Applying these values commonly suggests that the evaluation should examine the distribution of program outcomes and benefits. For example, individuals who hold a positive view of an educational intervention that has a beneficial overall effect might react negatively if the findings also showed that the intervention increased the achievement gap between students from high- and low-income families (Cook et al., 1975). A second general values issue likely to arise across programs is concern about human rights and dignity. For example, in the area of mental health services, commonly held values indicate it is important to minimize the use of seclusion, restraints, and atypical medications with undesirable side effects. People value fair and equal treatment of minorities, the disabled, and other groups, and violations of this value can influence the perceived success of a program—even a program that might, on average, have desirable effects. Third, the management of fiscal resources is also relevant to public support for programs and therefore to evaluations. Mismanagement of fiscal resources is not simply wasteful or fraudulent. It is a violation of the public trust—a violation of the honest and fair procedures that the public values (Lind & Tyler, 1998; Tyler & Lind, 1991). In short, analysis of values generally connected with social betterment suggests a set of criteria involving the equitable distribution of effects; human rights, dignity, and other program constraints; and fiscal management that is often important for evaluations.

Process Use. The notion of values inquiry also casts new light on what Patton (1997) has recently labeled the *process use* of evaluation.

Process use refers to the possibility that the procedures of carrying out an evaluation, and not just the evaluation findings, can influence sensemaking. From a sensemaking perspective, the existence of process use is not surprising: simply by framing questions, any effort at sensemaking can change the way people see the world around them (Weick, 1995). In particular the process and the act of selecting evaluation criteria can change the way that people look at a program, especially their views of what the program is meant to accomplish. From our perspective of assisted sensemaking, we see this not as a process use but as a finding that results from values inquiry, however informal. This is not just a matter of terminology. If these effects are construed as process use, evaluators may see them as incidental or perhaps as desirable side effects. If viewed as findings, however, they are subject to the standard criteria of rigor and bias minimization. Process use may not provide as much assistance as expected to sensemaking about social programs unless it is based on defensible procedures and solid findings.

Public Versus Private Policies and Programs. In the complex and lengthy path from needs to social betterment, democratic institutions arbitrate the cacophony of values and beliefs held by different individuals, social units, and organizations. Although simply recognizing this does not itself provide specific guidance to evaluators, it lays the groundwork for an evaluation approach. By assessing, simulating, or stimulating the natural valuation processes that occur in democratic institutions, including those processes that involve the media and public, values inquiry can aid in the processes of enumerating, sorting, and screening relevant values. Values inquiry is a way of probing the extant and emerging values in democratic deliberations for the purpose of selecting the effects that should be evaluation criteria. In this way, it provides an operational guide for evaluators, indicating how they should tentatively construe social betterment as they collect information that can be fed back to the actual democratic institutions that must seek it.

Admittedly, values inquiry is not a panacea. The potential exists for preferences to contaminate measures of values. Perhaps, though, this is not too severe a problem. In a democracies, even simple preferences can have some standing, assuming they are selected through proper procedures and leavened with the vision of the common good. Even with its limitations, values inquiry may be the best approach evaluations have to modeling the pathway to social betterment and collecting the information that will aid in sensemaking about social betterment.

Of course not all evaluation takes place in an explicitly democratic context. Of particular interest in the United States and Western Europe is the commonplace use of evaluation in the private sector. We believe the information presented in this chapter can be applied with very little translation by evaluators in much of the private sector. Consider such recent trends in business philosophy and management practice as the efforts to flatten the hierarchical structure in organizations, the initiatives to empower frontline employees as participants in decision making, the reconceptualization of consumers and the public as stakeholders, and the efforts to realize values other than the bottom line. Social trends suggest that the democratic model outlined earlier in this chapter may fit well with private sector organizations, at least those on the cutting edge of such practices.

Of course it is not clear what percentage of businesses fit this new model. Moreover, certain normative considerations that are inherent in modern democracies, such as each citizen's having a vote and a voice, are not necessarily intrinsic to private sector organizations. Private sector owners and managers, in principle, can deny the relevance of minority opinion. They can ignore conditions that workers see as problems as long as these do not violate laws or regulations or impair the bottom line. To the extent that private sector organizations have a traditional, hierarchical view of decision making, authority, and power, a focus on democratic social betterment and values inquiry may not fit well. Instead, evaluators may work more efficiently by focusing on Patton's notion (1997) of intended use by intended users. Nevertheless, the framework for evaluation practice described in the next three chapters should be helpful to private sector evaluators even in these circumstances.

Conclusion

The view of social betterment presented in this chapter can enhance understanding of the role of evaluation is society. It also has important implications for evaluation practice, as summarized in the following box.

The path to social betterment in democracies (and in philosophically similar private sector organizations) is complex and imperfect. Human needs are malleable. They reflect what people value, not simply the requirements of subsistence. Evaluation, accordingly, must be concerned with values, not simply with validating factual or causal claims. Evaluators then confront the issue of which values and whose values should guide the choice of criteria. The lack of a formal definition of needs has caused some to descend into relativism. Fortunately, there is an option between "nothing works" and "anything goes." The option is to recognize that democracy, through its processes and institutions, arbitrates value choices that are too complex to be formally derived. It is through such democratic processes that needs are legitimated, social problems identified, programs and policies selected, and the substance of social betterment defined. Values are intrinsic to these processes but are not necessarily apparent through natural valuation, so values inquiry has an important place in evaluation. Values inquiry can reduce bias in the selection of evaluation measures and increase the probability that the selected effects will reflect on salient issues of betterment.

The goal of social betterment also reminds us that human rights and dignity are important criteria for evaluating programs and policies, as are the distribution of effects and the proper handling of financial resources. The goal of social betterment allows evaluators

Selected Practice Implications of Social Betterment

1. Evaluations should be judged not in terms of utilization but in terms of
   a. How well the evaluator determines what information can best serve social betterment in context.
   b. What quality of information is obtained.
   c. How well the findings are disseminated to relevant democratic institutions, program personnel, and the public.

2. In both planning and reporting, the evaluator should have a broad view of who is involved, including the public.

3. In choosing criteria by which to judge a program, the evaluator should be aware that
   a. Program goals are generally not adequate.
   b. Systematic values inquiry is preferred.
   c. Circumstances may reduce the need for systematic values inquiry, if there is consensus that a particular set of outcomes well represents the needs a program is meant to address.

4. Social betterment should drive the choice of an evaluation's purpose.

5. When assessing merit and worth, evaluators should go beyond examining program effects and also study the way these effects are distributed, and how well the program satisfies valued procedural issues including human rights and dignity.

to acknowledge the relevance of those directly affected by a program and at the same time avoid the trap of creating a special interest group that sets the evaluation agenda. A concern for betterment also reminds us that utilization is not sufficient as a motivation for evaluation. Use may be most likely when the values that underlie the evaluation reflect the interests of those in positions of power. These are the individuals who can most readily use evaluation results. But they are not the only evaluation audience through which democratically based social betterment occurs. By using values inquiry as a guide in evaluation planning, evaluators can design evaluations highly relevant to social betterment. This social betterment is the ultimate end of evaluation, and informing democratic institutions is the means to achieve it.

3

Defining Evaluation Purposes

Evaluation exists to improve the way that programs and policies function by providing information that can be used in democratic institutions to advance social betterment. If an evaluation is to aid in sensemaking about a program or policy, a series of decisions must be made about how the evaluation will be structured and carried out. These decisions will in turn affect the extent to which the evaluation provides useful information for improving, overseeing, selecting, or understanding public policies and programs. In the previous chapter, we discussed the rationale for using values inquiry as a guide for many key evaluation decisions, such as the selection of outcomes to measure. In this chapter we address another overarching concern, the selection of the general purpose of the evaluation. Social betterment is the ultimate purpose, but various types of evaluation have the potential to support this overall goal. Therefore evaluators should also consider more immediate reasons why people engage in sensemaking about policies and programs; we call these reasons evaluation *purposes*.

Four Purposes of Evaluation

We identify four primary purposes for which evaluation findings can be employed: assessment of merit and worth, program and organizational improvement, oversight and compliance, and knowledge development. The *ultimate* purpose in carrying out most evaluations is to improve social conditions, but social betterment is a distal objective, mediated by democratic institutions and many interests and constituencies. More immediate, more proximal purposes need to be identified to drive the design and conduct of evaluation toward this ultimate goal. Identification of the immediate purpose can help evaluators make decisions about an evaluation's specific form.

An evaluation may be directed toward one of these purposes or (especially if it has a large budget and long time frame) multiple purposes. Indeed, of the skills that evaluators and evaluation program administrators can develop, among the most valuable is the ability to create an evaluation that can serve more than one purpose well (a process we discuss in some detail in Chapter Five). At the same time, evaluators need to clearly distinguish these four purposes. Most evaluation studies serve primarily one or two of them because attempting to do everything with limited resources can lead to doing nothing well, and because trade-offs among the purposes must often be considered if multipurpose evaluations are to be successful.

Although we do not emphasize it here, we recognize that motives other than those implied by the four purposes can also underlie an evaluation. For example, administrators may solicit an evaluation because they are required to do so by legislative mandate or by external funding agencies. Moreover, the motives underlying an evaluation are sometimes less than pure. Evaluations are sometimes commissioned to delay a decision, to duck responsibility for making a decision, or to improve public relations for a weak program (Weiss, 1998)—or even to try to torpedo a program (Suchman, 1967). Our focus is not on these uses of evaluation as a political tactic. Instead, we focus on four legitimate purposes to which the sensemaking of evaluation can contribute. Careful planning in light of these four purposes should maximize an evaluation's ability to contribute to sensemaking. This can hold true even when the evaluation originated as a political tactic.

Distinguishing the Purposes

Evaluators have long recognized that evaluation can serve different purposes. Scriven (1967) made the now classic distinction between formative and summative evaluations. *Formative* evaluations are those designed to facilitate program improvement, whereas *summative* evaluations are those intended to provide a definitive judgment of program or policy's merit and worth. Formative evaluation is exemplified by midterm course evaluations that provide feedback about things a teacher might do differently to try to improve a class. Summative evaluation is illustrated by *Consumer Reports*–type findings that offer a bottom-line judgment on the merits of some product.

Since Scriven introduced the distinction between formative and summative evaluation, evaluation scholars have identified a third possible purpose of evaluation, knowledge development (see especially Patton, 1997, on three uses of evaluation findings, and Chelimsky, 1997, on three perspectives on evaluation). When knowledge development is its primary purpose, an evaluation focuses on developing or testing (or both developing and testing) general propositions about such matters as the causes of social problems, the solutions to social problems, and the processes of policymaking, even though the knowledge may not directly improve or judge the specific program or policy being studied. Although some consensus may be developing among evaluation scholars in defining these three purposes of evaluation, there is enough divergence in previous definitions to lead us to suggest four purposes rather than three, adding oversight and compliance as a separate category.

The Four Purposes Illustrated

During the 1990s, so-called boot camps became a popular alternative to prison and other criminal sentences in many U.S. states, especially for juvenile offenders (Austin, Jones, & Boylard, 1993). Boot camps are modeled after military training centers. The underlying rationale is that the hard work of the boot camp will decrease participants' subsequent motivation to commit crime and will also improve their personal skills, which will in turn lead to enhanced success in a life without crime. As a way of understanding the four evaluation purposes, consider the kinds of questions that interested parties might ask after the first states have implemented boot camps.

Some questions will deal with the *merit and worth* of boot camps. Legislators, who must decide whether to renew and expand the program, will want to know: What are the effects of the boot camps? In particular, do they seem to reduce recidivism more than traditional sentences? Considering their costs, are boot camps worth it? Answers to these questions are likely to be important also for legislators in states that are considering boot camps, for the public, and for judges who are sentencing eligible defendants. Most of these groups will also want to know: Are the effects larger for some groups than for others? Are there different types of boot camps, and if so, is one type better than the others? Defendants, their families, and their advocates (for example, the American Civil Liberties Union) may also want to know whether the rights of those assigned to boot camps are violated.

Other questions will relate to *program and organizational improvement*. These will probably be of primary concern to boot camp managers and staff as they consider ways to do their jobs better. But these questions will also, though perhaps less directly, be of interest to all others who want the program to be a success. What are the program's apparent strengths and weaknesses? Are there impediments that can be removed? Do some components, such as physical training, seem more important than others? Does implementation follow generally accepted practices or conform to best practices (if such standards exist)? Are any actions needed to increase participation (such as educating judges about this sentencing option), to improve staff skills (such as training staff on the developmental needs of adolescent offenders), to modify eligibility criteria for participation (such as excluding violent offenders), or to internally reallocate program resources (such as increasing psychological services and eliminating costly Outward Bound sessions)? What additional information do program managers and staff need to improve operations?

The purpose of *oversight and compliance* will also generate questions. These will be of special interest to those with specific responsibility for ensuring that the program is operating according to its mandates, such as agency directors and legislators. The public and the press may also want to know about this. The general question for this purpose is: Does the program comply with statutes, rules, regulations, and other mandates for its operations? A variety of specific questions may follow. Do those referred to boot camps all meet the specified eligibility criteria? Have staff been screened and trained as they are supposed to be? Are safety and health requirements followed?

Still other questions fall under the rubric of *knowledge development*. Some of these will be related to boot camps only by convenience. For example, a criminal justice researcher may try to test labeling theory as it applies to recidivism. A methodologist might wonder if she can illustrate a new statistical procedure with data from the boot camp evaluation. Other knowledge development questions may be more directly related to boot camps: Can one develop a well-supported theory of boot camps as a treatment alternative? Does the boot camp experience contribute to a broader theory of the causes and treatment of criminal behavior? Can it lead to better ways to think about what works in criminal justice?

Many important questions will fall at the intersection of two or more evaluation purposes. In particular, the question of why the program works relates both to the assessment of merit and worth and to knowledge development and may also be important for program improvement. Before getting to more complicated questions such as this, it is important to better understand each of the four individual purposes.

The Four Purposes Defined

In this section we address the characteristics of the four purposes in greater detail.

Assessment of Merit and Worth. The evaluation purpose of assessment of merit and worth refers to the development of warranted judgments about the effects and other valued characteristics of a program or policy—and thus about a program or policy's value. By *effects* (or *outcomes*, a term we use synonymously), we mean the actual consequences of a program or policy, intended or unintended, positive or negative. For example, in an evaluation of a prekindergarten program, one might look for any effects on children's social skills, on their school readiness, and on parents' educational aspirations for their children, to mention but a few. Our definition also refers to *other valued characteristics*. The merit and worth of a program depends in part on whether it safeguards participants' (and others') rights and liberties. Programs that discriminate in hiring, violate privacy, or degrade participants are less meritorious and worthy than programs that do not. Although these other valued characteristics could conceivably be treated as effects, we prefer to highlight them separately because evaluators who focus primarily on effects often neglect to investigate practices that might indicate incursions into democratically established and protected rights.

We also distinguish between merit and worth. *Merit*, as we use the term, refers to the quality of a program or policy in terms of performance, and *worth* refers to the value this performance brings to the larger social good (Patton, 1997; Scriven, 1993). Consider an AIDS/HIV intervention. Its merit might consist of its success in reducing risky behaviors such as needle sharing or unprotected sex. The discovery of a vaccine for HIV would not necessarily alter the merit of the program—which might still function well at reducing the same behaviors—but it would presumably reduce the worth or value of the program to society.

As we mentioned, assessment of merit and worth corresponds to what Scriven (1967) called summative evaluation. Although it is now common to use the phrase *determination of merit and worth* in describing this evaluation purpose, we prefer the term assessment of merit and worth. The distinction is not trivial. *Determination* implies a role for evaluation that cannot be justified. It suggests coming to a fixed answer or settling a question. The very origins of the word suggest *coming to an end*. In evaluation, these connotations are unfortunate and undesirable. For one thing the limits of evaluation argue against using a term that implies finality. The history of evaluation practice teaches that the criteria for merit and worth can be slippery and subject to change—and that this can be a good thing (consider our example showing that the criteria used to judge preschool programs have expanded over time; Barnett, 1995). And even if the criteria for merit and worth were stable and well known, evaluation methods would remain fallible. In addition, evaluation information is not the end of the process of judging merit and worth. Although evaluation can provide assessment information that is useful to democratic institutions as they make sense about policies and programs, as they define merit and judge worth, this is very different from expecting evaluation to *determine* merit and worth (see also Stake, 1997).

Program and Organizational Improvement.   When the evaluation purpose is program and organizational improvement, efforts are made to provide timely feedback designed to modify and enhance program operations. Formative evaluation (Scriven, 1967), as we mentioned, is the precursor term. When an evaluation is aimed at program improvement, it is likely to provide information about program effects and especially processes. Relative to an assessment of merit and worth, this evaluation is likely to have less concern with methodological rigor and validity and more concern with timeliness of information. Also, feedback is likely to be directed to program staff, the individuals who will make adjustments in program operations (see, for example, Wholey, 1983).

There are various models of program improvement. Following Scriven (1993), one approach to program improvement involves a comparatively casual and swift assessment of merit and worth, with the results presented to program staff who can then use this feedback to establish the need for program modifications. The metaphor Scriven suggests (1991, p. 169), which he credits to Bob Stake, is of the cook tasting the soup before the guests arrive and making timely adjustments. Another approach is analogous to the method of the auto mechanic, who does not judge the value of a car relative to alternative cars or other means of transportation but instead tinkers with the carburetor to try to enhance this car's performance. This type of improvement-oriented evaluation often focuses on identifying program elements that are not meeting expectations, examining alternatives, and choosing one of these alternatives. In a third approach to program improvement evaluation, program operations are compared to some supposed standard of best practices. In yet another approach, program staff are helped to a common understanding of the program and its desired outcomes through *evaluability assessment* (Rutman, 1980), the construction of program theory (Bickman, 1987), or a form of *developmental evaluation* (Patton, 1997). The evaluator's hope is that the new, shared view of the program will lead to better program services. In whatever form it takes, program improvement evaluation often provides information on current operations, outputs, and outcomes.

Chelimsky (1997) points out that some evaluators do not focus so much on improving a specific program as on improving organizational capacity to set policies, design and administer programs, and evaluate. We see this as similar to program improvement; the difference is that the objective of improvement is addressed from a broader, systems perspective. Thus program and organizational improvement evaluation includes much of what Patton (1997) refers to as developmental evaluation. It also addresses concerns about sustainability, an issue that arises with some frequency in so-called developing countries, where the question is whether service delivery organizations have the infrastructure to deliver services in the absence of continuing external support (Bamberger, 2000). (In further discussions of this purpose, we occasionally use *program improvement* as shorthand for program and organizational improvement.)

Oversight and Compliance. Evaluations with the purpose of evaluating oversight and compliance estimate the extent to which a program meets specified expectations such as the directives of statutes, regulations, or other mandates, including requirements to reach specified levels of performance. Traditionally, oversight and compliance evaluations focus on such issues as whether the program services being delivered are the services that have been authorized (McLaughlin, 1975), whether program clients meet established eligibility criteria (U.S. General Accounting Office, 1998b), or what percentage of the target population is being served (U.S. General Accounting Office, 1998a). Such evaluations can help meet program sponsors', funders', and the public's need to oversee the program and hold staff and administrators accountable. Recently, measurement of performance indicators has been more widely adopted as means of extending oversight from strictly procedural issues to outputs (such as the number of clients served) and outcomes (such as clients' performance) (Newcomer, 1997). For example, several U.S. states have set standards for public schools to meet, and hold the schools accountable for reaching them.

Oversight and compliance evaluations can indicate whether a program is meeting formal expectations and, if they have an outcome monitoring component, can also show what level participants are achieving on outcome measures. Still, such evaluations do not in and of themselves give a strong warranted assessment of merit and worth. They typically do not sort out the extent to which the program is responsible for the outcomes. Thus outcomes might be at a desirable level due to an improved external environment, such as a growing economy, rather than due to program effectiveness. Conversely, a program may operate in full accord with legislation and regulations and still not be effective.

Knowledge Development. Knowledge development refers to efforts to discover and test general theories and propositions about social processes and mechanisms as they occur in the context of social policies and programs. For some scholars, the world of social policies and programs is a valuable laboratory for developing and testing hypotheses and theories. The researcher interested in knowledge development may not be concerned with the specific program or policy per se but may be using it primarily as a venue that allows the investigation of some disciplinary research question. Alternatively, knowledge development can be a valuable adjunct to other evaluation purposes and can in some cases make major contributions to social betterment.

Knowledge development can focus on a wide variety of research questions involving large social science theories or on *small theories* of local programs (Lipsey, 1993), depending on the researcher's interests. For example, scholars of public administration might use evaluation work to develop general theoretical propositions about the implementation of social programs (Scheirer, 1987). Other scholars might develop a general classification system to describe the different types of services delivered in some area of human services, such as assisted living programs for the elderly (for example, Conrad & Buelow, 1990). Yet others might attempt to develop a theory of the treatment types that are effective for different types of clients in a program area, as Lipsey (1997) has in his meta-analysis of juvenile justice evaluations. Or an evaluation might allow a novel use of some research methodology, as in the use by Henry and Gordon (2000) of independent sample surveys in an interrupted time series design to evaluate the effectiveness of a public information campaign.

Evaluation Traditions

The four evaluation purposes have evolved in association with various general traditions in the field of program and policy evaluation. The assessment of merit and worth is associated with an evaluation tradition that Shadish, Cook, and Leviton (1991) call the *manipulable solution theory of practice*. With prominent advocates such as Donald Campbell (1969b), this tradition has dominated much of the modern history of evaluation. It focuses on identifying programs and policies that work, typically by estimating the effect of the program or policy on outcomes considered to be important. One example of evaluation in this tradition comes from the early 1980s, when the city of Minneapolis was the site of an evaluation of a revision in police policy about domestic assaults, that is, fights between husbands and wives (or other domestic partners). Standard policy at the time was to end the fight and separate the spouses but not to arrest the assailant. A randomized experiment, a potentially powerful method for causal analysis, was carried out to see the effects of an alternative policy (Sherman & Berk, 1984). When a domestic assault meeting eligibility requirements occurred, the investigating police either followed the standard policy, or arrested the assailant, depending on a random schedule. Rates of reassault were estimated from police records and from interviews with victims. The results of the evaluation favored the new policy of arresting domestic assailants (however, this result has not replicated in follow-up evaluations at other sites) (Sherman, Smith, Schmidt, & Rogan, 1992). In terms of evaluation purposes, what is noteworthy is that this evaluation was carried out to try to judge the relative merit of competing policies.

The evaluation purpose of oversight and compliance is associated with a less visible but still important tradition, epitomized in much of the work carried out by the U.S. General Accounting Office (GAO) on behalf of Congress, which is interested in assessing the extent to which policies and programs follow the directives of statutes, regulations, or other mandates. One example is a study Congress asked GAO to conduct on the earned income credit (EIC), a tax credit available to employed persons who meet established low-income guidelines, with different eligibility cutoffs depending on family size. A stated objective of the EIC is to provide an incentive for work rather than welfare. Potential questions of oversight and compliance involve the percentage of eligible taxpayers who apply for the EIC, the pattern of taxpayers' EIC use over time, and the changes in income and other outcomes that follow that use (U.S. General Accounting Office, 1997).

The purpose of program and organizational improvement is associated with several evaluation camps that fall within what Shadish, Cook, and Leviton (1991) call the *stakeholder service theory of practice*. One important version of this approach is captured in the work of Wholey and his colleagues (Wholey, 1979, 1983; Wholey, Scanlon, Duffy, Fukumoto, & Vogt, 1970). Wholey emphasizes the use of evaluation to guide program managers' efforts to administrate and revise programs. He focuses on program managers and staff as a stakeholder group that can deliver incremental improvements, and designs monitoring systems that can help them accomplish this. Another stakeholder service approach is reflected in the work of Patton (1997) (discussed in Chapter One). Patton's *utilization-focused evaluation* is well encapsulated in its motto, "intended use by intended users." Patton discusses how to identify the key stakeholders for an evaluation and determine their key information needs. Success in evaluation, from this perspective, lies in providing the information that satisfies those needs. Although in principle this could involve any of the four evaluation purposes, it appears that in practice stakeholders usually tell utilization-focused evaluators that they want program and organizational improvement. Similarly, the more recent trend of *empowerment evaluation* appears to consist mostly of efforts to teach program staff (and perhaps participants) to collect information for program and organizational improvement.

This purpose is exemplified by one component of an evaluation (Affholter, 1994) of the Intensive Crisis Counseling Program (ICCP) in Florida. In the ICCP, professional counselors under contract with the program offered intensive, short-term, home-based family counseling, with the expressed goal of reducing abuse, neglect, and placements in emergency shelters and foster care. During the evaluation, outcome data, such as the number of families remaining intact, were examined for each counselor. Staff then investigated counselors who had poorer outcomes. They discovered, for example, that one contractor had stopped doing service delivery, beyond the initial assessment, in the families' homes. By leading to changes in the way services were delivered, the evaluation was used for the purpose of program improvement.

Finally, the knowledge development purpose is associated with what Shadish, Cook, and Leviton (1991) call the *generalizable explanation theory of practice*. This approach, advocated by Cronbach (1982), focuses on developing explanations about why programs and policies have their effects, under the assumption that such explanations are useful to program planners and staff. One general offshoot of this approach emphasizes program theory (for example, Bickman, 1990; Chen, 1990; also see Pawson & Tilley, 1997). The knowledge development purpose is also associated with the tradition present in a number of different academic disciplines of using program and policy evaluation as a vehicle for testing theoretically relevant hypotheses. The knowledge development tradition is illustrated by Lipsey and Wilson's summary (1993) of the results of 302 meta-analyses of the efficacy of psychological, educational, and behavioral treatments. This study was done largely to assess the accuracy of the common claim that when it comes to social interventions, "nothing works" (for example, Martinson, 1974). Each of the 302 meta-analyses had statistically combined a large number of individual evaluations in some treatment area, resulting in an *effect size* that would indicate in statistical terms how much better an intervention group did than a control or comparison group. Lipsey and Wilson found a striking tendency for positive average effects. Eighty-five percent of the meta-analyses had effect sizes of 0.20 or larger. Lipsey and Wilson's review leads more to the conclusion that "everything works" rather than that "nothing works." At least it appears to be the case that there is an average positive effect for most interventions that persist long enough to be the subject of a meta-analysis. Lipsey and Wilson also attempted to contribute to knowledge development in the area of evaluation methodology by examining whether different types of research designs were associated with smaller or larger effects. In terms of purpose, the point is that although Lipsey and Wilson's study is based on evaluations, it was not designed to directly aid in overseeing, improving, or assessing the merit and worth of any particular policy or program. Instead, it was a general attempt at knowledge development.

Table 3.1 summarizes some key attributes of the four evaluation purposes, presenting the focus, a typical methodology, the usual audience, and associated evaluation traditions for each. The fact that for each purpose, different traditions have evolved and experienced long-term survival suggests that each purpose has value for assisting natural sensemaking, at least in certain conditions. From a commonsense realist perspective, which gives conceptual standing to lessons from practice (Putnam, 1990), this association between evaluation purposes and long-term practice traditions helps justify our distinction between the four purposes.

The fact that different traditions have evolved in association with the different purposes also suggests a possible problem. As Chelimsky (1997) argues, because they come from various traditions, evaluators differ sharply in their beliefs about the general purpose of evaluation. Some evaluators believe that generally the assessment of merit and worth is *the* purpose; others believe that generally program and organizational improvement is preferred; and so on. We contend, however, that the purpose(s) of an evaluation should be determined, not by an evaluator's predisposition, but by the evaluation's potential contribution to social betterment. This leads to the question of which of the four purposes best contributes to sensemaking support for democratic institutions and processes, and under what conditions.

Social Betterment and the Selection of Evaluation Purpose

As we have stated, the field of evaluation is premised on the belief that evaluations can contribute to social betterment, primarily by providing information that can support the deliberations, choices,

TABLE 3.1. Some Key Attributes of the Four Purposes of Evaluation.

	Assessing Merit and Worth	Program and Organizational Improvement	Oversight and Compliance	Knowledge Development
Focus	Support of judgment about value	Enhancement of program services	Compliance with formal expectations	Generation or testing of social science theory
Typical mode of inquiry	Causal analysis and values inquiry	Description, with timely observation and feedback	Description, including program activities and outcomes	Classification and causal analysis
Usual audience	Democratic institutions, the public	Administrators and program staff	Legislators, funders, the public	Social scientists, "conventional wisdom"
Evaluation tradition	Campbell's experimenting society (1969); the manipulable solution approach (see Shadish, Cook, & Leviton, 1991)	Wholey (1983) and feedback to managers; much of the stakeholder service approach (see Shadish, Cook, & Leviton, 1991)	GAO and state legislative oversight agencies	Cronbach (1982) and Chen (1990) program theory; the generalizable explanation approach (see Shadish, Cook, & Leviton, 1991)

and actions taken in democratic institutions. Recall also that evaluation's role is not limited to public deliberative processes such as debates in legislatures. Evaluation can be also influential in the administrative units that carry out policies and programs. Administration by public employees is an important part of the social betterment process, and in some ways it has the most proximate influence on social problems. With this in mind, in this section we consider the general conditions under which each of the four evaluation purposes might best aid sensemaking needs and capacities in a democracy. In other words, we discuss the function that each evaluation purpose serves. (In Chapter Five, we discuss more nuanced, contextual factors that can influence the selection of an evaluation's purpose.)

Assessment of Merit and Worth

The fundamental rationale for assessing merit and worth is that doing so contributes to democratic deliberations about which major course of action to choose. Information about merit and worth helps when a decision must be made about adopting a new program or about selecting one of a set of alternative policies or about continuing an existing program or policy. How can democracies make informed choices about charter schools, welfare reform, and so on without information about merit? Of course decisions can be made without evaluation findings, and evaluation findings may not determine decisions. But the decisions are necessarily less well informed, less reasoned, without evidence of merit and worth. An assessment of merit and worth thus represents the highest contribution evaluation can make when democracies face a major fork in the road about which (if any) policy or program to adopt or drop. Given the centrality of democratic deliberations and choices to the social betterment process, and given the potential contribution of assessments of merit and worth to these deliberations, it is not surprising that many evaluators hold this purpose in high regard. Some even *define* evaluation solely in terms of assessing merit and worth (for example, Scriven, 1993).

In light of this key role for evaluations that assess merit and worth, why would one ever carry out an evaluation that emphasized another purpose? The primary reason is that the times when institutions confront major policy course changes are relatively rare. Democratic institutions have limits on their ability to deal with pressing public issues (Hilgartner & Bosk, 1988). Legislatures can consider only so many major policy initiatives at once. Administrators cannot drop their focus on service delivery to reconsider all possible policy prescriptions. The media cannot keep the public informed if policies on transportation, education, the environment, health care, Social Security, employment, and training are all being considered for wholesale change at once. At best, a small number of major changes can be at the forefront of the public agenda at any time (McCombs & Zhu, 1995). But this does not mean that the remaining policy and program areas ought to go without evaluation. Instead, other evaluation purposes should rise to the fore, especially in the short run.

A second reason for giving priority to other evaluation purposes is that the timing may in other ways be bad for the assessment of merit and worth. Perhaps not enough is known yet about how to deal with a social problem or about how to get a program running smoothly. Or perhaps a good deal is known, but a number of compelling assessments of a program's merit and worth already exist. In either case the relative value of evaluations with other purposes would increase, at least for a while.

Program and Organizational Improvement

When program and organizational improvement is the primary evaluation purpose, the evaluation usually emphasizes timely feedback to modify and enhance program operations. This purpose of evaluation can serve social betterment by improving the options available for democratic consideration and selection. Under what conditions does program improvement best serve social betterment, and conversely, when can program improvement be a *disservice*? On the one hand, program improvement efforts should be avoided when they will preclude the timely assessment of merit and worth needed for reasoned deliberative choices. For example, advocates of Project DARE, a drug abuse resistance education program, have tried to fight off evidence that the program is ineffective by contending that they have continued to improve it (Gorman, 1998). Of course, programs can and should be improved, and it is appropriate for democratic decisions to be revised when evidence of merit and worth changes. But in the case of DARE, our sense is that claims of program improvement activity were used, perhaps disingenuously, in an attempt to fend off persuasive evidence that the program does not reduce substance abuse.

On the other hand, if program improvement work can be done *prior* to an assessment of merit and worth, social betterment is doubly served. Evaluation resources are often sufficient for this work because the front-end work for the assessment of merit and worth— planning, reviewing documents, constructing a program theory, testing instruments— can do double duty as the foundation for program improvement. Such sequencing of purposes, which has been built into some evaluation funding, can also help evaluators avoid the sin of premature assessment of merit and worth (see, for example, Sanders, 1999). Currently, unfortunately, evaluations conducted to stimulate program improvement are often not followed by assessments of merit and worth (Rog, 1985).

Program improvement also serves social betterment when, following an assessment of merit and worth, a program is adopted in another jurisdiction and steps are then taken to improve it. For example, a natural experiment (Rog, 1994) might be undertaken to investigate whether outcomes differ as a function of variations in services across sites of group delivery. If some service packages or types of service delivery are found to be more effective, they can be encouraged or mandated. Thus program effects may be enhanced at a time when it is unlikely that the program itself will be seriously scrutinized for termination or replacement.

Oversight and Compliance

When an evaluation focuses on the purpose of oversight and compliance, it assesses the extent to which a program meets formal expectations found in statutes, regulations, or other mandates. Oversight and compliance studies tend to focus on the fidelity with which a program is implemented. Fidelity here often includes both adherence to specific program mandates and to externally established procedures, such as generally accepted accounting practices or requirements for equal opportunity in personnel decisions. Thus this purpose often motivates performance measurement and monitoring. In general, oversight is an important function especially for legislatures, courts, and higher administrative levels, which are supposed to ensure that policies are carried out properly and, increasingly, that outcomes are at expected levels. One-shot performance reviews and ongoing monitoring inform those with responsibility for oversight whether a policy is on track or needs some tweaking, without requiring the intense scrutiny of an assessment of merit and worth and without consideration of wholesale changes.

Under what conditions does evaluation best serve deliberative democracy by emphasizing oversight and compliance? First, evaluations with this purpose contribute well when some democratically selected program or policy has documented merit and worth and its effectiveness could suffer from poor compliance to established procedures. Consider programs to immunize poor children against childhood diseases. The effectiveness of vaccination against childhood diseases is well established. Program failure to comply with the rules and regulations could reduce program effectiveness, scope, and efficiency. Accordingly, oversight and compliance appears to be precisely the right evaluation purpose.

Second, there is social value in avoiding waste and fraud in social programs and in having the dictates of law and other democratically established mandates followed. Careful stewardship of financial resources is obviously important. Of course evaluations focusing on finances are often conducted by experts such as auditors who are in fields closely related to evaluation (Wisler, 1996). Other important mandates include, but are not limited to, protecting individual rights, providing equal opportunities to members of protected groups, and avoiding services that unnecessarily threaten clients' or others' dignity.

Finally, evidence from oversight and compliance evaluations may be valuable when combined with other evaluation purposes, especially the assessment of merit and worth. A good assessment of merit and worth that produces negative findings may indicate poor implementation rather than a flawed program theory. Evidence that the program was implemented as directed may be collected as part of an assessment of merit and worth, but it may also come from a prior or concurrent oversight and compliance evaluation.

Knowledge Development

Knowledge development—the effort to construct and test theories and propositions about social processes and mechanisms as they occur in the context of social policies and programs—can aid in the long journey to social betterment. It can contribute to general deliberations about social problems and their proposed solutions— for example, by increasing people's understanding of the dynamics of the population in need and by explaining the underlying mechanisms by which programs and policies operate. Knowledge development is especially likely to move to the fore when very little is known about a social problem. And evaluators should be vigilant in looking for other opportunities to contribute to the knowledge base. Nevertheless, knowledge development should most often be a secondary rather than a primary evaluation purpose. First, in many cases, scholars in sociology, psychology, political science, education, health, and so on are in the best position to develop and test fundamental theories about human needs and social problems. Also, funds other than those budgeted for evaluation are often available for knowledge development.

In evaluation, there is special value to those forms of knowledge development that complement another evaluation purpose. In particular, the exploration of underlying mechanisms and testing for moderators of program effects is likely to add greatly to an assessment of merit and worth (Mark, Henry, & Julnes, 1998; Pawson & Tilley, 1997). Moreover, knowledge gained from experience with evaluation can lead to general propositions about obstacles to successful program implementation (see, for example, St. Pierre & Kaltreider, 1997). At the same time, thoughtful judgment is needed to ensure that adding a knowledge development component does not seriously impede the primary evaluation purpose, which presumably has a more direct linkage to social betterment.

There is a potentially important instance in which knowledge development is likely to be the primary evaluation purpose. Some evaluations that look like assessments of merit and worth may in reality be better thought of as knowledge development. As noted previously, assessments of merit and worth serve democratic institutions that must make major program or policy choices, but sometimes evaluation is mandated when no such choice is forthcoming, perhaps for symbolic or political reasons. Some evaluators, especially those with academic research interests, may be inclined to do an evaluation that looks like an assessment of merit and worth even when no one is likely to be listening to the results in the immediate future. This choice is at best questionable when another purpose, such as program improvement, could be of benefit. But this approach can serve knowledge development, with the results enlightening discussions somewhere down the road or contributing to a subsequent meta-analysis designed to identify and explain the best program strategies for social betterment (Lipsey, 1997).

Exhibit 3.1 summarizes the generic ways in which social betterment drives the choice of evaluation purpose.

Relationships Among Purposes

So far this chapter has discussed the four purposes individually, but the reality of their application is far more complex. Metaphorically, evaluators might think of evaluation purposes as defining where they want to go in a dark room, thereby determining where they want to point a flashlight. If they happen to possess a powerful flashlight, which they point at a particular target, they are likely to illuminate some of the other objects in the room. Likewise, evaluations

EXHIBIT 3.1. How Social Betterment Drives Evaluation Purpose.

Social Betterment Consideration	Evaluation Purpose
• Democratic deliberations are needed about what course of action to take (for example, choosing a policy to meet a newly legitimized need or choosing between alternative programs).	→ Assessment of merit and worth
• A program of known worth could suffer from poor compliance. • A program might not be meeting established expectations and mandates or exercising sound financial stewardship. • It is necessary to rule out failure to implement as the explanation of failure to produce outcomes.	→ Oversight and compliance
• Efforts to enhance program operations will not inappropriately delay or invalidate assessment of merit and worth. • The program is generally judged of high worth and is not likely to undergo wholesale change.	→ Program and organizational improvement
• Mechanisms or moderators can be studied and will add to an assessment of merit and worth. • Learning that will contribute to the broader field can be added at low marginal cost to achieving other purposes.	→ Knowledge development

that emphasize one purpose may indirectly contribute to another. In addition, a single evaluation can combine two or more purposes, and a series of evaluations can be planned to address different purposes.

Contributions of One Evaluation Purpose to Another

An evaluation that directly emphasizes one purpose may also indirectly serve other purposes. For example, a credible assessment of merit and worth will often also indirectly stimulate program improvement. If program staff are simply informed about how well or (especially) how poorly a program is doing, this often leads them to seek ways of doing better. Although probably less frequent in practice, an assessment of merit and worth can also have spin-off benefits for the two other purposes. It can indirectly contribute to knowledge development, as illustrated by Lipsey and Wilson's synthesis (1993) of meta-evaluations. And it can sometimes help satisfy the concerns that motivate an oversight and compliance evaluation. If it is clear that a program effectively reduces the social problem it was designed to address, the need to question its compliance with service delivery guidelines may be reduced.

Evaluations focused on oversight and compliance may also partially illuminate the other purposes. When a right way to carry out program activities is known, the findings of an oversight and compliance evaluation, showing that a program is being implemented incorrectly, may contribute to program improvement. In addition, when an oversight and compliance evaluation examines whether a program violates individual rights or involves fraud, it provides information relevant to merit and worth. Moreover, some evidence indicates that institutions are more likely to get the behaviors and outcomes that they monitor (Wood & Waterman, 1991, 1994). Evaluations that monitor behaviors that lead to reduced social problems can thus sometimes help produce the behavioral changes that will lead to better outcomes. Of course, "goal displacement" can also occur, whereby more important behaviors are reduced while more easily measured ones increase.

Multipurpose Evaluations

Beyond these incidental spin-offs from one purpose to another, a single evaluation can be explicitly designed to directly address more than one purpose. Consider efforts to identify and to test the underlying mechanisms responsible for a program or policy's effects. When successful, they answer questions about whether or not the policy works and why. Some writers on evaluation purposes (Chelimsky, 1997; Patton, 1997) have stated that the study of mechanisms is a form of knowledge development. Evaluations that probe underlying mechanisms are likely to be relevant to social science theories about the causes of and treatments for social problems (Chen, 1990; Pawson & Tilley, 1997). But they also contribute to the assessment of merit and worth. Evaluation cannot adequately test underlying mechanisms without also assessing a program's effects on outcomes. (It is, however, possible to omit some valued outcomes because they have not been identified by prior theory, and this is a potential danger of being too theory driven.)

Series of Evaluation Studies

In some cases, evaluation purposes are combined in a series of evaluation studies. One common and often desirable sequence involves a series of evaluation studies that address, in turn, the purposes of program improvement, assessment of merit and worth, and oversight and compliance. Once ways of improving the program have been identified and implemented, the merit and worth of the presumably improved and well-implemented program are assessed, and finally, assuming the program is meritorious and worthy, program activities are monitored to verify that the program is still being carried out in the way found to be effective.

Conclusion

We have identified four possible purposes of evaluation: assessment of merit and worth, program and organizational improvement, oversight and compliance, and knowledge development. Although other pragmatic concerns, including some less than glorious, can sometimes motivate an evaluation, this fourfold set of purposes functions well as part of a vocabulary for planning evaluations in the service of social betterment. Different purposes and combinations of purposes are appropriate under different circumstances, and in all cases, considerations related to social betterment should drive purpose choice.

Assessments of merit and worth have a special role because they provide the information most useful for democratic deliberations intended to choose the best means to use in seeking desired ends. Oversight and compliance evaluation serves well when some democratically selected program or policy has documented merit and worth and its effectiveness could suffer from poor compliance to established procedures or when inadequate attention may be given to human rights and expenditure controls. Program and organizational improvement evaluation serves social betterment well—as long as it is not a ruse for avoiding consideration of merit and worth. It is often most useful when a social programs enjoys solid support and is not likely to be considered for wholesale change. Knowledge development is best seen as a purpose to be used in conjunction with other purposes. In particular, the study of underlying mechanisms can be a valuable adjunct to an assessment of merit and worth. Knowledge development can also motivate rigorous estimation of program effects during the interstices between the active attention to a program or policy within democratic institutions.

This framework of evaluation purposes contributes to a sensible way of thinking about evaluation. Together with the framework of inquiry presented in the next chapter, it provides a language evaluators from different traditions can use to communicate better and to understand each other's stance in the broader whole of evaluation. Even more important is its use in the planning of an evaluation. Although subsequent chapters present more nuanced and more complex guidelines for the choice of an evaluation purpose, the schematic summary in Exhibit 3.1 is an effective starting point for making judgments about the relative priority of the evaluation purposes in a given case. This framework is also applicable to the private sector. For example, a private company evaluating a training program might be concerned with assessing its merit and worth, with improving it, or with ensuring its compliance with regulations, and certainly there are researchers who have tested some pet theory in the context of evaluating a company's training program.

Selecting an evaluation purpose is of course not the end of evaluation planning. Once the evaluator has an evaluation purpose or combination of purposes in mind, he or she must turn to inquiry methods.

4

Specifying Inquiry Modes

Once the purpose of an evaluation has been identified, it is time to consider what methods to use to collect information that might aid democratic efforts at social betterment. *Inquiry modes* lie at an intermediate point between evaluation purposes and the specific methods that are used to examine a program or policy. They comprise clusters, or functional groupings, of methods that have evolved to support people's different natural sensemaking capacities. Evaluators often jump directly into the choice of a specific method (usually the method they are best trained in). We believe that evaluation planning proceeds better when evaluators first think about the general type of inquiry method needed to support a specific aspect of natural sensemaking.

We argue here that the inquiries most evaluators have traditionally carried out under the umbrella of program evaluation fall into three distinct modes: description, causal analysis, and to a lesser extent, classification. In addition, the theory of evaluation as assisted sensemaking calls for the inclusion of another family of methods that has been used less often, or at least less systematically, in many past approaches to evaluation practice—values inquiry, the empirical or formal study of the values that people hold about social programs and their effects, and that are embedded in them. In this chapter, we discuss each of four modes of inquiry in detail, including the extent to which each inquiry mode can, on average, fulfill different evaluation purposes.

The Four Inquiry Modes

All four modes of inquiry have evolved as collections of assisted sensemaking techniques that enable humans to compensate for the limits of natural sensemaking. Individuals usually cannot observe all program sites or observe program outcomes for all consumers, for instance. Furthermore, individuals' untrained observations are likely to be biased in any number of ways. Although assisted sensemaking techniques are themselves fallible and have inherent flaws, they can nevertheless overcome many limitations of natural sensemaking, limits that can result in what Patton (1997) calls a "beguiling distortion of reality, awesomely selective perceptions, stupefying self-deception, [and] profane rationalization" (p. 3). The modes are discussed in detail in Chapters Seven through Ten. In the following sections, we introduce each mode.

Description

Description refers to a family of methods commonly used in evaluation to measure (1) program resources (noting, for example, inputs to the program, such as staff levels), (2) services delivered (showing, for example, the amount and type of services and the means of delivery), (3) program clients and their characteristics (revealing, for example, how many clients, with what demographics), (4) program context (assessing, for instance, the size, demographic composition, and economic state of the community in which the program is offered), and increasingly, (5) outcome variables (revealing outcome levels but not whether outcomes are attributable to the program). Descriptive methods can also be used to measure almost anything related to a program or policy, including the subjective experience or meaning experienced by participants.

Many different methods can be used for description. In evaluation, description frequently relies on management information systems or other administrative data or on direct on-site monitoring of actual service delivery. The on-site techniques range from highly structured direct observation to less structured, more emergent methods. Interviews, focus groups, and surveys can be used. As exemplified by the Government Performance and Results Act (GPRA) and the performance-based budgeting occurring in many states (Melkers & Willoughby, 1998), *performance measurement*, also called *monitoring*, seems to be the most rapidly growing form of descriptive inquiry in evaluation. However, with few exceptions (for example, Wholey's work, 1979, 1983, 1987), performance measurement has been largely ignored in evaluation theory.

Classification

Description stays at the level of observable or "directly measurable" attributes (for example, attitudes and knowledge). *Classification* is intended to tap deeper structures. Classification methods are used to assess underlying structures and categories and to determine to which category an entity belongs (Julnes, 1999). In the context of evaluation, classification is used (1) to identify the categories into which clients, services, programs, times, settings, or effects fall; and (2) to assign specific cases (of services, programs, individuals, settings, or outcomes) to general categories or groupings. The categories themselves reflect a presumably more fundamental level (or levels), and cannot be directly observed or measured. Instead, they must be inferred from patterns of observable characteristics. In evaluation a number of important tasks involve classification, as illustrated by these two questions: Is the Bank Street preschool program child centered or teacher directed (Marcon, 1992, 1994b)? Is a particular local preschool site truly an example of the Bank Street curriculum? In addition classification might identify the components

(Wholey, 1994) or elements (Cook & Shadish, 1986) that make up a given program.

In short, in evaluation (as elsewhere), classification involves two steps (Bailey, 1994). First, a classification system must be developed, usually inductively. This system may also be referred to as a taxonomy or a category system. In this step, the characteristics that define each class are also determined. Methods such as case studies and factor analysis can be used to develop a classification system. In her educational research, for example, Marcon (1992, 1994a, 1994b, 1999) has developed a classification system consisting of three groups of teachers (and therefore, in most of early childhood education, three groups of classrooms): teacher directed, child centered, and middle of the road. She has also developed a set of fourteen survey items that can be used to assign teachers to one or another of the three groups. In the second step of classification, the evaluator determines whether a specific case falls in one class or another. Generally speaking, the attributes of the specific case are compared with the patterns of characteristics that define the categories, and some decision rule is applied. For example, over two hundred sites for the Georgia Prekindergarten Program have been classified into the three categories established by Marcon (Henderson, Basile, & Henry, 1999).

Causal Analysis

Classification assists the natural human tendency to go beyond the level of simple description by inferring underlying categories. The inquiry mode of *causal analysis* also supports a natural sensemaking activity that goes beyond description: the tendency to make causal inferences. Causal analysis refers to a variety of methods used to investigate the causal relationships set in play by a program or policy. In evaluation, causal analysis primarily involves estimating the impact of a program on valued outcomes. For example, one might assess whether the Bank Street preschool program has such effects as cognitive gains among children and increased expectations among parents. Causal analysis of effects goes beyond the descriptive measurement of outcomes because it must rule out alternative interpretations of how the outcomes occurred so that they can be justifiably attributed to the program. Causal analysis therefore generally requires more complex procedures than description (comparison groups and controlled assignment to groups are perhaps the most widely discussed procedures but a number of others are available).

Another important objective of causal analysis is the identification of the mechanisms that underlie any effects. For example, several studies have shown that preschool programs have positive effects on children's staying on grade level and on their avoiding assignment into special education. But it is also useful to know whether this is because such programs raise parents' and teachers' expectations or because of some other underlying mechanism (Zigler & Muenchow, 1992). The evaluation of underlying mechanisms can support efforts to make sense of the likely effects of policy alternatives. In addition, having a good explanation of why effects occur, should facilitate efforts to generalize, that is, to use the findings in other settings (Cronbach, 1982; Cook, 1993; Mark, 1990).

Values Inquiry

Description, classification, and causal analysis are usually applied in service of the representational side of sensemaking. That is, these assisted sensemaking techniques are generally used to help people gain a more sensible and more accurate representation of the world. *Values inquiry*, the fourth inquiry mode, assists natural valuation. It refers to a variety of methods that can be applied to the assessment of the values surrounding a social policy and its effects. Systematic techniques have been developed for unearthing values and for analyzing the assumptions behind them and their limitations. In large part values inquiry involves measurement of the extent to which various stakeholder groups, including the public, value various possible outcomes or attributes of a program or policy. For example, an evaluation of a preschool program might examine the extent to which parents, program staff, and the public value such possible outcomes as short-term cognitive gains, social skill development, reduced school dropout rates, reduced delinquency, and a narrowing of the gap between advantaged and disadvantaged children's performances. Surveys could be used to obtain ratings and rankings of the potential outcomes. Alternatively, heterogeneous groups could be formed to deliberate about the possible outcomes and how they might be weighed and rated. Or values stances could be derived through the application of some formal framework (for example, feminist theory or critical theory).

Our view is that values, and especially systematic inquiry about values, have received inadequate attention in most evaluation writings, at least from those who emphasize such traditional, representational sensemaking activities as classification, causal analysis, and description. Given the important role of values inquiry in evaluation, we emphasize it in this book. However, because values have up to now held a rather limited role in the received view of evaluation, the methods of values inquiry in evaluation are not as extensive or as highly evolved as the methods of inquiry directed at the representational side of sensemaking.

Table 4.1 summarizes the focus and common methods of the four modes of inquiry and names a major evaluation figure whose work emphasizes the use of each mode.

Inquiry Modes and Natural Sensemaking

Each of the four inquiry modes has analogs in natural sensemaking. For example, people naturally make use of causal inferences in everyday life (Heider, 1944), and the inquiry mode of causal analysis refers to a cluster of systematic methods designed to improve and extend this natural human capacity. Likewise, the systematic methods of classification have an analog in categorization, which is a natural activity for humans (for example, Rosch & Lloyd, 1978) and underlies human cognition and action. Inquiry modes are *defined* not by their data sources or by any specific attribute (includ-

TABLE 4.1. Some Key Attributes of the Four Inquiry Modes.

	Description	Classification	Causal Analysis	Values Inquiry
Focus	Measuring characteristics of clients, services, and outcomes	Developing categories and/or assigning cases to them	Estimating effects of program; identifying mechanisms	Identifying value positions of stakeholders and the public
Typical methods	Performance measurement; observation of program operations	Taxonomies of program types; cluster analysis	Randomized experiments; case studies	Group deliberations; surveys of the public or stakeholders
Illustrative user	Joseph Wholey	Mark Lipsey	Donald T. Campbell	Jennifer Greene

ing whether their methods are quantitative or qualitative) but as functional groupings around the aspect of natural sensemaking that they assist.

In addition, the systematic inquiry methods in each mode all *depend on* natural sensemaking. Natural categorization, for instance, underlies *any* systematic inquiry, whether it involves description, causal analysis, or values inquiry (for example, when doing program description, evaluators may naturally categorize some people as *clients* and others as *staff*). Although assisted sensemaking methods depend on many aspects of natural sensemaking, this does not diminish the validity or utility of the distinctions among the inquiry modes. For example, although natural categorization might underlie any other inquiry mode, the assisted sensemaking techniques that have evolved to systematically carry out classification, such as cluster, factor, and content analysis, can usefully be set apart from the methods in other inquiry modes. The formal inquiry modes have far less overlap than do the corresponding natural sensemaking tasks.

Still, the boundaries between inquiry modes can sometimes seem blurry, as is true even of useful classification schemes (Aronson,

Harré, & Way, 1995; Putnam, 1990). And a single data source may be used in support of different aspects of natural sensemaking. To take but one example, descriptive outcome monitoring data could at some point be used for causal analysis in an interrupted time series design (Mark, Reichardt, & Sanna, 2000) or in a causal model (Scheirer, in press). But these are still clearly methods of causal inquiry, designed to assist the natural human tendency to make causal inferences, regardless of the data source. We believe that the blurriness between inquiry modes will often seem greater for qualitative than for quantitative methods. This is because a researcher using a specific qualitative method will often move fairly seamlessly from support of one natural sensemaking capacity to support of another. For example, observational methods might be used, in one sequence or another, for description, classification, causal analysis, and values inquiry. We contend, however, that an evaluator can identify which of these inquiries is going on at any time.

Another complexity arises because values inquiry is intrinsically connected with the other inquiry modes, as would be expected given our commonsense realist rejection of the traditional fact-value dichotomy (Putnam, 1990; also see Chapter Six). Accordingly, the methods of values inquiry overlap in important ways with methods used in other modes. One response to this overlap, and to the rejection of the fact-value dichotomy, would be to argue that issues of value should be subsumed under the other three inquiry modes. Given the special place of values in our view of social betterment, however, we believe that values inquiry requires independent status as a distinct mode, not to segregate it in practice but to ensure that it receives sufficient attention in evaluation planning and practice.[1]

---

1. Another alternative would be a cross classification of inquiry modes (description, classification, and causal analysis) and inquiry domains (representation and valuation). In this two-by-three matrix, each mode could bear on both representations of the world and the valuing that people do. The mode of *formal inquiry*, encompassing model-driven analysis of programs according to, for example, feminist or Rawlsian theory, could also be included (producing a two-by-four matrix). Although avoiding the overlaps of the four-mode system we are using, this approach results in some essentially empty cells (for example, causal

As Aronson, Harré, and Way (1995) state, "No hierarchy is so complete that it is predetermined how we should use it to deal with marginal cases" (p. 24). Similarly, the existence of some marginal cases does not, we believe, threaten the usefulness of our distinctions. Furthermore, realist philosophy provides a parallel structure that supports and grounds the four inquiry modes.

Realism, Practice, and the Rationale for the Four Inquiry Modes

Contemporary realists often refer to the existence of a reality that is structured, hierarchical, and embedded (Bhaskar, 1975). In large part this means that unobservable phenomena underlie the things we all perceive and experience. Beneath the surface, so to speak, there are structures (for example, at one level of analysis the element oxygen will be found). There are also underlying generative mechanisms (such as combustion). And these underlying structures and mechanisms give rise to what we perceive and experience (for example, fire). The distinctions between the level of experience, underlying structures (or categories of things), and underlying mechanisms (or causal processes) can also be illustrated in the context of preschool program effects. A child may experience certain events in preschool, such as being given a choice among several things. Some time later she may have the experience of answering questions on a test in first grade. Unknown to the child, there are underlying mechanisms through which some things may cause others. For example, being given structured choices during preschool (the cause) may lead to higher scores on cognitive tests in first grade (the effect) because such structured choices may trigger increases in children's

---

analysis is rarely applied to valuation issues, and formal inquiry is rarely applied to representational ones). In addition, the two-by-four classification might, even more than our fourfold system, seem to codify the old, discredited (Putnam, 1990) fact-values dichotomy. Our four-mode system, although less tidy in a traditional sense, also appears preferable precisely because its overlaps correspond to the evolved patterns of practice in the real world.

internal motivation (the mechanism) (see Entwhisle, 1994; Marcon, 1999). The underlying mechanisms are unobservable but give rise to observable, experienced events. Also unknown to the child, there may be meaningful groupings of preschool classes as, for example, into teacher directed or child centered (Marcon, 1994a, 1999).

In short, then, realists presume a differentiated and stratified world, in which (1) the events that people experience are the result of (2) underlying structures and (3) underlying mechanisms. As summarized in Table 4.2, these attributes of the world correspond to three of the inquiry modes. First, the methods of causal inquiry have evolved to probe underlying mechanisms. For example, randomized experiments can, under optimal conditions, rule out all but the most likely explanations for the occurrence of some outcome. Second, the methods of classification have been created to study underlying structures. For instance, cluster analysis can be used to categorize local projects into groupings that share common characteristics. Both causal analysis and classification focus on phenomena beneath the surface, not directly observed but inferred. In contrast, the inquiry mode of description focuses on things that can be observed, recorded, or measured (such as the number of children served by a pre-K program and the time the children spent with math manipulables), without the same level of effort to "go beyond the data."

Values inquiry corresponds to a different aspect of contemporary realism, natural valuation, which we described earlier as one of

TABLE 4.2. The Relationship Between Key Realist Concepts and Inquiry Modes.

Realist Concept	Inquiry Mode
Experience	Description
Underlying structures	Classification
Underlying mechanisms	Causal analysis
Natural valuation	Values inquiry

the two major components of sensemaking. Judging the worth or value of something is a natural human activity (Putnam, 1990). People not only develop representations of the world around them, they also make value judgments about myriad aspects of it. When humans observe events, such as social conditions, they naturally make judgments that some are better than others, that some are more desirable than others, that some are necessary for the "common" good (Berlin, 1998). Values inquiry extends these natural capacities.

Although we derived the four inquiry mode system not from realism but from our review of methods used in practice, we are gratified by the ease with which the system also maps onto realist concepts. Thus, we believe that realism supports the system of four inquiry modes. However, the greater value of applying realism to our practice framework is that in conjunction with evaluation purpose, it can guide the selection of an inquiry mode for a particular evaluation.

Choosing Inquiry Modes in Light of Evaluation Purpose and Realism

The planning of an evaluation, we hold, should proceed from (1) an analysis of the decision context related to social betterment to (2) the selection of an evaluation purpose (or set of purposes) to (3) the selection of an inquiry mode. In this section, we examine the selection of an inquiry mode in light of evaluation purpose and realism.

What Quality of Inquiry Is Required in a Particular Case?

As we shall see, different inquiry modes may be used for any one given purpose. Mode 1 might do an excellent job for that purpose, mode 2 a decent job, and mode 3 a poor job. But is it always necessary or desirable to use the *best* inquiry mode for the job? Most people would agree that you don't need to use the best wine for cooking and that you don't need to get the best available security system for a hovel. Despite this commonsense recognition, many evaluators, policymakers, and others seem to have trouble recognizing when they need a Cadillac evaluation and when a VW Bug evaluation will do. The following box presents some guidelines to help evaluators, stakeholders, staff, and others in judging the quality of inquiry method needed for an evaluation. We emphasize, however, that the details of applying these guidelines may be different in different cases and that practicing evaluators are likely to have or to develop more refined judgments suited especially to their practice areas.

Guidelines for Judging the Quality of
Inquiry Methods Needed

Guideline 1: If a higher quality approach is no more costly, always go with it. If a higher quality method is as feasible and cheap as a lower quality one, why choose the lesser one? This guideline always trumps the others. Of course costs are rarely going to be equal, but in some cases the cost of a better approach will not be socially significantly more than a less desirable approach.

Guideline 2: Higher quality answers are more important to the extent that the wrong answer is costly. Not all decisions have equally important consequences. For example, a minor change in the way a program is implemented is less likely to have major consequences than is the program per se. Consequently, lower quality methods may suffice for evaluating the minor program tweak than for evaluating the program as a whole. Further, wrong decisions are not equally costly. For instance, it is probably more important to get the right answers about a statewide preschool program than about a local school district's in-service program for teachers. The absolute costs are greater for the statewide preschool program, as are the opportunity costs (the things that could be done if the statewide program were not funded) and the potential harm from undesirable side effects. Of course, as Yogi Berra is reported to have said, "It is difficult to make predictions, especially about the future," and reaching decisions about the ultimate and varied costs of a wrong decision is indeed an imperfect art. Nevertheless, evaluators and others should address the likely cost of a wrong answer during evaluation planning. Sometimes this issue can be adjudicated through the process of values inquiry. For example, program staff and clients can speak to the costs of implementing or maintaining an ineffective or harmful intervention.

Guideline 3: Better quality answers are needed to the extent the consequences of a decision cannot be observed and reversed in a timely fashion. Imagine a policy change in a big city police department that reduced the number of officers on the street. *If* timely information about the new policy's effects (for example, whether crime rates increased) is to be obtained and *if* the policy could readily be reversed, then lower quality information can suffice initially to put the policy in action. If a bad decision can readily be fixed, there is less pressure to be sure the decision is right. Conversely, if the consequences will not be known for a long time (for example, the record keeping and reporting system is slow) of if the decision is not readily reversible (for example, because the revised budget would make it infeasible), it then becomes important to have a higher quality evaluation initially.

Guideline 4: Good prior evidence often reduces the quality needed for later evidence. If, for example, rigorous evaluations have demonstrated that a drug and alcohol abuse program has merit and worth in 200 schools, the 201st school to adopt the program is likely to be satisfied with a lower quality assessment of merit and worth, if any.

Of course, this guideline has exceptions. If there are good reasons to question the generalizability of prior evidence, then high quality answers may be required regardless. For example, if the 201st school differs in important ways from the previous 200, new high quality evidence may still be required. Quality prior evidence may also not be enough if evaluation results in the area meet with continued resistance and findings are needed that are compelling enough to sail against the tide of public opinion.

Guideline 5: To the extent there is uncertainly or dissent about the factors in these guidelines, higher quality methods may be required. For example, the more uncertainty that exists about the consequences of being wrong (guideline 2), the greater the need the need for a higher quality approach is likely to be (Boruch & Rindskopf, 1984).

From Evaluation Purpose to Inquiry Mode

There are not any hard-and-fast, one-to-one correspondences between evaluation purpose and inquiry mode. Purposes can be pursued in different ways, and methods are not limited to the service of a single purpose. This is true in most areas of life. You can use a wrench whether your purpose is to change a bike tire, steady a desk leg, or keep papers from blowing off the desk. Flour might be used to bake a cake, coat chicken for frying, or whiten a child's hair for a school play. Purpose does not inherently imply method. Nevertheless, there are some associations in practice between the four evaluation purposes and the four inquiry modes. Although these linkages are not intrinsically necessary, it can be argued that they have evolved in practice for generally sound reasons. Some, we believe, contribute more to social betterment under specific circumstances. Thus the fact that more than one inquiry mode can support a single evaluation purpose does not imply that anything goes when it comes to selecting an inquiry mode. In the remainder of this chapter and in the next, we lay out the reasoning behind using a particular inquiry mode for a particular purpose. Given the priority that we place on the assessment of merit and worth, we address this purpose in somewhat more detail than the others.

The Quality of Different Inquiry Modes for Assessing Merit and Worth. Table 4.3 suggests a ranking for the quality of different inquiry modes for the assessment of merit and worth. These rankings suggest the *average* quality of each mode for assessing merit and worth; not every method subsumed in a mode will be of equal quality. In general, causal analysis provides the highest quality assessment of merit and worth. For most social programs and policies, the key issue regarding merit and worth is whether the program or policy has particular desirable effects and does not have undesirable effects. Getting causal inferences right is therefore typically quite important, so that one does not spend limited resources on ineffective programs. How positively we value welfare reform, for example, is likely to depend on whether it causes an improvement or a decline in the well-being of poor children and on its other effects.

In at least some cases causal analysis should be supplemented with some descriptive inquiry to achieve a truly high-quality assessment of merit and worth. Because violations of rights and dignity may not be readily measured in a causal inquiry, the descriptive adjunct would assess whether clients' rights, access to equal opportunity, dignity, and other social values were violated. As discussed earlier, judgments about the merit and worth of programs and policies depend in no small way on these important considerations.

In principle, classification can provide a high-quality assessment of merit and worth *when certain conditions are met*. For example, once we know the price of gold, we learn the value of a metal nugget when we determine, first, that it is gold and, second, how much it weighs. We do not need to do an experiment in order to see the effect of gold nuggets on financial transactions or on net worth. Similarly, classification can effectively assess merit and worth when a strong system exists for classifying local projects as members of a program category already known to be effective. However, this requires a strong and generalizable prior linkage between category membership and effectiveness, and we believe that this condition is unlikely given the current state of knowledge in most areas of social programs and policy. If, as is far more likely in current practice, the linkage between category membership and outcomes is not

TABLE 4.3. The Quality of Different Inquiry Modes for Assessing Merit and Worth.

Inquiry Mode	Quality on Average for Assessment of Merit and Worth	Comments
Causal analysis, with descriptive study of rights and dignity	★★★★★	Although the optimal feasible method, it may not be needed in all cases (see guidelines for quality of methods of inquiry).
Causal analysis alone	★★★★	Adequacy depends on whether outcomes have been well chosen and on whether undetected violations of rights and dignity might occur. If other evidence on rights and dignity exists, this mode is excellent.
Classification, when link between category membership and outcomes is strong	★★★★★	Excellent in theory, if conditions are met. But this will rarely happen in current state of practice.
Description	★★↬	Limited because of uncertainty that the program causes the outcomes, but may suffice in some important circumstances. Will be better if descriptive data can be used in causal analysis.
Classification, when link between category membership and outcomes is weak or absent	★	Generally inadequate. But commonly a useful adjunct to other inquiry modes, to provide more nuanced information (for example, about differential effects)
Values inquiry	NA	Although not really a method for assessing merit and worth per se, it is important for guiding selection of outcome measures and for aiding in valuation of findings.

well established, classification alone is a weak inquiry mode for assessment of merit and worth.

The most likely use of classification for the assessment of merit and worth is in conjunction with other inquiry modes. Classification of program subtypes, clients, settings, and outcomes into groups can lead to a more finely nuanced assessment of merit and worth, which may better reflect the complex, open-system world and also stimulate better sensemaking. For example, Rog (1991) classified interventions for homelessness by profiling them in terms of their referral sources, their target populations, and the services they provided. When such uses of classification are combined with other inquiry modes (for example, causal analysis) for assessing merit and worth, the resulting information will often be more useful than the information from the other modes alone.

Description is generally not a strong method for the assessment of merit and worth. As we have seen, description as an assisted sensemaking technique does not strive to penetrate the surface level of events and experiences, so description alone is not usually adequate when it is important to get the underlying causal relations right, as is commonly the case for assessments of merit and worth. For instance, a newly developed performance measurement system would not allow causal analysis about the effectiveness of a program as a whole, especially when many other factors in the environment may influence the level of outcomes. Performance measurement does not provide a high-quality assessment of merit and worth because it generally "does not attempt to identify the extent to which the program caused the outcomes" (Hatry, 1997, p. 42) and, further, does not directly address "how and why questions" (Newcomer, 1997, p. 10). Keep in mind, however, that as previously noted, data from description can provide the grist for the mill of causal analysis, as when performance data are used in an interrupted time series analysis of the effect of a new policy. Careful thought about such possibilities will be important for the evaluator planning for long-term use of a performance measurement system.

Nevertheless, democratic institutions and processes sometimes need only an imprecise, rough assessment. It may be enough to know that important outcomes are moving in the right direction, even if the movement cannot be attributed with any confidence to the program. The worn expression, "If it ain't broke, don't fix it," conveys the sort of satisficing logic (Simon, 1957) that allows findings from performance measurement systems to sometimes suffice as rough assessments of merit and worth. Take the example of the school performance reports produced in many states. If a report shows high levels of student achievement and attainment along with few threats to student and teacher safety and with positive school-community relationships, this may be sufficient to lead parents, the school board, and the community to judge the school meritorious even though the school may not be entirely responsible for these outcomes. It appears that in practice, methods often can be applied to attribute merit and worth to specific individual programs (for example, a phonetic reading program) far more readily than to complex, multifaceted systems (for example, public education). Fortunately, satisficing logic may suffice more often in the latter cases.

An increasingly important situation in which such logic is used is the evaluation of multipronged community-level interventions. In such cases, confident causal analysis of each prong's effects, or even of the prongs' joint effect, may be difficult at best. And the relevant decision may be whether parts of the intervention need to be modified or whether the targeted social problem seems to be improving in the face of the intervention as a whole. In such cases, description in the form of performance measurement may suffice for the assessment of merit and worth. This is also sensible in light of the guidelines presented earlier. In particular, in multipronged community assessments, performance measurement systems can provide timely feedback about the apparent direction outcomes are going, and adjustments can be made as needed (see guideline 3). Thus the highest rated inquiry modes in Table 4.3 are not always needed—or even appropriate.

Values inquiry by itself does not assess a program's merit and worth, but it may be conducted simultaneously with other inquiry modes that can assess merit and worth (House & Howe, 1999). As we have seen, values inquiry can support and enhance the natural valuation that is at the core of the translation of *findings* about merit and worth into *judgments* about how valuable these outcomes are to the individual and society. Democratic deliberations should be enhanced, for example, by the presence of explicit evidence about what outcomes others, especially members of groups less vocal in deliberation, hold as most important for a program. For instance, causal analysis may be used to assess merit, and values inquiry used to assist in deliberations about worth. However, in some circumstances an evaluator might forego systematic assisted sensemaking for values inquiry and instead rely solely on democratic institutions and processes to translate findings about merit and worth into judgments about the value of a policy. How are the evaluator and others to decide when systematic values inquiry is most important? In addition, if values inquiry is to be carried out in an evaluation, how is one to decide what level of quality is needed? The following box offers some guidelines.

Guidelines for Determining When High-Quality
Values Inquiry Is Important

High-quality methods for empirical values inquiry are important to the extent that

1. There are likely to be differences in the way program outcomes are valued.

2. The values stances of various key stakeholder groups and the public are not well known.

3. Concerns such as consistency with previous evaluations or mandated attention to certain outcomes would not override the findings of values inquiry.

4. Social conditions support thoughtful deliberations, publicly or by appropriate representatives, about the proper course of action.

As we have been emphasizing, the assessment of merit and worth is an important evaluation purpose because such assessments can contribute greatly to democratic choices about what means to use in trying to achieve social betterment. Of course, the assessment of merit and worth will not be the primary purpose of every evaluation study. Indeed, major choice points in the road to social betterment may be relatively infrequent. Therefore, it is also important to consider the decision-making process for selecting an inquiry mode for the other purposes.

The Quality of Different Inquiry Modes for Program and Organizational Improvement. When program and organizational improvement is the primary evaluation purpose, the evaluation usually emphasizes timely feedback that can be used to modify and enhance program operations. As outlined in Chapter Three, various models of program improvement exist. The approach suggested by Scriven (1967) sees program improvement as involving a kind of mini-assessment of merit and worth. That is, a relatively casual and timely assessment of merit and worth is conducted, and the results are reported to program sponsors and staff, who can then use this feedback to establish the need for program modifications. For this approach, any of the methods discussed for the assessment of merit and worth can be employed. For example, causal analysis can provide a mini-assessment of merit and worth in the service of program improvement by examining which of two (or more) possible program alterations best facilitates desired outcomes. In the case of a statewide prekindergarten program, knowing the relative effectiveness of each of the state-approved curricula could lead to program improvement by allowing the state to remove approval from the least effective curriculum. In addition, knowledge about underlying mechanisms will often lead to program and organizational improvements. For example, if is shown that preschools' positive effects come from increasing parents' expectations, then preschool programs could direct more effort toward this mechanism. Usually, though, lower quality methods are used so that less costly findings can be provided in a timely way for sponsors and staff to make any needed improvements. For example, a relatively weak and low-cost causal analysis method, such as a natural experiment (Rog, 1994), can provide information about which of two methods for delivering services is more effective.

Another approach to program and organizational improvement is analogous to the task of an auto mechanic, who does not judge merit and worth but makes or suggests modifications likely to enhance performance. Evaluations of this form often focus on diagnosing the parts of the program that are causing problems, considering alternative approaches to these parts, and deciding which change to pursue. Description is the most likely inquiry mode for this approach to program and organizational improvement. Evaluators can use ongoing information from monitoring, in particular, to assess the need for revisions and their likely nature. Wholey's approach to evaluation (1979, 1983), in which performance measurement systems are developed for managers' use in revising program operations, illustrates this technique. This emphasis on performance monitoring for the purpose of program improvement is also present in the Government Performance and Results Act, the federal law that calls for performance monitoring in virtually all U.S. federal agencies by the year 2000 (Newcomer, 1997). This approach is also illustrated by much of the quality improvement movement. Morrell (2000), for example, discusses descriptive methods borrowed from industrial engineering that can be used for the purpose of improvement.

Another approach to program and organizational improvement, which overlaps the others conceptually, involves comparison to some explicit model. The model is often described in terms of presumed best practices to which the program should aspire (Bickman, 1985). Any discrepancy between actual program practices and the model is taken as evidence of the need for program revisions. When there is good evidence that the best practice model has demonstrable merit and worth, then this is a form of assessing merit and worth via classification (and addressing program improvement at the same time if program strengths and weaknesses are identified relative to the successful model). However, our sense is that often the so-called best practices are in large part a subjectively determined set of practices that specialists think *should* be related to desirable outcomes, even though good evidence is lacking (Bickman, 1985). In such cases the result can be only a program and organizational improvement effort, not an assessment of merit and worth.

Finally, values inquiry can feed into the preceding approaches to program and organizational improvement or can constitute a separate approach by itself. It can contribute to improvement by clarifying the program aspects that matter most and thereby suggesting the aspects to improve. It can also contribute by identifying the program characteristics and potential outcomes that are most important to service recipients or to others such as service providers and taxpayers. Finally, the literatures on evaluability assessment (for example, Rutman, 1980), on the formative use of program theory (Bickman, 1990), and on developmental evaluation (Patton, 1997) all suggest that better service delivery can result from evaluation processes that lead program staff (and others) to examine what matters about a program and to decide what outcomes are most important. In this use, values inquiry stands alone as a program improvement effort.

Table 4.4 suggests a ranking for the quality of each inquiry mode for program and organizational improvement, oversight and compliance, and knowledge development.

The Quality of Different Inquiry Modes for Oversight and Compliance. When evaluations have an oversight and compliance purpose, the motivating question is whether the program is following specified rules and regulations and in other ways meeting expectations. This question can usually be answered well without any attention to underlying mechanism or structure. Accordingly, methods from the inquiry mode of description are quite appropriate for this purpose. Descriptive methods are more concerned with

TABLE 4.4. The Quality of Different Inquiry Modes for Program and Organizational Improvement, Oversight and Compliance, and Knowledge Development.

	Oversight and Compliance	Program and Organizational Improvement	Knowledge Development	Comments
Description	★★★★	★★★★★	★ to ★★★★★	Can show whether a program is following mandates, and can contribute to program and organization improvement in several ways.
Classification	★★★	★★★★	★ to ★★★★	Good for oversight and compliance when program types are mandated. Can be excellent for program and organization improvement when comparison is to best practices that truly are worthwhile.
Causal analysis	★★	★★★	★ to ★★★★★	Generally not relevant to oversight and compliance. Can be very strong for program and organization improvement, but the best methods are usually more costly and slower than appropriate. Lower quality causal methods can be a best buy for program and organization improvement.
Values inquiry	★★★★	★	★ to ★★★★	Might help development of fidelity criteria for oversight and compliance, but not their assessment. Can be ideal for program and organization improvement in cases when much uncertainty or disagreement about program mission exists, and can aid in focusing other modes for this purpose.

Note: The rankings for knowledge development indicate that each inquiry mode may be either good or bad for this purpose, depending on the question of interest.

events and experience than are methods for classification or causal analysis, which focus on unobservable underlying structures and mechanisms. One-time or, preferably, ongoing performance measurement systems are among the descriptive methods best used for oversight and compliance. By assessing whether services are delivered in intended ways to intended clients, monitoring serves this evaluation purpose well.

In some cases the inquiry mode of classification can do a high-quality job of satisfying the purpose of oversight and compliance. For example, classification methods can be used to demonstrate that a local project fits into some mandated program category. For instance, regulations might specify that Montessori schools are approved for a statewide pre-K program. Montessori schools have a specified curriculum and physical layout, and local schools could be classified according to whether they fit this model. In some instances, an evaluation might blend methods of description and classification, with description from a performance measurement system used to classify local projects according to their fit with a program type.

Conversely, causal analysis and values inquiry will usually not provide a high-quality oversight and compliance evaluation. The key questions of oversight and compliance involve fidelity to some established model of program delivery or to externally established procedures (such as accounting procedures), not cause and effect, so causal analysis will simply not be terribly relevant (other than in the very limited sense of demonstrating that some organizational factor affects compliance). Values inquiry also is not directed toward establishing such fidelity and so is generally not relevant to oversight and compliance. Values inquiry might address the extent to which stakeholder groups and the public were concerned about fidelity, although this would be an unlikely use of evaluation resources. The point at which values inquiry could be genuinely useful for oversight and compliance is during the *development* of the mandates. But description and, if there is a program model, classification are the preferred modes for oversight and compliance evaluations.

The Quality of Different Inquiry Modes for Knowledge Development. It is difficult to specify the quality of the different inquiry families for knowledge development—it depends on the nature of the knowledge the evaluator or researcher is trying to develop. Causal analysis can contribute very well to some knowledge development work, say, about the role of incentives in human behavior (McSweeney, 1978) or about the types of interventions that are most effective for different types of juvenile offenders (Lipsey, 1993, 1997). However, different inquiry modes are more effective for other types of knowledge development work. For example, initial research on the temporal pattern of welfare use would be well served by good description (from an ongoing performance measurement system perhaps) but not by causal analysis methods. Classification too can be used for knowledge development—for example, in efforts to determine whether there are different subgroups of welfare recipients or different categories of the homeless (Kuhn & Culhane, 1998). Values inquiry may be used to point up gaps or oversights in the values that are commonly held about a public program or about social programs in general. This approach might be motivated by the desire to know more about the public's view of social problems and their implications. Thus values inquiry could be used to test theory-based hypotheses about the relationship between individuals' values and their preferred policies. In short, any of the inquiry modes can be of either high or low quality for knowledge development, depending on the research question.

Review: Inquiry Modes for Program Improvement, Oversight and Compliance, and Knowledge Development. For program improvement, different approaches are associated with different inquiry families. For the mini-assessment of merit and worth an evaluator can use any of the inquiry families appropriate for assessing merit and worth; however, given cost and timeliness concerns, the lower quality approaches will most commonly be used. For the auto mechanic approach, description will usually be the inquiry mode of choice. For the best practices model approach, classification is the likely inquiry mode. Values inquiry can contribute to any of these program improvement approaches, or it may function on its own. High quality in oversight and compliance evaluations can be achieved with description or, if fidelity to a model is an issue, with classification. Causal analysis and values inquiry will usually be of limited relevance to oversight and compliance. Finally, in the case of knowledge development, any inquiry mode may be high or low in quality, depending on the research question.

The guidelines offered in this chapter for determining the needed quality of inquiry method apply to all evaluations regardless of purpose. This is true even when the inquiry mode selected is one that on average does a high-quality job for the purpose in question. For instance, the inquiry mode of description usually provides high quality for the purpose of oversight and compliance. However, evaluators have a range of options in implementing a descriptive study, and some are of higher quality than others. Therefore judgments must be made about the level of quality needed in the specific method (or combination of methods) selected from the mode of description. As the guidelines state, higher quality inquiry methods should be chosen to the extent that the higher quality method is no more costly, getting the wrong answer would be socially costly, the consequences of a decision cannot be monitored or a decision cannot be readily reversed; and good prior evidence is lacking.

Conclusion

In this chapter we have identified and discussed four inquiry modes from which evaluators can select methods: description, classification, causal analysis, and values inquiry. These inquiry modes correspond relatively directly to key realist concepts.

This framework of inquiry modes can enhance evaluators' understanding of evaluation and its role. It can lead evaluators to think about methods in relation to the aspect of natural sensemaking that they support, rather than in terms of stale distinctions such as quantitative versus qualitative. In conjunction with the frame-work of evaluation purposes, it can help evaluators view the broad expanse of the field and recognize where their and others' traditions are located. For example, Campbell emphasized the purpose of as-sessing merit and worth and the inquiry mode of causal analysis. Wholey emphasized program and organizational improvement as a purpose, and description as an inquiry mode. Thinking about such different traditions in respect to the four evaluation purposes and four inquiry modes can encourage evaluators to appreciate the rich diversity of evaluation.

At least as important, the framework of inquiry modes comes together with evaluation purposes, the goal of social betterment, and concepts of realism to provide considerable guidance for plan-ning evaluations. Evaluation purpose, together with considerations of social betterment and realism, provides guidelines for the selec-tion of inquiry mode, and a major focus of this chapter has been the relative desirability of each inquiry mode for a given purpose.

At this point, the pieces of the puzzle of evaluation planning are coming together. First, the evaluator reviews circumstances related to social betterment (Chapter Two). Next, he or she selects one or more evaluation purposes, a choice ultimately driven by the goal of social betterment (Chapter Three, especially Exhibit 3.1). Then, the evaluator selects one or more inquiry modes, based on evalua-tion purpose and informed by realism (as described in this chapter). Values inquiry will typically be an important adjunct to whatever inquiry mode is chosen, especially with respect to setting the crite-ria for judging a program or policy.

The sketch in these first four chapters of the process of planning an evaluation is an oversimplification in many important respects. In practice the process often involves iteration between the steps. Practical considerations may also place initial limits on what we have listed as a later stage (for example, the use of some inquiry mode may be infeasible). In addition, greater understanding about which purpose will best serve social betterment may emerge over time, with more experience with the program being evaluated or with changes in stakeholders' and agencies' agendas. Evaluators should also be open to serendipity, to the unexpected opportunity, as when Rog (1999) saw that in an evaluation of a program for homeless families, she could contribute to knowledge development by measuring the extent to which clients experienced violence. In short, the key to success in the process of evaluation planning often is making adjustments and replanning.

The discussion this far has also generally oversimplified the process by focusing mostly on one purpose and one inquiry mode at a time. In truth, evaluations often are meant to serve several purposes simultaneously. The complex choices facing evaluators when both evaluation purposes and inquiry modes can be multiple are addressed in the next chapter.

PART TWO

Linking Betterment, Evaluation Practice, and Realism

5

Planning Evaluations

After a successful evaluation is completed and the findings released, its construction in terms of purpose and inquiry modes can appear, especially to novice evaluators, to be the product of divine inspiration. In reality, the planning of a successful evaluation usually requires painful laboring over which purposes can and cannot be fulfilled and over which inquiry modes can and cannot be brought to bear. It usually requires creativity in considering how a budget can be stretched and how a given method might serve multiple purposes. Successful evaluation planning is likely to require discussions with many parties about numerous trade-offs.

In the previous chapters, we began to put together the pieces of the puzzle of evaluation planning. We described how considerations of social betterment can guide the choice of evaluation purpose, and how the choice of inquiry mode can be guided by purpose and by the strength of the evidence required for the information needs at hand. Now we address further complexities in the puzzle of evaluation planning. Judgments must be made but not just about a single evaluation purpose. Rather, evaluators and others must decide whether an evaluation should serve more than one purpose and, if so, which combination of purposes to pursue. Judgments must also be made not just about a single inquiry mode to use but about which modes to combine or to use in sequence. No wonder the planning of evaluation is often thought of as an art (Cronbach, 1982).

In this chapter, we provide guidance for planning these complexities of successful evaluations. However, because the requirements of evaluation planning are complex and require great attention to the details of a specific case, we do not attempt to offer formal prescriptions. Quality evaluation planning cannot proceed from a paint-by-numbers kit. But neither is it necessary for evaluators to start with a blank sheet of paper and no direction. Thus we intend this chapter to be viewed as guidelines, suggestions, and examples designed to support and strengthen the ability of evaluators and others to work through the key judgments of evaluation planning. The art of evaluation planning is not arbitrary. The puzzle pieces must be put together skillfully and thoughtfully to create an evaluation that can serve social betterment well.

In this chapter we also elaborate on our previous discussion of social betterment by examining more specific details of the policy environment, that is, the circumstances into which the evaluation findings will be cast. These and similar contextual details should influence judgments about whether multiple evaluation purposes are required and, if so, which combination of purpose is most important for sensemaking needs. This will in turn influence decisions about the combinations of inquiry modes that may be required. Of course, planning must be for the sensemaking needs of tomorrow, and so professional judgment, expert opinion, and even intuition play a role in assessing how the environment might look when the evaluation findings are ready.

Assessing the Policy Environment

Each evaluation purpose corresponds to a different type of information need that arises as democracies (and most other institutions and organizations) strive to achieve social betterment through policies and programs. Thus the selection of purpose should be keyed to the policy environment. Evaluators should pay particular heed to choosing the purpose that will result in the type of information of greatest importance in the anticipated policy environment. In this section we review four policy environments, that is, four contexts into which evaluation findings commonly are intended to be of use. Although multiple processes may be occurring in a specific case, our focus is on the dominant process that democratic institutions are engaged in in each environment.

Stable Policy Environment

For the most part, the policy environment can be characterized as *stable*, with few major shifts under active consideration at any given time. This state of affairs has been captured by the term *incrementalism* (Lindblom, 1968; Lindblom & Cohen, 1979), which suggests that changes are usually small and occurring at the margins rather than deep and pervasive. As indicated by the decreasing volatility in budget allocations, incrementalism has increased in the years since World War II (Jones, True, & Baumgartner, 1997). Public education, highway maintenance, Social Security, mental health service delivery, and most other policy areas change infrequently from year to year in terms of core assumptions and programs. The Georgia Prekindergarten (Pre-K) Program is an interesting example of how stable policies can become. In November 1998, Georgia voters approved a state constitutional amendment requiring that the Pre-K Program receive priority in the expenditure of state lottery proceeds. This constitutional amendment virtually guarantees continuation and, more generally, a stable policy environment for the Pre-K Program. Although a constitutional mandate for program stability is an extreme example, it cannot be overemphasized that stable policy environments are likely to predominate at any given time, with major disjunctures in policy correspondingly rare.

In stable policy environments, evaluation information is most likely to contribute to social betterment when it assists in improving a previously chosen course of action. Therefore the assessment of merit and worth is far less likely than other evaluation purposes to be of value, and the purposes of program and organizational improvement and, to a lesser extent, oversight and compliance are more likely to lead to social betterment. Questions relevant to program staff and to clients will relate to the potential desirability of modest changes in service delivery, within the overall assumptions and provisions of the policy. Questions relevant to policymakers will focus on the extent to which program operations comply with laws and regulations, looking at such issues as whether a target population is receiving mandated services. When the policy environment is stable, the choice between these two evaluation purposes depends on the relative importance of these two audiences and their concerns. For the Georgia Pre-K program, program improvement concerns are at the forefront, as program personnel seek to refine the program. Specific program and organizational questions of current interest include identifying better approaches to service delivery.

Although policy environments are usually stable, incrementalism sometimes gives way to more wholesale reform, or at least to debate about major reforms. Public education is usually stable from year to year but recent debate has focused on major reform in the form of educational vouchers for students to use to attend the school of their choice. Mental health service delivery is usually stable from year to year but faced a major reform in the deinstitutionalization of the mentally ill, as well as continuing challenges in the wake of this reform. Assessments of merit and worth can fuel such discomforts with existing policies and can sometimes contribute to destabilizing a stable environment. Performance measurement systems that demonstrate poor student performance in terms of standardized test scores and high school graduation rates can fuel the fire for vouchers and other educational reform, for example. If, however, an assessment of merit and worth shows that expectations for positive outcomes are not being realized or that negative side effects are sizable, but does not point to a viable alternative, and if there are no competitors on the horizon, the result can be mainly frustration and dissatisfaction. Policy theorists have noted that problems must be linked to proposed solutions to gain traction and move through the policy processes (Kingdon, 1995). Thus, in a stable environment, assessments of merit and worth have a lower probability than other purposes of bringing pay-offs in improved social conditions, though they may plant seeds for challenges to the status quo at a later point. Knowledge development may be more important than an assessment of merit and worth in such instances, because it may lead to the creation of an alternative program or policy that will some day challenge the current one.

Competitive Policy Environment

From time to time, innovative policies and new programs or methods for service delivery arise on the public agenda as potential replacements for existing policies and programs. In addition to educational vouchers and the deinstitutionalization of mental health service consumers, recent examples include limits on the length of time an individual can receive welfare assistance and privatization of correctional facilities. Alternatives such as these challenge the assumptions on which the existing policies were based and create competition in the policy environment. Advocates often claim that an innovation has more positive intended effects and fewer negative side effects than the existing policy. In many cases the competition is about the means to the same agreed-on end, but in some cases the innovation involves value shifts, sometimes implicit or deeply buried ones. For instance, although agreeing on the general value of education, educational voucher programs supplant the traditional values associated with providing a universal system of free public schools.

Whether involving a shift in values or not, newly proposed policy solutions vary in terms of how new and untested they are. Sometimes the new policy has already been implemented in other jurisdictions. In other cases the policy is still theoretical and untested, at least on the scale now proposed. When actively choosing a new course of action, policymakers may consider whether to move quickly to full-scale implementation or to begin with a more limited trial program. In any event, when new and competing policy alternatives are being examined, typically the desired information is an assessment of merit and worth. The central question posed in this environment is, In comparison to the existing policy, how does the new one perform? Usually, the new alternative must perform better than the existing policy on one or more valued outcomes or perform as well at a lower cost to justify the change and the associated risk of adopting something new. In an environment with competing policies or programs, then, head-to-head comparisons of merit and worth can contribute valuable information to democratic deliberations about which course of action to choose. Again, such situations are relatively rare relative to the stable policy environment in which program and organizational improvement is the preferred purpose.

When democratic institutions are struggling with the choice of one course of action or another, evaluation purposes other than the assessment of merit and worth are less likely to provide relevant information. Still, they can contribute to betterment in this environment. Knowledge development can be especially important, at least in those cases that require the study of the underlying mechanisms through which a newly proposed program or policy has its effects. Findings from an oversight and compliance evaluation may show whether the current policy has been implemented in accordance with the program mandates, and these findings may shed light on whether the lack of positive results is due to inherent problems in the course of action or to implementation problems that can be resolved. In addition, program and organizational improvement evaluations may reveal program enhancements for whichever course of action is chosen. But in a competitive environment all of these purposes are likely to be of secondary value in the debate if an assessment of merit and worth is available.

Opportunities for Funding Options in the Environment

As we noted, an assessment of merit and worth is less valuable when the existing policy is not being directly compared to a potential replacement. Even if mental health treatment programs are shown to produce no discernible effects in an evaluation, what can be done with the information? How can betterment be served? Canceling treatment is a logical option but not a humane or politically viable one. A decision has already been made to offer treatment for the illness, and in the immediate time horizon, findings do not directly support an alternative course of action by consumers or policymakers. Whereas competition in the policy environment drives an interest in assessment of merit and worth, the absence of competition usually provides evaluators with a rationale for considering other purposes as primary.

Exceptions occur when there are viable funding options and when the social problem can be better specified or understood. Sometimes funding options are asymmetrical, such that funding increases are possible but not decreases (or vice versa). For example, if mental health treatment programs are shown to be effective, then funding for them might be increased to expand coverage to those currently untreated. However, the converse is probably not true. Even if these programs were shown to be ineffective, it is unlikely that policymakers would substantially decrease funding. Similarly, no one advocates closing public schools even if few are happy with the general performance of students. Conversely, negative findings might spark an increase in basic research funding, to try to develop the knowledge foundation that will lead to new treatment approaches for the mentally ill, for example, or negative findings might lead to pilot tests of innovative treatment modalities. Even in the absence of strong competitors, an assessment of merit and worth might influence funding options when they exist, and therefore it might be the most valuable purpose. In other cases, cutting funding from an ineffective program may be a real option, and again this would call for an assessment of merit and worth.

At the same time, in the past many evaluators operating in a context of no competition between program alternatives appear to have grossly overestimated the likelihood of real funding options. Research indicates that budgetary shifts have dampened in recent years, indicating stability rather than large funding swings (Jones, True, & Baumgartner, 1997). In addition, evaluators have often assumed, implicitly at least, that a Cadillac assessment of merit and worth would inform the decision to implement a funding option, and they have created massive and extensive causal analyses. Again, in reality often no realistic funding option has been available because the social problem still exists, because it cannot be ignored, because of the absence of alternatives, and because the political commitment to do something precludes change. When there are no competing alternatives and no funding options exist, program and organizational improvement may provide a clearer course to social betterment. The ability to create and manage an expensive evaluation should not excuse an evaluator from making hard-headed judgments to distinguish those evaluation design options that are more likely and those that are less likely to put society on the road to social betterment.

New Policy or Program Environment

Newly established policies or programs are an interesting case. In some instances a new program is in fact a pilot program, which may or may not be implemented more widely, depending on its initial performance. For these pilot programs, assessment of merit and worth once again rises to the fore. Solid information on merit and worth is needed to sort out the strengths of the new course of action and to make decisions about whether to expand the program's scope. (This subtype of new program may be also be seen as a special instance of a competitive environment.)

Newly established programs other than pilot programs are often vulnerable to criticism, even when no viable alternatives for wholesale change are rising to the public agenda. Thus this environment often leads to the evaluation purpose of program and organizational improvement. Program improvement can be especially important for new programs, which may still have weaknesses in organizational capacity or inconsistencies between program goals and the existing mission of the agency, or service delivery challenges. Oversight and compliance evaluations can also be beneficial through their search for discrepancies between operations as mandated and operations as implemented.

Guidelines and Examples

Table 5.1 illustrates the relative priority of each of the four evaluations purposes in the four policy environments. In individual cases, a thoughtful exploration of the policy environment and a careful probe of the relevant parties' values may suggest a different priority. We suggest, however, that the burden of proof should fall on evaluators and evaluation sponsors to rule out the highest priority purpose shown here before selecting another. Although Table 5.1 is not a final resolution of the selection process, it stands as a point of departure for the discussion of evaluation purpose. At the very least these guidelines should offer a clear reminder that the selection of purpose should not be driven by the methodological or theoretical interests of the evaluator but by the likelihood that the evaluation will support the pursuit of improving social conditions. Evaluation sponsors often weigh in heavily on these issues, but clients and other stakeholders also have interests. Evaluators should seek to reduce bias and to provide balance in the selection process by using the values inquiry methods discussed in Chapter Ten.

Sorting out the status of the policy environment in the first place also requires careful assessment and judgment, which generally means that differences of opinions will occur. For instance, the Georgia Pre-K Program was the first universally available developmental program for four-year-olds in the country. The program is relatively recent (established in 1993) and even more recently codified in the state constitution (1998). Views about the policy environment and about the evaluation purpose that will best serve social betterment depend on the perspective from which people view the program. From the perspective of program administrators and staff in Georgia, the most direct route to betterment is probably program improvement. There is little chance the program will be eliminated. Its environment is unusually stable. So program

TABLE 5.1. Selecting Priority Purposes for Anticipated Policy Environments.

Stable Environment	Competitive Environment	Shifts in Funding Environment	New Policy or Program Environment
1. Program and organizational improvement	1. Assessment of merit and worth	1. Assessment of merit and worth	1. Program and organizational improvement *or* assessment of merit and worth
2. Oversight and compliance	2. Knowledge development (about mechanism)	2. Program and organizational improvement	
3. Knowledge development		3. Knowledge development	2. Oversight and compliance
4. Assessment of merit and worth	3. Program and organizational improvement *or* oversight and compliance	4. Oversight and compliance	3. Knowledge development

administrators and staff are likely to be concerned with how they can modify service provision to maximize program benefits. For program detractors, many of whom view the program as "free babysitting," compliance with statutes is an important issue. Critics' complaints often revolve around whether program sites are delivering services in a way intended to stimulate social and emotional benefits or whether they are just standard day-care facilities that provide economic incentives for removing children from their families at public expense. If critics could plausibly make the case that funding options exist (for example, that funding might be eliminated if the program were shown to be ineffective), the existence of those options would support an assessment of merit and worth. From the perspective of other states or of the federal government when considering adopting a similar program, questions related to merit and worth prevail: Are the services for four-year-olds improving their educational and social outcomes later on relative to those who had not attended the prekindergarten program? Depending on whose perspective you take—program staff, program detractor, or

policymaker or citizen in another jurisdiction—a different evaluation purpose may appear to most directly support betterment.

As this example illustrates, disagreements may exist about the
information that is most important for social betterment in a specific case. In the stable environment Georgia Pre-K Program example, what is the most pressing information need—for the program
improvement favored by program staff or for the oversight and compliance preferred by program detractors? Are there really any plausible funding options for this new but stable program? To what
extent should the interests of those in other states, for whom universal pre-K may become a competitor to current policies, influence
an evaluation funded by Georgia taxpayers? Is there truly any serious competitor for the current policy or program?

The complexities in choosing an evaluation purpose arise for at
least three reasons. First, if two people disagree in their assessment
of the policy environment, they will probably differ in their evaluation priorities. For example, what a legislator views as a pilot program, a local staff member may see as a stable program without
competition—and these discrepant views would suggest different
evaluation purposes. Second, even where there is consensus about
the nature of the policy environment, disagreement may occur
about evaluation priorities, as we have noted in the case of newly
created programs. And third, many contextual factors can enter
into judgments beyond those we have discussed.

Fortunately, in practice evaluators often find ways to adapt to
such complexities by conducting evaluations that fulfill more than
one purpose. In the remainder of this chapter, we present some
options that arise when multiple purposes and multiple inquiry
modes are combined in an evaluation.

Overview of Single- and Dual-Purpose Evaluations

We begin the exploration of multipurpose evaluations with a wide-
ranging display of single- and dual-purpose evaluation strategies,
and with discussion of the contexts in which each is most likely to

contribute and how. Although evaluators could plan an evaluation to meet all four purposes and although such an evaluation might conceivably accomplish its multiple objectives, we have limited our discussion to evaluations designed to meet at most two purposes. We do this for both pragmatic and philosophical reasons. Pragmatically, the array of permutations would be mind boggling if we considered every combination of single, twofold, threefold, and fourfold purposes. In terms of evaluation philosophy, the decision making required to serve three or four purposes is likely to be overly ambitious and inadequately disciplined. A theory of omnipurpose evaluations would promise too much. It might also divert evaluators from some hard choices. When everything is thought to be possible, there is no need for priorities. Without focus, no purpose may be given adequate attention. Thus the results from an omnipurpose evaluation can fail to provide information that can be used for *any* deliberations about how social conditions can best be improved. Instead, evaluation effectiveness typically depends on determining the one or two purposes most likely to serve betterment in a particular context.

When a single purpose is chosen as the priority, we refer to the evaluation as having a *pure* purpose. A pure purpose evaluation may indirectly contribute to some other purpose, but this will be an unplanned benefit not an intention. In contrast, dual-purpose evaluations, designed to address two purposes, are an important fixture on the evaluation landscape. Changes occur in social conditions. Agendas shift after elections. The appointment of new officials makes future information needs notoriously difficult to predict. In addition, those with different roles in democracies (for example, legislators, program staff, and clients) can have different information needs, even if the players and agendas remain constant. In the unkempt world of democratic policymaking, dual-purpose evaluations increase the probability of contributing to betterment. They allow evaluation planners to better serve multiple masters in unstable circumstances and to hedge their bets about future information needs while maintaining some sense of priorities.

In similar fashion, endless strings of inquiry modes could, in principle, be put together to produce information concerning the chosen purpose. However, resources and time constrain this possibility. Our tack here is to consider the sequences of inquiries evaluators are most likely to use, sequences limited for the most part to two or three modes. Sequences should not be multiplied to extend so far into the future that they strain the capacity and, indeed, credibility for anticipating distant information needs. At some point, course-correcting feedback from the institutions using the information is likely to be required.

Despite these restrictions in our discussion, it should give evaluators concrete ideas about sequences, and with experience, evaluators should be able to extend the suggestions offered here, for example, by stringing together pure and dual-purpose evaluations to provide more comprehensive information about a policy or program.

A Matrix of Possibilities

Table 5.2 presents various combinations of primary and secondary evaluation purposes along with the pure purpose options. The shaded cells contain the pure purpose options. The primary purpose defines the columns in Table 5.2 and the secondary purpose defines the rows. The matrix is not symmetrical (that is, the entries above the diagonal are different from those below) because of the distinction between primary and secondary purposes. For example, the top right cell denotes evaluations that have the primary purpose of knowledge development and the secondary purpose of assessing merit and worth, while in the bottom left cell, the priorities are reversed. The italicized cells in the upper left quadrant present the purposes (single and combined) to which we believe most evaluation practice and evaluation theory has been dedicated. On the other hand, the cells in the lower right quadrant appear relatively infrequent in evaluation practice.

TABLE 5.2. Primary and Secondary Combinations of Evaluation Purposes.

Secondary Purposes	Primary Purposes for Evaluation Planning			
	Assessment of merit and worth	*Program and organizational improvement*	*Oversight and compliance*	*Knowledge development*
Assessment of merit and worth	Scriven's Minimal Theory Evaluation (1997a) "Black-box" randomized experiments	Performance monitoring (Wholey, 1994), with pattern over time used as rough assessment of merit and worth Natural experiments using performance indicator data to attribute outcome differences to program elements (Peisner-Feinberg & Burchinal, 1997)	Classification of program sites into required model when evidence exists of model's efficacy (Henderson, Basile, & Henry, 1999) Natural experiments using performance indicator data to assess impact of adherence to specific regulations	Theory testing that happens to occur in an evaluation context
Program and organizational improvement	Theory-driven outcome evaluation, using insider theories of service delivery (McClintock, 1990)	Process evaluation (Scheirer, 1994) Logic modeling (Wholey, 1994b) Developmental evaluation (Patton, 1997)	Compliance monitoring with recommendations (for example, U.S. General Accounting Office, 1998b) High Stakes Performance Accountability Systems (Ladd, 1999)	Development of classification system for programs based on effectiveness (Marcon, 1999)

Oversight and compliance	Standards-based accountability with information to overseers (Behn, 1997)	Low stakes accountability systems with feedback to administrators, staff, overseers, and public (Henry, 1996a)	Performance audits (Jonas, 1998; Divorski, 1996)	Studies of the relationship of controls or incentives to behaviors and outcomes
Knowledge development	Disciplinary theory–driven evaluation (Pawson & Tilley, 1997) Analysis of distribution of effects (Friedlander & Robins, 1997)	Identification and validation of best practices	Performance monitoring with side study of organizational learning or the proper construction of monitoring systems	(Not evaluation per se but research in the policy sciences and in disciplines such as psychology and political science)

Alone and in combination, the purposes of assessment of merit and worth and program and organizational improvement have pre-occupied the field—arguably because they are the purposes with the most direct linkages to social betterment. If evaluators assist demo-cratic institutions in choosing between policy alternatives on the basis of meritorious results, society benefits. If evaluators assist orga-nizations, be they public bureaucracies, private companies, or not-for-profit agencies, in improving the delivery of the chosen policy alternatives, once again society benefits. Because of their tight link-ages to social betterment, program improvement and the assess-ment of merit and worth have consumed most of the intellectual capital and most of the financial resources dedicated to evaluation. Prominent theorists, such as Scriven and Campbell, seem to weigh in more on the side of assessment of merit and worth. Other evalu-ation gurus, such as Patton and Wholey, tilt in the direction of pro-gram improvement. Still others, such as Chelimsky and Weiss, seem to recognize both as priorities, depending on circumstances. From our perspective, the pursuit of either pure purpose can be justified based on the policy environment and the certainty with which information needs can be anticipated, as discussed previously. But in the great majority of the cases, we believe one of these evalua-tion purposes should be selected as the primary purpose and the other should be incorporated as secondary. (Or under circumstances we describe later, one should be chosen as the primary purpose and either oversight and compliance or knowledge development selected as a secondary purpose.)

Looking Inside the Matrix

Let us consider some specific combinations. As noted in the second cell of the first column of Table 5.2, when an assessment of merit and worth also tests a theory about which of the program processes and components produces the desired effects, it will likely give rise to information that will be useful in modifying the program. The assessment can still estimate the size of the effects produced by the program. In addition, by encouraging program personnel (and perhaps others) to make their program theory explicit and by probing the accuracy of the links in that program theory, the evaluation should suggest possible avenues for program improvement.

When program improvement has priority and assessment of merit is secondary (the first cell in the second column), natural experiments or other inexpensive forms of causal analysis can be conducted to examine whether the pattern of variation in outcomes is partially attributable to different characteristics of the program. Through comparisons between groups receiving alternative versions or amounts of the program's services, the effect of program variants may be roughly estimated. At the same time, other, perhaps more rigorous comparisons can be made (involving patterns of outcomes over time and comparisons with those not participating in the program) to obtain an adequate assessment of merit and worth of the program as a whole. Some performance measurement systems are well equipped for evaluations with this combination of purposes, especially when socially accepted criteria and standards can be acceptable benchmarks for merit and worth. For example, school accountability systems in Texas, North Carolina, and Kentucky have set criteria for low performing or unacceptable schools. These criteria may suffice as rough indicators of merit and worth, while the performance monitoring system also provides program staff and others with information they can use toward program improvement. (Note also that this example illustrates that it may be easier for society to define what is clearly unacceptable than to define what is acceptable. Similarly, it may be easier for decision makers and others to accept the results of a rough assessment of merit and worth when it focuses on identifying unacceptable performance.)

The cells in the lower left and the upper right quadrants of Table 5.2 illustrate how it is possible to join knowledge development and oversight and compliance together with each other and with the other two purposes, the "heavy hitters" of assessment of merit and worth and program and organizational improvement.

Such combinations are, we believe, the next most frequent area of evaluation practice, after evaluations that give primacy to assessment of merit and worth and program improvement, alone or in combination.

Two traditions, both alive and well within the field of evaluation, illustrate the importance of these other combinations. First, legislative program evaluators at the state and federal levels frequently focus on oversight and compliance. One widely recognized responsibility of legislative bodies is oversight of the executive branch's administration of their legislative mandates. The General Accounting Office and legislative agencies in at least forty states (Jonas, 1999) now conduct evaluations that generally give priority to oversight and compliance. This purpose is often combined with an assessment of merit and worth or with program improvement to provide more comprehensive and more useful information to legislators and others about, respectively, the extent to which the program is working as anticipated and better ways of achieving the desired program results. (Legislative objectives are often used to define merit in these evaluations.) When oversight and compliance is combined with program improvement, the resulting evaluation may offer recommendations for refining the relevant legislation or suggest additional directives for the program.

In the second tradition, evaluators in academic settings or in think tanks often pursue knowledge development purposes. Although knowledge development may be combined with any of the other purposes, it is perhaps most commonly joined with assessments of merit and worth. The general value of knowledge development as a primary or secondary purpose is that the new knowledge it generates may have long-term benefits arising from testing underlying mechanisms, providing a new classification system for the types of programs in operation, assessing the distribution of effects across different groups of program participants, testing the benefits of competition in providing public services, or validating best practices in some program area. Knowledge development studies such as these may in turn guide program improvement, inform the assessment of merit, and produce knowledge that has application beyond the circumstances at hand.

Although we have not addressed each of the cells in Table 5.2 in detail, the practices listed in most cells should be familiar to evaluators. The critical questions at this point are how to decide which combination of purposes should be addressed in a given evaluation and what combination and sequence of inquiry modes may be necessary to address the multiple purposes at hand. It is to these two questions we now turn.

Dual Purposes: Contexts and Methods

In this section we focus in turn on each of the four purposes as the *primary* purpose of an evaluation. We consider that purpose as a pure purpose, and we consider it in combination with each of the other purposes.

Tables 5.3 through 5.5 summarize this information for the first three purposes discussed. In a sense, each expands on one of the first three columns of Table 5.2. These tables are intended to be quick references for evaluators planning an evaluation or an evaluation program. They address the common situations in which each of the evaluation purpose options is employed, the primary inquiry mode(s) used with each option, and the common methods applied in each case. Note that we have not attempted to list *every* situation that might be found or *every* inquiry mode or method that might be used, however well or poorly, for a given purpose. Evaluators should of course go through the judgment process discussed in Chapter Four of choosing the appropriate inquiry mode for the evaluation in question.

When Assessing Merit and Worth Is a Priority

Three attributes are common across the four pure and the dual-purpose options with assessment of merit and worth as the primary purpose. First, these options are most commonly called for in situations in which there is strong interest in comparing net effects, that is, in assessing how well a program stacks up against a competing program. Second, values inquiry is likely to be the first mode of inquiry in evaluations that place highest priority on the assessment of merit and worth. As we have seen, values inquiry should reduce bias in the selection of outcomes to be measured and should raise any issues of human rights or of procedural infractions that require attention. In many circumstances, an assessment of merit and worth cannot be adequately performed without formal values inquiry. When values are well known through natural valuation processes or when the issues have been well defined through deliberations, formal values inquiry may not be necessary as the initial mode of inquiry (see the values guidelines box in Chapter Four). But even in these cases, values inquiry might be appropriate later in the evaluation process to see whether different values have emerged through people's experience with the program or with changes in conditions.

The third attribute associated with the primary purpose of assessing merit and worth is the typical use of causal analysis as an inquiry mode. It is part of the most likely inquiry sequence for the pure assessment of merit and worth and for all combinations with such assessment as the highest priority. Recall, however, from the previous chapter, that in some circumstances descriptive methods such as performance measurement will suffice for the assessment of merit and worth and in some cases may even be more appropriate, especially for obtaining a sense of the collective worth of complex, multipronged public measures to improve social conditions.

Having seen the commonalities across the four options, let us turn to the differences. Pure assessment of merit and worth is the ideal that Scriven seems to have in mind when he advocates *minimalist theory* approaches. His logic seems compelling, and it may in fact be quite compelling for marketplace decisions (decisions made in the *market* rather than the *forum*, to use Elster's 1997 terminology); however, the contribution to social betterment of a pure assessment of merit and worth is limited. The addition of a sec-

ondary purpose usually produces a greater pay-off for one's investment of resources. Each of the combinations of purposes summarized
in Table 5.3 adds information that may be useful for realizing program benefits or for short-circuiting negative side effects. Each also
adds methodological complexities to the already complex endeavor
of the likely inquiry modes: values inquiry and causal analysis.

Adding program improvement to the assessment of merit adds
attention to the possibility of identifying more effective service
delivery methods, aligning service delivery methods with the
requirements of individuals who benefit most from them, or developing a taxonomy of best practices from evidence indicating a linkage between some practices and more positive effects. Alternatively,
the assessment of merit and worth may be carried out with data,
perhaps from a performance monitoring system, that also allow program staff and others to search for possible opportunities for, and
sources of, program improvements.

Adding oversight and compliance as a secondary purpose raises
another set of issues. Usually with this combination of purposes,
values inquiry and causal analysis are combined with a descriptive
exercise with the goal of examining compliance with program
mandates and the preservation of valued responsibilities, rights, and
liberties. Alternatively, classification might be added to the values
inquiry and causal analysis to assess whether the program offerings
fall into an approved category. Moreover, some care is required with
the combination of assessment of merit and oversight and compliance when the data used for these two purposes overlap. Fears about
being found to be out of compliance may hinder the collection of
data needed to assess merit and worth.

Finally, consider the case in which knowledge development is a
secondary purpose to the assessment of merit and worth. Although
the knowledge development component could focus on any of a
variety of things, often the concern will be with underlying mechanisms. Why effects occur is not a question for the pure assessment
of merit as in Scriven's minimal theory model. But such explanation may be crucial in providing needed support for reasoning

within deliberative institutions. The case has been made that knowledge development in the form of explanation can be an important aid to generalization (Cronbach, 1982; Mark, 1990). That is, explaining effects is important if one hopes to make the inferential leap that similar effects are likely to occur in the future or in another setting. With knowledge of why a program works, one may, for example, avoid attempts to export it to situations in which its desirable effects are not likely to be realized (Pawson & Tilley, 1997). This alone seems an adequate argument for employing this combination rather than the pure assessment or merit and worth. Certainly, developing tests of competing mechanisms requires expertise, thought, and time. But the marginal costs of adding such tests to the expense of values inquiry and causal analysis may be sufficiently low to justify this step. (Table 5.3 summarizes the main points in this section.)

When Program and Organizational Improvement Is a Priority

Combinations of purposes that include program improvement present some opportunities that are too often missed in evaluation, especially in the addition of a secondary focus on merit and worth. The literature on performance measurement and monitoring includes many recommendations in favor of this combination (for example, Chelimsky, 1997; Henry & Dickey, 1993; Scheirer, in press; Wholey, 1994, 1997), but few examples are actually available (Harkreader & Henry, in press). Evaluations that emphasize this dual purpose usually give a rough-gauge assessment of merit and worth based on descriptive outcome data and place more emphasis on using these descriptive data for program improvement. In some cases, extra steps are taken, such as trying to demonstrate a predicted sequence of changes, in an effort to increase confidence that the program is responsible for the observed outcomes (Harkreader & Henry, in press; Scheirer, in press). Another way to join the purpose of assessment of merit and worth to program improvement is to add a

TABLE 5.3. Primary Purpose: Assessment of Merit and Worth.

	Assessment of Merit and Worth (Pure Purpose)	Assessment of Merit and Worth Combined with Program Improvement	Assessment of Merit and Worth Combined with Oversight and Compliance	Assessment of Merit and Worth Combined with Knowledge Development
Common situations	Desire to estimate net effects for intended outcomes and for side effects central to deliberation and decision; desire to describe relevant issues of rights and dignity. Typically performed when resources and service delivery routines are well established.	Desire to assess net effects (intended and unintended) is most important, but the specification of the most effective service delivery approach is also in question.	Desire to assess net effects (intended and unintended) is most important, but ability or willingness to implement the intervention is also in question.	Desire to assess net effects (intended and unintended) is most important, but why a program works, moderating influences, or methodological testing are also important.
Likely inquiry mode sequences	Values inquiry then causal analysis; or causal analysis then values inquiry.	Values inquiry then causal analysis with classification or with description of program.	Values inquiry then causal analysis then description or classification.	Values inquiry then causal analysis with other modes required to address knowledge development.
Common methods	Randomized experiments; quasi-experiments; modeling natural variation; qualitative observations or mixed methods with iterative pattern matching logic. For valuation processes: focus groups; survey of criteria defining program success.	Same as for the pure purpose plus classification of best practices or performance monitoring to identify possible alternatives to current practices.	Same as for the pure purpose plus monitoring of compliance with requirements or classification (to assess compliance with required program model).	Same as for the pure purpose plus principled discovery and competitive elaboration of underlying mechanisms; analysis of distribution of effects for minorities.

natural experiment (Rog, 1994) or other weak form of causal analysis to the descriptive inquiry that is central to program improvement.

Knowledge development as a secondary purpose to program improvement will often focus on the development of best practice frameworks. The objective is to demonstrate the linkage between specific variants in service delivery and better outcomes. Service delivery information and outcome data will usually come from the same descriptive performance measurement system used to support program improvement. The linkages between service delivery and outcomes will be examined further with natural experiments or case studies, with the results contributing to the literature on best practices. Of course other forms of knowledge development can be added to an evaluation that places priority on program improvement. To take but one example, the performance measurement system used primarily for program improvement in a mental health center might also provide data to test "revolving door" hypotheses (that is, hypotheses about the extent to which clients return for new rounds of treatment).

One addition in particular requires considerable caution. The combination of the purpose of oversight with program improvement is ripe for conflict. Program operators may feel pressure to bias data to comply with performance standards, thus threatening the validity of the program improvement efforts that rely on these same data.

Finally, note that the role of values inquiry may differ for evaluations that place the highest priority on program improvement and for those that give priority to assessing merit and worth. Stakeholder participation has long been recognized to have two related but separate benefits for evaluation: identification of important effects and buy-in of stakeholders who may later use the findings (Bryk, 1983; Weiss, 1983). The former benefit is paramount when values inquiry is included in methods sequences for assessments of merit and worth; the latter predominates in evaluations that emphasize program improvement. Obviously, when the two purposes are combined, regardless of which has priority, both benefits are important. In addition, when program improvement is the pure purpose, values inquiry may be used by itself as an inquiry mode. The idea here is that assessing the values that various parties hold about a program can in and of itself suggest steps toward program improvement. For example, if an outcome that was ignored by the program designers is in fact highly valued, revisions to the program may be needed to bring services in line with highly valued clients' needs. (This section is summarized in Table 5.4.)

When Oversight and Compliance Is a Priority

Evaluations that set out oversight and compliance as a priority have at least until recently been considered the backwater of the field. Compliance with rules and regulations seemed to be the province of auditors and inspectors general (Wisler, 1996). Still, for many observers, oversight and compliance is the most direct approach to operationalizing the idea of accountability. Discussions of the need for accountability can be traced at least to *The Federalist.* As noted in paper number 47, oversight has its roots in the doctrine of the separation of powers. But other evaluators see the general notion of accountability as a justification for all types of evaluations (Chelimsky, 1997), without tying it directly to inquiring about the extent to which the program complies with statutory mandates.

Several recent trends have brought oversight and compliance evaluations more into the foreground. First is the development of active, professional evaluation units in state legislatures and at the U.S. General Accounting Office (Chelimsky, 1991; Jonas, 1999). These units have used oversight and compliance as a base from which they have also addressed other evaluation purposes. Their evaluations are frequently used in deliberations and as a basis for subsequent action. In the process many of these units have carved out an important role in legislative institutions. Second, serious questions have been raised about the relationship between regulations and performance. Regulations were previously considered supports for performance. They were seen as controls that would improve the delivery of services and result in increased benefits.

TABLE 5.4. Primary Purpose: Program and Organizational Improvement.

	Program and Organizational Improvement Combined with Assessment of Merit and Worth	Program and Organizational Improvement (Pure Purpose)	Program and Organizational Improvement Combined with Oversight and Compliance	Program and Organizational Improvement Combined with Knowledge Development
Common situations	Desire to improve program foremost; also desire to see if program outcomes are reaching expected levels and if negative side effects are occurring.	Delegation to program insiders to act when presented with evidence of strengths and weaknesses or to act based on accepting a shared vision of program.	Data collection methods for program improvement can capture compliance information at little additional cost.	Identification of strengths and weaknesses can be extended by classifying programs or assessing effectiveness of structural variations in the program or best practice models.
Likely inquiry mode sequences	Description then causal analysis or causal analysis (values inquiry may follow or precede).	Description then values inquiry; or values inquiry then description	Description	Description then causal analysis; or classification then causal analysis
Common methods	Process evaluations that include outcome measures; natural experiments; natural valuation, often implicitly modeled with program managers and staff.	Performance monitoring, with managers and staff deliberating on changes needed based on monitoring data, and natural valuation implicitly modeled with program managers and staff; values inquiry (as in developmental evaluation).	One-shot monitoring; ongoing performance measurement (high stakes accountability may bias data also used for program improvement).	Development of taxonomy of best practices; description of practices in operation; natural experiments to try to link best practices to better outcomes.

However, the more contemporary view is that regulations often impede performance (for example, Chubb & Moe, 1990). This view has strengthened the need for information on the actual impact of various rules and on whether they help or hinder performance. Finally, the interest in performance monitoring and results-based budgeting has forged linkages in both legislatures and administrative agencies between oversight and outcomes. Schools have led the way in the adoption of performance reporting and performance expectations that are tied to rewards and sanctions. Local government reinvention and the Government Performance and Results Act have spread the institutionalization of this movement far beyond the schoolhouse (Newcomer, 1997).

Oversight and compliance evaluations always examine compliance with existing rules and regulations, and they may also examine compliance with the attainment of formally established performance objectives. Performance measurement systems that provide information on the strengths and weaknesses of a unit's performance but do not provide a comparison against expected levels of performance do not meet our definition of oversight and compliance. However, performance systems that do both are a volatile mix, especially when program improvement is the primary objective (Henry, 1996a). As we suggested in discussing program improvement as the primary purpose, high stakes accountability, with sanctions and rewards, may inhibit evaluated units' cooperation with data requests, may increase strategic manipulation of data to improve the appearance of performance in the absence of actual improvement, and may diminish the internal use of performance data for improvement.

Pure oversight and compliance evaluations allow doubts to remain about whether compliance translates into the desired outcomes. Compliance with rules brings no assurance of improved social conditions. Such uncertainty is a major reason that pure oversight and compliance evaluations have been shunned by many in the field. It also accounts for the contemporary reinvention of oversight and compliance to include outcomes and other performance measures. Oversight and compliance evaluations can be combined with other purposes to provide information for both legislative and executive branch institutions to fulfill their roles in establishing *and* carrying out social policies and programs. Oversight and compliance is often a primary purpose both when programs are new and when they are well established. Newly established programs often undergo compliance checks (see General Accounting Office, 1999, on empowerment zones). Well-established programs are often subject to episodic review to provide oversight information to legislative committees and commissions. These may be low-cost, one-shot reviews (Bezruki, Mueller, & McKim, 1999), but of late, ongoing performance measurement systems have often been instituted to provide periodic feedback to both administrators responsible for service delivery and legislators responsible for oversight.

Among the combinations of purposes with oversight and compliance as the primary purpose, the most potent adds the secondary assessment of merit and worth. Improving outcomes, protecting the rights of stakeholders, and enhancing equity in ongoing programs are potential objectives for this combination. Often this combination is planned when there are deliberations about deregulation and also concerns about the ramifications of removing operational controls on those delivering services. Contemporary arguments often hold that red tape needs to be eliminated to allow program staff to concentrate on results (see, for example, Gore, 1993). But will deregulation actually result in less administrative diligence, reduced levels of desired outcomes, increases in negative side effects, problematic inequities in service delivery, or intolerable restrictions on stakeholders' liberty? For example, are limits on first-grade class size important for educational outcomes or should the restrictions be removed to allow schools to become more innovative? By adding the assessment of merit to oversight and compliance, evaluators may be able to analyze the effectiveness of specific current rules and estimate the impact of removing them selectively. Natural experiments that contrast sites that follow certain rules with sites that do not may be the most obvious method, especially as performance measurement systems are developed to provide comparable information across program sites.

If program improvement is pursued as a secondary purpose in oversight and compliance evaluations, a number of concerns are raised. On the one hand, as noted earlier, most of these have to do with the possibility that high stakes accountability systems will create incentives to manipulate data strategically. On the other hand, adding measures of good practices to oversight measures may provide managers and others with data for focusing their efforts toward program improvement. This combination of purposes does not necessarily include the validation of the good practices by demonstrating a relationship to good outcomes (this occurs when program improvement is the top priority). Rather, in this case, internal or external expert opinion is more likely to define good practices. Measures such as "percentage of open cases with no face-to-face contact in a month" for parole system evaluations, or "percentage of lead teachers with degrees in early childhood education" for evaluations of preschool programs are illustrative. Frequently, descriptive inquiry is used in such evaluations. Results may be provided for each evaluation purpose to different audiences or the same results may be put to use by these different audiences. Thus the teachers and parents on a school improvement team may use information on grades and standardized test scores in a different way than the local school board as it exercises its oversight responsibilities.

The final combination involves the addition of knowledge development to an oversight and compliance evaluation. This combination is most likely to occur when evaluators or other stakeholders have a direct interest in better understanding the relationship between policy or administrative controls on the one hand and the behaviors of those charged with the carrying out the policy on the other. Indeed, research in this area has found support for the bean counters' axiom that what is monitored is done (Wood & Waterman, 1991). This combination of purposes is relatively rare, but it may increase as performance measurement systems for oversight become more common and more comprehensive in examining effects. An exemplar of this combination is Robert Putnam's work (1995) on the effectiveness of regional authorities in Italy. For over twenty years, Putnam and his colleagues collected data on the operations and outputs of authorities in regions similar to states in the United States or provinces in Canada. These authorities were established in the 1970s, and Putnam was able to begin data collection before the actual start-up. His data are mainly descriptive, but he first determined the structural components of the authorities' outputs and then set up competitive tests between alternative mechanisms that might explain authorities' success or failure. He has found that a region's social capital largely explains the success of its regional government. In short, working from descriptive data for processes and outcomes, Putnam enhanced the state of knowledge about why some democratic institutions succeed and others fail. (Table 5.5 summarizes this section.)

Can Knowledge Development Be a Priority?

Evaluation has often been said to be a practical endeavor, a means for improving social conditions. Without question, there is a time and a place for evaluations that intend to promote social betterment by assessing merit and worth, by improving programs, or by contributing to oversight and compliance. But can an evaluation place sole or primary priority on knowledge development and still be an evaluation? Again, without question, knowledge development can contribute to social betterment. Indeed, some have argued that knowledge development is more likely to stimulate betterment than is the more applied route, such as evaluation (Rule, 1978).

Our position can be stated succinctly. Knowledge development can be a valuable secondary purpose for evaluation, even in some cases a primary purpose, but not the pure purpose. The addition of a knowledge development function in the form of a test of mediating mechanisms, for example, can greatly enhance an assessment of merit and worth. And without a doubt, pure knowledge development has its place in the specialty areas that overlap with evaluation.

TABLE 5.5. Primary Purpose: Oversight and Compliance.

	Oversight and Compliance Combined with Assessment of Merit and Worth	Oversight and Compliance Combined with Program and Organizational Improvement	Oversight and Compliance (Pure Purpose)	Oversight and Compliance Combined with Knowledge Development
Common situations	Deregulation is an expected issue in adapting a policy, but uncertainties exist about the effects of removing specific requirements.	Information is needed to align monitored regulations with good practices, performance-oriented oversight or management.	Periodic or episodic check is needed to provide routine oversight information for ongoing policy or program.	Interest in developing understanding of how variations in adherence to rules influence behavior and performances.
Likely inquiry mode sequences	Description then causal analysis; or description then classification then causal analysis.	Classification then description.	Description (one shot or performance measurement).	Classification then description; or description then classification; or description then causal analysis.
Common methods	Performance monitoring for natural experiments; development of taxonomies of compliance; setting standards adjusted for risk factors.	Development (by inductive or deductive classification) of groupings of practices to be monitored.	Traditionally, process-oriented reviews; now include outcome indicators and other indicators that inform equity and liberty concerns.	Classification of oversight structures; description or classification of variations in compliance with mandates; perhaps coupled with natural experiments to analyze effects.

For example, psychologists and early childhood education experts can and should study the learning process in preschoolers, and the results might inform subsequent evaluations of preschool programs. But basic theory development and theory testing, divorced from the assessment of merit and worth or program improvement or oversight and compliance is, in our view, not an appropriate focus in the field of evaluation.

Especially for evaluations conducted by those in academic settings and in think tanks, knowledge development may be the primary purpose. Nonetheless, evaluation should not be conducted for purely knowledge development purposes.

Planning Evaluation Programs

With so many sole and dual purpose evaluations, and with so many possible sequences of inquiry modes, a single evaluation can provide much flexibility and a wide range of options. But this flexibility and the many options increase the challenge of evaluation planning. In this final section we address this challenge in terms of the planning of programs of multiple, sequential evaluations.

Even solid evaluation findings from a well-planned evaluation, with findings that are relevant to the overall goal of social betterment, may not meet all the information needs that one wants an evaluation to address. Consider two scenarios.

An evaluation finds that a new science curriculum works better on the average than the unplanned array of curricula currently in place. But other questions then arise: For what types of children is the new curriculum more effective than the current one? For African Americans, Hmong, those with special needs, those who are gifted? What makes the curriculum work better? What if anything might teachers do to improve the new curriculum as they adopt it to their classrooms? Are some schools or some classrooms within a school more successful with the new curriculum than others? Why? Are the positive results visible only on standardized tests, or do teachers see improvements in students' motivation and critical thinking skills? Are there long-term effects on students' entry into scientific and technical fields?

In several rural communities in Central America, women's resource investment banks were begun by philanthropic agencies as demonstrations. The women and their families report having better living conditions in terms of stable food supplies and adequacy of housing after a few years of capital accumulation and financing of small business start-ups. More children in these villages are attending school and are staying in school longer. But other questions arise: Are certain types of financing more effective for certain types of women? Are there any negative side effects for the villagers? How do the women and their families feel about the changes in social conditions? What, if any, other changes have they experienced as a result of their participation in the program? Are there shortcomings in the program that can be remedied? Will the strategy work in Asian countries? Can conditions in urban areas benefit from similar investments?

These scenarios call attention to the fact that the search for social betterment is an ongoing, never-ending enterprise. No single evaluation, no matter how carefully planned, can provide all the information that can assist sensemaking about a program now and in the future. Thus it is generally preferable to think in terms of a series of evaluations, an *evaluation program*, to answer the emerging questions of those who must make choices in the pursuit of betterment. Evaluations can proceed from exploratory to confirmatory, from net effects to moderated effects. Performance measurement can provide a sense of the magnitude of a social problem whereas causal analysis can assess a specific program's contribution to reducing the problem.

Perhaps the classic evaluation program follows a sequence from program and organizational improvement to assessment of merit and worth to oversight and compliance. The initial evaluation of program and organizational improvement ensures that the program is indeed operating and that the operations have been fine-tuned. Assessment of merit and worth provides information on whether the program works or not. If it does, it is then important to monitor the operations to ensure that the services found to work are continued. Of course the logic of this or other sequences can be defeated by the facts of the case. Program weaknesses may not have been shored up before the assessment of merit and worth begins. Or the program's merit may be dubious, eliminating the value of compliance checks.

Despite such complexities, those who sponsor evaluations should consider the benefits of an evaluation program. The evaluation purpose and inquiry methods can be targeted to the information need of the moment. The program can be flexible, informed by the questions arising in democratic institutions as the findings from each evaluation are disseminated and discussed. An evaluation program also avoids having a single evaluation that must attempt to bear the burden of being all things to all people.

Conclusion

Planning an evaluation is a complex process that requires an analysis of the policy environment, matching the purpose to the information needs in the anticipated environment, and selecting appropriate modes of inquiry. The assessment of merit and worth, one of the two most called upon purposes in the field, functions best when a course of action is to be chosen (a competitive environment) and the alternative actions are known, and is also important when funding shifts are plausible even in the absence of competitors. Program and organizational improvement is most likely to be relevant when policies and programs are likely to change only at the margins (a stable environment). And these marginal changes are not insignificant. Correcting caseworkers who are not delivering services effectively or retraining preschool teachers who are inadvertently using developmentally inappropriate practices, for example, can produce significant benefits.

In many cases, evaluations will be planned to meet more than one purpose rather than a pure purpose. Limited resources and the existence of many unanswered questions require evaluations that cover as many issues as possible. We have described the permutations of evaluations that have two purposes. Skillful evaluators will find it possible to address more purposes, but in most cases attempting too much will result in accomplishing too little. Evaluators do well not to oversell or overreach.

To finish evaluation planning, an evaluator must move from evaluation purpose and inquiry mode to the selection of specific methods. Judgments about whether a Cadillac or a VW beetle method is required should follow the guidelines and suggestions presented in Chapter Four. Full discussion of the methods themselves begins in Chapter Seven. Before turning to these specific methods, though, we discuss realism and its implications for evaluation. As we outlined earlier, the philosophy of realism provides the rationale for the four inquiry modes; thus it supports the discussion of the methods in each inquiry mode in Chapters Seven through Ten. Realism also helps evaluators understand the nature of the contribution that evaluation can make to sensemaking about policies and programs.

6

Integrating Realism and Assisted Sensemaking

In the preceding chapters we detailed a framework that evaluators and others can use in planning evaluations. Social betterment motivates that planning and, more generally, motivates the field of evaluation. For at least some evaluators, motivation is not enough, however. These scholars and practitioners believe that evaluation theories should also deal with justification, that they should identify and explain a basis for their claim that evaluation (or other systematic inquiry) can provide sound information. In this chapter we discuss the realist theory that we believe helps provide a justification for evaluation. Moreover, realism is useful as more than justification. It also offers a coherent view of how people go about making sense of the world, including the world of social policies and programs. A philosophical foundation can enhance the understanding that evaluators and others have about the nature and role of evaluation. As that foundation, realism can contribute enormously to evaluators', stakeholders', and administrators' way of thinking about evaluation and its role as an assisted sensemaking endeavor.

There are additional reasons why considering this foundation, or paradigm, is a worthwhile undertaking. First, such philosophical foundations do matter. Although a chosen foundation will not completely determine an evaluator's activities and interpretations, it will influence them. Evaluation, like much of the social sciences, has to date been dominated by two opposing views of how systematic inquiry can help people understand the world. One is a validation paradigm based on logical positivism and its subsequent variants, especially logical empiricism. The other is an interpretivist paradigm, which has offspring such as social constructivism (Caracelli & Greene, 1997; Julnes & Mark, 1998; Reichardt & Rallis, 1994). The practitioners and theorists within each paradigm have developed procedures to counter what they see as the most serious threats to establishing justified conclusions. Although reasonably successful in avoiding these threats, the procedures have also committed each paradigm's followers to positions that entail other serious inadequacies.

Recognizing these inadequacies, many evaluators have become disenchanted with the paradigm wars of recent decades and are ready to move on (for example, House, 1994; Smith, 1997). One desirable role for a theory of evaluation, then, is to chart a path that bypasses past controversies and is more consistent with the basic assumptions that most evaluators actually bring to their practice. One could simply try to ignore the philosophical base for practice, but this can create other problems, including leaving the door open for a resumption of the paradigmatic wars. To date, the paradigm wars have been resolved only in the sense of an armistice that allowed the methodologies of both sides to be accorded a place in the practice of evaluation (Cook, 1997; Datta, 1994b). The second reason why defining a philosophical framework seems worthwhile is that an explicit, appropriate conceptual foundation for evaluation can help evaluators and theorists organize and extend the many lessons now available from practice.

Thus in the remainder of this chapter we present a realist perspective in support of the practice of evaluation. We describe relevant aspects of current realist philosophy and some implications for evaluation.

Realism for Assisted Sensemaking

Realism is a perspective with much to offer both the practice and the theory of evaluation. In this section we summarize our realist stance, identifying our position as a variety of what has been called *commonsense realism*. We then describe several other core realist ideas with implications for evaluation, including antiformalism, natural sensemaking, stratified levels of analysis, antireductionism, and openness to alternative explanations.

A Commonsense Foundation

We can crudely summarize the commonsense realist foundation for evaluation as asserting that

- There is a real world confronting evaluators. What people observe in this world is the result of real but not directly observable causal mechanisms and underlying structures.

- Humans have evolved sensemaking techniques. Although these *natural* techniques generally lead to a workable understanding of the world, they have limits and flaws.

- Although there is a real world "out there," some important aspects of it are socially constructed. Therefore our understanding of the world inevitably involves constructions.

- It makes sense to talk about the accuracy of statements, even though no statement may fully convey all the details and complexity of a given situation.

- Some conditions are valued more than others, and so it is meaningful to talk about improvement and about social betterment.

- Social policies and programs have evolved in part to address social problems (that is, to pursue social betterment), and some are more effective than others or are more effective under particular conditions.

- Evaluation has evolved as a means of informing deliberations about social programs and policies, and by doing so evaluation can contribute to the attainment of social betterment.

- Some approaches to evaluation are more useful than others or are more useful under particular conditions, and realism can help evaluators and others select the more useful approach in a particular setting.

As realists, our belief about evaluators is similar to Meehl's about scientists: "As to realism, I have never met any scientist who, when doing science, held to a phenomenalist or idealist view; and I cannot force myself to take a nonrealist view seriously even when I work at it. So I begin with the presupposition that the external world is really there, there is a difference between the world and my view of it, and the business of science is to get my view in harmony with the way the world really is to the extent that is possible" (1986, p. 322). Likewise, we presume that the external world of policies and programs, practitioners and clients is really there; that there may be a difference between that world and people's view of it; and that the business of evaluation is to get people's view in harmony with the way the world of policies and programs really is to the extent possible.

But there are, as Harré (1986) for one tells us, *varieties of realism*. Some realists take extreme positions, such as denying the fundamental reality of everyday items such as tables (Sellars, 1963). The realism we advocate is a variety of commonsense realism. According to this view, commonsense experience of the world is allowed some standing when formal theories that attempt to provide systematic accounts of that experience are developed and evaluated. Rather than taking the formalist approach of deriving first principles from a particular philosophical position and then deducing best practices from these principles, the commonsense realist stance calls for a more subtle and interactive role for philosophical principles in supporting practice.

Antiformalism.   To emphasize lessons from practice over theory-driven principles is to reject what might be called the tyranny of formal models as the sole source of prescriptions for practice. Some realists have noted that this antiformalism means that inquiry may be guided by some formal logic, but need not be dictated as such. As Hilary Putnam (1995), a contemporary American realist, remarks: "[The] revolt against formalism is not a denial of the utility of formal models in certain contexts; but it manifests itself in a sustained critique of the idea that formal models . . . describe a condition to which rational thought either can or should aspire" (p. 63). For evaluators, this antiformalism means that the logic of evaluation may be *guided* by formal logic but need not be dictated by it.

It is a basic claim of commonsense realism that formalism has led to misconstruing both the goal and process of people's efforts to make sense of their world. As Harré (1986) notes, by "defining, even only tacitly, such cognitive phenomena as scientific knowledge in terms of truth and falsity, the demands placed on a community which has the task of accumulating some of 'it' are set in such a way that 'it' can never be achieved" (p. 4). Whereas formalism gives us truth as the goal, commonsense realism holds sound and justified sensemaking in high regard. That is, instead of holding that the goal of inquiry and theory development is to establish the truth value of various claims as though seen from a "God's-Eye View" (Putnam, 1990), commonsense realists hold that the goal is to allow judgments about the plausibility of the claims. Dropping ultimate truth as the goal of inquiry does not, however, equate with sanctioning *any* conclusion. Even though universal or absolute truth will not be the goal, criteria can be used to assess the strength of conclusions. Our realist antiformalism applies, then, to the traditional issues of epistemology, which are concerned with making factual claims about our world. For evaluators who prefer not to engage in the paradigm debates and related philosophical discussion, the message of commonsense realism should be somewhat comforting (and in keeping with their own tendencies). The practice of evaluation can and should go on, even though some classical philosophical questions about knowledge are not fully answered.

Commonsense realism applies antiformalism to values as well as facts (and rejects a rigid distinction between facts and values, as we discuss later). Although formal theories of valuation can be important in identifying key values stances and in framing a critical analysis of potential values positions, they are rarely adequate to serve as the sole or primary foundation for practice. More generally, "formal philosophic theories, such as Rawls's (1971) theory of justice, can serve to inform and critique our positions but need not be used to determine judgments in every evaluation, or how certain interests should be weighted in advance of the study" (House, 1995, p. 45).

Formal theories can help evaluators understand values issues, but they do not capture natural valuation. Natural valuation is the commonsense realist solution to restoring a sense of balance to value judgments, and it has this important implication for evaluation practice: rather than try to prove the validity of a single set of values for all contexts and then apply those values in all evaluations, it is better to carry out values inquiry as part of an evaluation.

The antiformalism of commonsense realism accords well with what sensible people and sensible practitioners have always done. As Gilbert (1998) put it, "While Descartes wondered whether he could truly know anything, his butcher chopped chickens and his banker counted coins. While Kant argued that he could truly know nothing, his barber made haircuts and his baker made muffins" (p. 124). While some philosophers have strived for a formal foundation for knowledge and while others have decried the possibility of such a foundation, the practicing evaluator down the block has provided useful information about social programs and policies.

Finally, endorsing antiformalism means that we offer the theory of evaluation as assisted sensemaking as a guide, as a support to practice, but not as a rigid, formal determinant. And as a further guide, and alternative to formalism, we offer the pattern-matching process emphasized by Campbell (1966). For us, the pattern-matching process is an important aspect of sensemaking, which we look at more closely now.

Natural Sensemaking. Rather than presuming the superiority of a particular formal logic, commonsense realists claim that humans, having evolved in a complex, open systems world, have developed *ways of knowing* that are generally appropriate for such a world (Tharp, 1981). The term *natural sensemaking* is used to describe these evolved tendencies to construct meaningful order. We use the term to differentiate what people naturally do from positivistic efforts to reveal laws and truth in order to see from a God's-Eye View. Natural sensemaking does not entail direct access to truth. "[A]ccuracy is nice, but not necessary. . . . Instead, sensemaking is about plausibility, pragmatics, coherence, reasonableness, creation, invention, and instrumentality" (Weick, 1995, pp. 56–57). The concept of sensemaking has been popularized by Weick (1979, 1995), although our overall view of sensemaking differs somewhat from Weick's, who focuses on organizational management. For instance, as we focus on assisted sensemaking in evaluation we place a stronger emphasis on realism and on searching for effective interventions, and we place less stock in the power of self-fulfilling prophecies and in the tactic of taking any action than Weick appears to. Our view is also strongly influenced by Campbell's work on epistemology (1974b, 1977).

The following box presents some key attributes of natural sensemaking along with (in italics) the related characteristics of evaluation as an assisted sensemaking enterprise. Sensemaking is part of a naturalized epistemology, one that among other qualities has faith in the natural capacities of human sensemaking and rejects overly formal accounts of knowledge construction. But this faith in natural human sensemaking is accompanied by an appreciation also of natural sensemaking's limits. In using natural sensemaking, people can fall prey to inaccuracies for a variety of reasons. For example, they often see things as they expect them to be or as they want them to be (Gilbert, 1998). That is, natural sensemaking can be biased by expectations and desires. In the area of social policies and programs, this is a real danger, for most stakeholders have expectations and desires.

Even plausible accounts arising from natural sensemaking are not always accurate. Moreover, once people have generated an account, accurate or not, or endorsed it as plausible, they can be slow to revise their thinking even in the face of changed evidence. For example, Paulos (1998) describes a study in which participants were presented descriptions of two firefighters, one successful and

---

Key Attributes of Natural Sensemaking and Related Characteristics of Evaluation

1. Sensemaking is active. As Bartlett discussed in 1932, a person's understanding and memory of a new event depends on her existing cognitive structure. Even visual perception is actively constructed (Hoffman, 1998). When different cognitive structures are applied to the same situation, the outcomes of this sensemaking process may well be different. Thus two people observing the same program may reach different conclusions. *Evaluators should recognize the importance of probing and clarifying the value bases that lead different people to view programs and policies through different cognitive structures. Evaluators can also strive to report findings in a clear way, which may reduce any biasing effect from readers' or listeners' existing cognitive structures.*

2. Sensemaking is also active in the sense that it involves acting in, and on, the world. The term *enactment* is used in the literature on sensemaking to "preserve the fact that, in organizational life, people often produce part of the environment they face" (Weick, 1995, p. 30). *The policies and programs public officials and program staff develop are enactments of their sensemaking about human needs and*

social problems, and create part of the environments with
which they and clients deal. Evaluators too create measures,
perform observations, and in other ways act on the world of a
social program as part of the process of making sense about it.
Evaluation and even the very decision to evaluate can influ-
ence the policies and programs evaluators examine.

3. People tend to engage in sensemaking when something
   unexpected occurs, when there are obstacles to reaching
   goals, and when a situation demands thoughtful attention
   (Weick, 1995). *Evaluations are sometimes commissioned*
   when the unexpected occurs. More important, the reporting of
   evaluation findings can serve to break people away from busi-
   ness as usual and elicit their focused sensemaking.

4. Sensemaking involves defining what the question is, not
   just attempting to answer it. The way the question or
   problem is defined is part of the process of making sense
   (Weick, 1995, p. 189). *This aspect of sensemaking encapsu-*
   lates the recent notion of the process use of evaluation (for
   example, Patton, 1997). For instance, the process of selecting
   evaluation measures for a program can change the way people
   view that program.

5. Sensemaking "is a continuous alternation between evidence and explanations, with each cycle giving added form
   and substance to the other" (Weick, 1995, p. 133).
   Evaluators also need to carry out this iteration between data and
   explanations, as we discuss in some detail later under the rubrics
   of principled discovery *and* competitive elaboration.

6. Sensemaking generally involves an evolutionary process—
   people apply an explanatory account, judge its fit with the
   data, and retain accounts that have an adequate fit
   (Campbell, 1977; Weick, 1995). That is, accounts are
   retained if they seem plausible, and people may see an account as plausible even if it does not comport with the
   data as well as other potential accounts. *Evaluation can*

assist sensemaking by highlighting evidence and thus contributing to the evolution of better explanatory accounts. In a sense, evaluation adds an evidence-based selection mechanism to the process of natural sensemaking.

7. Sensemaking is often based on anecdotes, narratives, and other exemplars or accounts about how things operate. These serve as an important part of the cognitive framework that people apply to make sense. *The enlightenment use of evaluation probably operates in this way, as evaluation provides a kind of war story that later serves as a seed for natural sensemaking. In constructing reports of evaluation findings, evaluators should be mindful of the role of anecdotes and narratives in natural sensemaking. At the same time, evaluation should attempt to keep the vivid but unrepresentative anecdote from outweighing other, better evidence.*

8. Sensemaking is often social, and indeed, "arguing is commonplace in sensemaking" (Weick, 1995, p. 136). *This characteristic connects to the concept of deliberative democracy as a venue for sensemaking about policies and programs (see Chapter Two). It can also remind evaluators of the importance of meta-evaluation and other forms of critique (Campbell, 1986, discusses imbuing the field of evaluation with a "disputatious community of scholars").*

one not. Half the participants saw the successful firefighter described as a risk-taker, and half saw the unsuccessful firefighter described as a risk-taker. After the participants were asked to describe what makes a good firefighter in general, they learned that the two firefighters were fictitious creations of the experimenter. Still, there were persistent effects. Those who had been told that the successful firefighter was a risk-taker had constructed a plausible explanation why this would be so, and they continued to believe it. Those who had been told the opposite had also constructed a plausible account and continued to believe that account. Explanatory accounts persist in part because they can bias the search for and interpretation of further evidence (Gilbert & Osborne, 1989). Belief in an account can lead people to see the world as more consistent with that account. It is for such reasons that natural sensemaking often needs to be supplemented by assisted sensemaking techniques that strive for objectivity and openness to evidence (Datta, 2000; Scriven, 1997).

The concept of sensemaking links directly to realism. According to Weick (1995), the term sensemaking "invokes a realist ontology, as in the suggestion that something is out there to be registered and sensed accurately." But the concept also prevents a simplistic or naive realism by invoking "an idealist ontology, as in the suggestion that something out there needs to be agreed on and constructed plausibly" (p. 55; also see Campbell, 1991). This integration of sensemaking with commonsense realism may be especially appealing to those with qualitative leanings. The concept of sensemaking reminds us all that, while there is a real world out there, the act of trying to learn about it is a fully human project.

People's attempts to come to know the world are by necessity indirect and mediated in many ways. Still, as we have said, this does not mean anything goes. The commonsense realist, sensemaking view is that some accounts of the world are better and more accurate than others. No human theory has avoided revision in the face of continued inquiry, and no theory should be expected to do so. Some views about a social program are wrong, and they can be revised and improved. Bhaskar (1978) reminds us that only realists can take this view: "For it is only if the working scientist possesses the concept of an ontological realm, distinct from his current claims to knowledge of it, that he can philosophically think about the possibility of a rational criticism of these claims. To be a fallibilist about knowledge, it is necessary to be a realist about things" (p. 43).

Experiences, Underlying Mechanisms, and Meaningful Categories

Given that we all strive to make sense of a real world, what is the nature of that world? Contemporary realists often differentiate between the events people experience and the underlying structures and causal relations that give rise to those events. Both underlying mechanisms and structures are of interest: "Science, it is argued, is concerned with both taxonomic and explanatory knowledge: with what kind of things there are, as well as how the things there are behave. It attempts to express the former in real definitions of the natural kinds and the latter in statements of causal laws" (Bhaskar, 1978, p. 20). In Chapter Four, we illustrated the distinctions between the level of experience, underlying structures (or categories), and underlying mechanisms (or causal processes) in the context of a preschool program: underlying structures exist (such as the categories of teacher-directed and child-centered classrooms); underlying mechanisms also exist (such as the development of internal motivation) through which some things (such as being given choices among activities during preschool) may cause others (such as having higher scores on cognitive tests in first grade). The underlying structures and mechanisms are unobservable but give rise to observable, experienced events.

There are some important implications here for evaluation practice. The belief that programs and policies have their effects as the result of underlying mechanisms often has implications for the selection of measures. Consistent with an emphasis on program theory (for example, Bickman, 1990; Chen, 1990), it suggests that evaluators often should attempt to identify and measure possible mediators of program effects. For example, an evaluation of a preschool program might assess changes in the parents' expectations, parents' interactions with their children, educational resources parents make available for their children's development, teachers' assessments of and expectations for the children, and children's social behaviors because all of these have been implicated as possible mediators of preschool program effects. Such measures of expected underlying mechanisms can be very useful as evaluative criteria, especially when diagnosing possible reasons for program failures (Chen & Rossi, 1987).

The realist position that meaningful categories, or underlying structures, exist also has implications for evaluation practice. In particular, it justifies the search for program subtypes and other classifications (such as different types of clients). Once identified, these categories allow more refined sensemaking about programs and policies.

Many realists take seriously the notion of natural kinds (Bhaskar, 1989; Aronson, Harré, & Way, 1995) and assert that classification should identify classes of entities that differ from each other in fundamental ways, as types of elements, such as carbon and oxygen, do (Bhaskar, 1978), as molecular compounds do (Putnam, 1990), and as species of animals do (Aronson, Harré, and Way, 1995).

A potential objection can arise here, based on the point that programs are socially constructed and, it is sometimes argued, not subject to the same sort of analysis about structure and categories as other, natural items in the world. The commonsense realist response is that there are meaningful groupings of many things in the world, such as the distinction between teacher-directed and child-centered preschools (Marcon, 1999), even if the categorization scheme does not involve natural kinds like "carbon atoms." Although much of our social environment is socially constructed, once constructed it becomes real and can be analyzed in terms of structure and types. Speeding laws are a social construction, but they are in a very important sense real (as anyone who has paid a hefty fine for speeding knows). As mathematician John Allen Paulos (1998) observes, "Our relationship to manmade rules, as opposed to scientific laws and mathematical theorems, is somewhat similar to that of people addicted to placebos—we want, believe, and require them to work, and so they do" (p. 84). Moreover, states may have different types of speeding laws, which could be classified into groups. It may be easier to change speeding laws than the law of gravity, but both are out there, subject to our sensemaking efforts. For socially constructed entities, however, context may often be more important than for most natural laws.

Open Systems: Mechanisms in Contexts. The way that underlying mechanisms and meaningful categories play out in the social world is complex. In accordance with the open systems perspective developed over the past half century, most contemporary realists presume that causal mechanisms are sensitive to contextual influences. Thus programs that cause particular effects in one context may yield different effects in another (Bunge, 1997). Accepting this notion, evaluators turn from the question, Is the program effective? to the more textured, For whom is the program effective, in terms of which outcome variables, with what program elements, and under what conditions?

At the same time, commonsense realism does not believe that reality is so contextually complex and undifferentiated that there are no meaningful regularities to observe. To the contrary, realist sensemaking is driven by the belief that the world is sufficiently differentiated, because of underlying mechanisms and structures, that at least some of the patterns revealed by proper inquiry will have implications beyond the particular context in which they were observed. Indeed, were it not for such implications—for the usefulness of generalizing beyond the data observed—why would we humans have evolved our elaborate sensemaking capacities? Consequently, those who plan evaluations must make judgments about the value of increased specificity about contextual determinants of program effectiveness, compared to the value of more aggregated conclusions about average program impact. There are limits to the utility of increased specificity, and a major determinant of the most useful level(s) of aggregation in an evaluation should be social betterment. Values inquiry can also be useful in determining what level of aggregation will best serve those involved in the democratic search for betterment.

Stratified Levels of Analysis. Unlike positivists who have focused on constant conjunction between identified causes and effects, realists, believing that observed regularities are the result of unobserved underlying causes (Bhaskar, 1979), have focused on what are referred to as generative mechanisms that involve underlying structures. Realists view reality as "stratified. Events are explained by underlying structures, which may be explained eventually by other structures at still deeper levels" (House, 1991, p. 4).

Consider a social grouping such as a school. One could analyze the effects of school climate on school-level data about student achievement, attainment, and safety. Alternatively, one could study the structural elements of school climate by examining individual characteristics of teachers or students or the households from which the students are drawn. This second approach is often described, borrowing terminology from physics, as more molecular than the first, which is labeled as more molar. The more molecular approach focuses on entities (in this case, teachers, students, and families) that are embedded within entities the more molar (in this case schools). The fact that one analysis is molecular relative to another does not, however, establish it as fundamental to the other.

The realist notion of a stratified reality is relevant to the selection of evaluation criteria. To promote betterment in a stratified world, it may be important to understand program impacts at multiple levels, where they may be different or may even conflict. Georgia's HOPE scholarship program provides college tuition and fees for Georgia high school graduates who have earned a cumulative grade point average of 3.0 or better in high school and who attend college in state. This program may increase the human capital in the state by increasing the number of college educated residents. Most Georgia colleges and universities might benefit by having more and better prepared students attend. However, students might have their college choice limited by the economic incentives to stay in Georgia. Community colleges that previously attracted high-performing local students through lower costs might lose them to the more costly schools that students now find affordable. And other states might suffer from the loss of the high-quality Georgia students who otherwise would have crossed state boundaries to attend college. Considering the program from the point of view of such different levels might lead an evaluator to examine criteria such as in-state versus out-of-state postbaccalaureate employment that might not have emerged if only a single level such as the individual student were considered.

Further, the level of analysis adopted—whether individual, school, state of Georgia, or regional—might affect the value assigned to the outcome as people view different benefits and drawbacks. Sensemaking is enriched when evaluators select criteria representing multiple levels of the stratified social system. In principle, understanding will typically be enhanced by a combination of more molecular and more molar analyses. Although such multilevel assessments may increase the difficulty of making overall judgments about a program, greater problems will often result from assessments that produce overly simplified conclusions based on only one level of the stratified reality.

The desire to represent multiple levels quickly runs into practical limits, however. Funding and other resource constraints require choices. In addition, it is always possible to look "deeper." Any unit of analysis that evaluators might use can be decomposed into ever-more molecular units, and no level can be claimed as fundamental. The realist way out of this maze involves an antiformalist recognition that the choice of level(s) of analysis does not derive from some first principle from philosophy or science. Instead, that choice should derive primarily from relevant practice considerations. For evaluation, then, the right level of analysis is that which will best

inform democratic processes and institutions in their search for betterment.

Antireductionism: Emergent Order. Another useful theme of
commonsense realism also relates to the multiple possible levels of
analysis. Even though various levels may have implications for one
another, problems can arise in making deductive predictions from
one level to another. Two concepts are particular important in
understanding this difficulty: emergent order and downward causation. Emergent order has its origin in part in such work on evolutionary epistemology as the emergentist principle of Campbell
(1974a, 1974b). Campbell's emergentist claim is that "biological
evolution . . . encounters laws, operating as selective systems, which
are not described by the laws of physics and inorganic chemistry . . .
[nor by their] future substitutes" (cited in Munro, 1992, p. 119).
That is, evolution, through the dynamics of organic interactions,
has produced biological and social phenomena of increasing complexity that resist explanation in terms of more mechanistic or
molecular forms of analysis. These complex phenomena are characterized as emergent. For example, human social interactions are
complex phenomena that are not captured by the laws of Newton-
ian mechanics even though the laws of physics set certain limits on
human actions.

The concept of emergent order is further illuminated by the
related idea of downward causation (Campbell, 1974a; 1990). Old-
style reductionism assumed that the whole can be understood by
understanding its parts, and that accounting for the behavior of a
system is a matter of accounting for the behavior of its component
subsystems. The idea of downward causation is antireductionist and
posits instead that influences can be expected to occur in both
directions—upward from subsystems and downward from the
whole; every level constrains others. One can understand a professional association, for example, in part by understanding its members; but the nature of the association as a whole also has an impact
on those members.

Openness to Alternative Accounts.   It is because commonsense realists acknowledge that multiple levels of analysis can be adopted and
that one cannot move reductionistically from one level to another
that they also see as hopeless the positivist goal of finding the one,
true, fundamental account for any phenomenon. Evaluators trained
in sociology may frame an evaluation in terms of different underlying
mechanisms and different categorization schemes than a psycholog-
ically oriented evaluator would, for example, yet the two types of
accounts that result do not invalidate each other. Furthermore, different accounts— each valid—may be applied, depending on one's
purpose (Aronson, Harré, and Way, 1995). For example, physics
instructors might classify the members of a group of grandfather
clocks in terms of the attributes of their pendulums, antique collectors
might classify them based on maker and age, and interior decorators
might classify them by size and color. Like several contemporary
philosophers, Boyd (1990) suggests that it is possible "quite coherently [to] accept the pluralist conception of scientific categories even
within a single scientific discipline" (p. 189).

   This ability to acknowledge that more than one account can be
accurate is significant. It allows us to reject the search for positivistic, God's-Eye Truth without descending into hopeless relativism. A roadmap can be quite useful even if it does not capture all
the attributes of the area it shows, such as elevations or soil composition (Trochim, personal communication, 2000). It can still help
you if your goal involves driving from place to place. It will offer
much less help if your goal is to decide where to build a new road
(because terrain, soil conditions, and the like will be as important
as convenience of location). But this does not mean that there is no
truth, that all accounts are equal. One roadmap can be more accurate than another, even if no roadmap contains all information
about the area mapped.

   What does it mean, though, to say that an account is accurate,
or valid? Traditional views of validity and validity threats (for
example, Cook & Campbell, 1979) largely suffice as an answer.
A complementary view comes from Putnam (1981, 1990), who

summarizes his position this way: "to claim of any statement that it is true, that is, that it is true in its place, in its context, in its conceptual scheme, is, roughly, to claim that it could be justified were epistemic conditions good enough. If we were to allow ourselves the fiction of 'ideal' epistemic conditions . . . , one can express this by saying that a true statement is one that could be justified were epistemic conditions ideal" (1990, p. vi). By epistemic conditions, Putnam means the circumstances and ways in which we can "put nature to the test," and he illustrates such conditions in terms of the assertion, "there is a chair in my study." In this case, the ideal epistemic conditions would be met if you could be in Putnam's study, with adequate lighting, with nothing obscuring your vision, with no visual or mental deficiencies, and so on, to observe whether or not a chair is there. Of course, in evaluating social programs and policies, the ideal epistemic conditions are an ideal toward which we can only strive. Even when the available epistemic conditions are adequate, and we do get an accurate account, it will not encompass everything about the situation. For instance, an observation that there is a chair in Putnam's study, though accurate, would not capture everything about Putnam's study. So how are evaluators to judge which aspects of reality to try to capture? For that we must turn to values.

Getting Beyond the Fact-Value Dichotomy

Among the complexities of social life is that some outcomes are valued more than others, and that people often differ in the outcomes they value more. Those in the positivist tradition have long endorsed a strict dichotomy between fact and value. The basic claim has been that values are relative, subjective, and not amenable to scientific justification whereas facts are universal, objective, and open to logically warranted, firm conclusions. For many evaluators this distinction has been appealing in that it has allowed them to try to find out the facts about social programs, leaving others to worry about how those facts should be valued.

Several commonsense realist scholars have argued against the fact-value dichotomy. For instance, Putnam (1981, 1990) has made what is called the *companions in guilt argument*. The essence of this argument is that the reasons given for separating values from facts—that there are cultural disagreements about values, that value positions are historically conditioned, that there is no unequivocal scientific or logical account for what value is—all apply also to facts and to systematic inquiry itself. Therefore, "no scientific conclusion should be drawn from the fact that we cannot give a 'scientific' explanation of the possibilities of values until we have been shown that a 'scientific' explanation of the possibility of reference, truth, warrant, and so on, is possible" (Putnam, 1990, p. 117). In short, the positivist rationale for studying facts and ignoring values does not hold water.

Another reason for moving beyond the fact-value dichotomy, particularly for the field of evaluation, is the way in which facts and values are entangled in deliberations about social policies and programs (Putnam, 1990, p. 167). Holding different values often entails different views of the facts, as both psychologists (for example, Lord, Ross, & Lepper, 1979) and political scientists (for example, Free & Cantril, 1967) have demonstrated. Therefore, arguments about social policies and programs typically involve an intrinsic intertwining of facts and values (House & Howe, 1999). Reasoned arguments about the desirability of three-strikes-and-you're-out laws, welfare reform, bilingual education, and all other programs and policies do not rest solely on facts or solely on values, but on interlinked combinations of the two. In arguing against the fact-value dichotomy and seeing instead the entanglement of facts and values, realism supports our inclusion of values inquiry in our evaluation theory.

Realism, Social Betterment, and Evaluation Practice

One of the advantages of a philosophy of realism is that it supports the other components of the theory of evaluation as assisted sensemaking. We have discussed a number of these (summarized in the box at the end of chapter) in the course of presenting our philo-sophical foundation for our view of evaluation as assisted sense-making. In the following sections, we outline some additional linkages.

Realism in Support of Social Betterment

Contemporary realist thought also supports the attention we give to social betterment and the democratic processes through which that betterment is defined and sought. Particularly relevant are the views of Putnam (1990, 1995), who suggests that it is inappropriate to think of *solving* ethical problems in the same way that we think of solving mathematical puzzles or scientific problems: "The very words *solution* and *problem* may lead us astray. . . . I suggest that our thought might be better guided by a different metaphor—a metaphor from the law, instead of a metaphor from science—the metaphor of *adjudication*" (Putnam, 1990, p. 181). Putnam's view that ethical problems should be adjudicated is entirely consistent with the view that decisions about social policies and programs should be addressed through democratic institutions and processes.

Realism in Support of Systematic Inquiry

Realism also supports evaluation practice in general and evaluation as assisted sensemaking in particular. First, realism supports the distinction we have made among the four evaluation purposes. In Chapter Two, we saw that the four purposes correspond to different traditions that have evolved in evaluation practice. The common-sense realist perspective gives considerable standing to lessons from practice. From this perspective, the fact that the four purposes have been associated with different, long-standing practice traditions helps justify our distinguishing among them. Likewise, as discussed in Chapter Four, the four inquiry modes correspond to key realist concepts, and these correspondences can contribute to decisions about which inquiry mode is preferable in a given instance.

Realism also offers useful guidance for many other decisions that must be made in the process of planning and carrying out an evaluation. In addition to the implications summarized in the box on page 168, realism can contribute to systematic inquiry in terms of the choice of and role for qualitative and quantitative methods and in terms of the iteration between data and explanation.

Qualitative and Quantitative Methods, or, Commonsense Realism as a Base for a Lasting Peace Following the Paradigm Wars.

Evaluation, like most of the social sciences, has long been dominated by two opposing views of how people understand the world. In evaluation, these opposing paradigms have commonly been labeled for their predominant methodological approach. Thus the paradigm wars have often been called the qualitative-quantitative debate. The paradigms associated with quantitative and qualitative methods have long opposed each other, with each becoming ascendant for a time only to have its inherent flaws lead to the other's resurgence (Sorokin, 1957). Despite the inadequacies of each, they have dominated the debate over the proper foundation for evaluation, and fuel has been added to the fire as many evaluators have felt it necessary to choose one or the other.

The quantitative paradigm traces its intellectual history to Hume, Comte, and the logical positivists—staunch empiricists who sought to avoid claims that could not be substantiated by direct experience. The quantitative paradigm emphasizes objective reality. In program and policy evaluation this typically means an emphasis on the effects of a program or policy as measured through quantitative indicators. The qualitative paradigm, in contrast, developed largely from long-standing traditions in anthropology and some areas of sociology. The qualitative paradigm emphasizes meaning and subjective experience. In program and policy evaluation this typically translates into an emphasis on participants' experience of a program or policy as revealed through their own words.

Followers of the quantitative paradigm generally believe in an external reality about which different observers can reach agreement through common, shared methodologies. Followers of the qualitative paradigm, in contrast, sometimes deny that there is any reality separate from experience. Because differing interpretations are deemed equally valid, these constructivists talk not of reality but of multiple realities (Guba, 1990). Quantitative types commonly seek generalizable conclusions from evaluations. Qualitative types often do not place priority on generalization, questioning whether it is attainable, and instead focus on the particularities of a specific program as it occurred in a specific context. In the language of sensemaking, quantitative researchers emphasize the representational side (as in describing the effects of a program), and qualitative researchers emphasize the valuative side (as in identifying the meaning and value participants ascribe to their experiences). Although both qualitative and quantitative methods involve assisted sensemaking techniques, qualitative methods in general are closer to natural sensemaking whereas quantitative methods are more obviously constructed technologies.

Over the last two decades much intellectual capital has been spent in the ongoing, sometimes rancorous debate between adherents of each paradigm. Datta (1994b) suggested that a series of addresses by presidents of the American Evaluation Association "sent signals that seemed to indicate if not a state of war, then at least a condition of stridency. . . . One signal from the qualitative perspective said, 'Your paradigm is history.' A riposte from the quantitative perspective was, 'Don't call me a dinosaur, you innumerates.' And another signal could be read as saying, 'But we honor dinosaurs if they talk nicely'" (p. 53).

Some have argued that qualitative and quantitative paradigms cannot peacefully coexist. Lincoln (1990) argued that "accommodation between paradigms is impossible. The rules for action, for process, for discourse, for what is considered knowledge and truth, are so vastly different that, although procedurally we may appear to be undertaking the same search, in fact, we are led to vastly diverse, disparate, distinctive, and totally antithetical ends" (p. 81). Despite such contentions that accommodation is impossible, there is also a long history of calls for integration across the two paradigms (Cook & Reichardt, 1979). The voices calling for integration seem be predominating of late (for example, Caracelli & Greene, 1997; Datta, 1994b; House, 1994; Mark, Feller, & Button, 1997; Reichardt & Rallis, 1994; Smith, 1994, 1997). Even Lincoln and Guba (1994, p. 189) acknowledge at least the possibility of reconciling the paradigms. The question, however, is under what conceptual stand or paradigm the integration is to occur (Datta, 1994b; Smith, 1997). Answering this question is one of the central challenges now facing evaluation theory. Commonsense realism, with an appreciation of the human nature of sensemaking, offers an alternative paradigm that includes the best of the so-called qualitative and quantitative paradigms and avoids the most serious problems of each. It acknowledges both the representational and the valuative sides of sensemaking. In short, commonsense realism combines features that have drawn evaluators to one camp or the other, qualitative or quantitative.

The historical paradigms associated with quantitative and qualitative inquiry are not inherently necessary, and evaluators should not be bound by them in making method choices. Instead, the primary consideration that evaluators should use in choosing methods is, as we have been emphasizing throughout, the ability of the method, in the evaluation context, to contribute to social betterment by addressing the relevant evaluation purposes. Realist evaluators recognize that all methods are constructed sensemaking techniques, and all are fallible. In this light, social betterment is best served by qualitative methods in some situations, quantitative methods in others, and by a combination of these methods in many conditions. (Because each of the four inquiry modes contains both qualitative and quantitative methods, these methods might represent multiple modes or only one.) The task for evaluators, then, is to understand what types of information are required for the particular decisions at hand and how evaluation might improve sensemaking in deliberative processes and democratic institutions. Evaluators should not rely on a context-independent logic to guide their activities, but should instead base their practice on the context in which they work and the goal of social betterment. Rather than follow a qualitative or quantitative, or even a formulaic mixed-method tradition, evaluators should adopt a developmental perspective that considers the amount and types of support evaluation might supply that would be most useful for informing social decision making. For example, issues of representativeness and average effects may predominate when decisions are required about national or state policy. Legislative processes will be served in these cases if quantitative methods are in the foreground, supported as needed by qualitative adjuncts. In contrast, compelling narratives may be more useful for practitioners faced with decisions about how to match the right type of services to each client.

There are of course important differences between the quantitative and qualitative traditions. One key distinction, at least according to those who adhere closely to the interpretivist version of the qualitative tradition (for example, Smith & Hanushius, 1986), is that qualitative methods focus on meaning—on the subjective experience and interpretations of people, on what is perceived, on what people feel, on what they construe the world to be like. The interpretivist tradition also recognizes that the process of observing and participating in dialogues can influence what is said and thought, and how it is said and thought (Lincoln & Guba, 1985). Methods have been developed that attempt to focus on and in essence speed up such deliberative processes but still yield authentic expressions by people who have directly experienced the program. Validity of expression is a primary objective of many of those working in the qualitative tradition (Maxwell, 1996).

The quantitative tradition has developed from a different set of priorities. To a great extent, one can view the history of quantitative social science methodology as an attempt to invent procedures that go considerably beyond natural sensemaking techniques and the subjective experience of individuals. These methods—many of which have parallels in qualitative methods (Campbell, 1974c; Cook & Reichardt, 1979)—attempt to avoid or control for the bias that can lead to inaccuracies in natural sensemaking (Campbell, 1969b; Mark, Henry, & Julnes, 1999). Of course, methodological control procedures do not guarantee accurate answers. However, they are useful in reducing the risk of otherwise likely biases, such as the tendency for advocates of a policy to interpret their experiences so as to support their positive belief about the policy's benefits.

Realism affords evaluators the opportunity to include both qualitative and quantitative assisted sensemaking techniques. This may reduce the biases or, more accurately, blind spots in each tradition. Among evaluators using quantitative techniques, such biases often crop up in the selection of things to be measured. When values issues are seen as beyond the scope of quantitative evaluation methods, the possible program effects are often chosen without serious reflection. But how people experience a program, its role in their lives, and their relative preferences about its possible effects all matter in judgments about a program. It also matters what the public believes about and expects from a social policy. Biases can also occur in the selection procedures used to determine which (if any) directly affected individuals contribute to the deliberations on the valued aspects of public programs. By endorsing both quantitative and qualitative approaches, realist evaluators can remove the artificial distinctions between them and concentrate on the use of the least biased method for the purpose chosen in a particular context. Evaluators should attend to the most objective possible evidence about a program and to the least biased possible valuation of the program. Those biases that do exist should be acknowledged and where possible, subjected to further investigation by methods that do not have the same biases.

Exploratory Versus Confirmatory Approaches. A perennial controversy in evaluation—related in part to the qualitative-quantitative debate—is whether more is gained by exploratory analyses or by confirmatory analyses. From the realist point of view, an important determinant of analysis choice should be the current knowledge about the mechanisms likely to operate in a specific context.

Two general approaches can be described that involve exploration and confirmation (Mark, Henry, & Julnes, 1998). Principled discovery refers to procedures that are not driven by a priori explanatory models but that have their starting point in the data, with the evaluator looking for patterns of events and experiences. Competitive elaboration refers to procedures appropriate when one begins with an explanatory model in mind. In other words, an inquiry or phase of an inquiry can start with data or it can start with explanations. Although sometimes treated as distinct, these two approaches are both part of a larger process and can—and should—be integrated within a single evaluation (Julnes & Mark, 1998).

Indeed, iterating between exploration and confirmation is often a key aspect of success in evaluation (Julnes, 1995). Just as such iteration is important in natural sensemaking, in the assisted sensemaking of evaluation it is generally needed to both supply warranted information to democratic institutions and probe the complexities of an open system world, with stratified levels and emergent properties. Accordingly, iteration between exploration and confirmation is given considerable attention in subsequent chapters, especially in Chapter Nine.

Conclusion

To endorse realism is to risk two critical reactions. Adherents of the quantitative tradition often react with a scholarly version of "Duh!" Their point is that in some ways, to endorse realism is rather unspectacular, for it is only common sense to acknowledge that there is a world out there. The second reaction often comes from qualitative scholars who fear that realism is positivism dressed up in natural fiber leisure wear (the modern equivalent of sheep's clothing). Their point is that things are more complicated than is suggested when one says there's a real world out there, that our understandings of that real world are intrinsically tied to the world in our heads and to the social world. We cannot address all of the finer points associated with these two forms of objections in a single chapter. But our hope is that readers are persuaded that our form of commonsense realism has value, with worthwhile implications for evaluation, and that the integration of sensemaking with commonsense realism incorporates social construction yet also explicitly retains a belief in and desire for better representations of the external world.

Some noteworthy implications of commonsense realism for the planning of an evaluation are summarized in the following box.

Realism also supports key aspects of the planning framework presented in preceding chapters. In particular, it provides justification for the distinctions drawn among the four evaluation purposes and among the four inquiry families. Realism also provides guidance on the selection of an inquiry mode.

The variety of realism portrayed in this chapter also has substantial implications for the way people think about evaluation, its sensemaking potential, and its role. Realism paints a fairly complicated picture of the world. It is a world of multiple levels, in which the stuff of experience is the result of unobservable underlying mechanisms and structures. It is a world of open systems, such that programs and policies that are effective in one context may not be effective in another. It is a world of emergent properties, in which understanding at one level of analysis may not account for the complexities of another level. It is a world in which facts and values are intertwined, and in which formal models are inadequate to provide specific direction toward social betterment in concrete situations. It is a world in which any representation is necessarily incomplete, but a world in which it is nevertheless possible to speak of the strength of, warrant for, and the limits of any given representation.

But realism also paints a hopeful picture, and one that complements and converges nicely with the other components of evaluation as assisted sensemaking. Progress is not inevitable, but social betterment is possible. Democratic institutions provide forums and vehicles for the adjudication, if not the solution, of the complex value-laden issues of social policies and programs. Values inquiry, motivated by concern for social betterment, can guide many of the

Selected Practice Implications of Realism

- The realist concept of underlying mechanisms, consistent with the literature on program theory, suggests that evaluators should often attempt to identify and measure possible mediators of program effects.

- The realist position on meaningful categories justifies the search for program subtypes and for other classifications (for example, of different types of clients) that allow more refined sensemaking about programs and policies.

- Commonsense realism supports both consideration of context and the possibility of generalizing, through its rejection of the assumption of context-invariant effects and its rejection of the claim that reality is so contextually complex and undifferentiated that there are no meaningful regularities to observe.

- The antiformalism of commonsense realism supports carrying out values inquiry as part of an evaluation rather than trying to apply a common set of values in all evaluations.

- Realism also supports values inquiry through its rejection of the fact-value dichotomy and its recognition of the entanglement of facts and values.

- Realism supports the view that general considerations related to social betterment, and systematic values inquiry in particular should drive many decisions about an evaluation, including

  The level(s) of aggregation to focus on when seeking more refined conclusions.

  The preferred degree of molecularity in explanatory accounts.

  The appropriate mix of qualitative and quantitative methods.

- Antiformalism suggests that any theory of evaluation should be thought of as a guide, as a support to practice, and not as a rigid determinant.

decisions that must be made in the planning and conduct of an evaluation. Lessons from practice can also guide the way in the absence of formal, first principle models. Practice can move beyond the traditional paradigms of the quantitative-qualitative debate. And, as the very concept of sensemaking reminds us, although there is a real world out there, the act of trying to learn about it is a fully human project.

The formal inquiry methods that we use in this effort are constructed technologies that can supplement and correct biases in everyday sensemaking. In the remaining chapters, we examine the specific methods that make up each of the inquiry modes, and consider their strengths and weaknesses. This discussion of methods rounds out the planning framework for evaluation presented in previous chapters. In well-planned evaluations, evaluators move from considerations of social betterment, to consideration of evaluation purposes, of inquiry modes, and of the specific details of methods. These methods need to be examined individually in terms of their potential and limitations for assisting sensemaking in the commonsense realist world of policies and programs.

PART THREE

Four Inquiry Modes

7

Description

What percentage of elementary students missed more than ten days of school last year? Are students with frequent absences different from those with few absences? What percentage of children of former welfare recipients have no coverage for medical care? Has this percentage been steady, or has it been changing over time? What services are actually being delivered in a program designed to rehabilitate the credit records of low-income families and move them toward home ownership? Is this program serving the population specified in the enabling legislation? Has home ownership increased in economically depressed neighborhoods in the area? Has home ownership increased among program clients? Has one racial or ethnic group had a greater increase in home ownership than another?

Parents, service recipients, citizens, legislators, administrators, and service delivery personnel have questions such as these on their minds. To answer these and similar questions, evaluators use methods from the inquiry mode of description. They describe the activities of programs, their surrounding contexts, and the resources involved; they describe the characteristics of clients in the programs; and they describe the clients' or the community's standing on short-term and long-term outcome measures. Descriptive methods have always been used in information gathering but have received greater attention in evaluation in the last twenty years or so, for at least three reasons. First, this growing emphasis builds on a long-standing focus on description in qualitative evaluation (Stake, 1967), a tradition that has become increasingly mainstream in the field (Cook, 1997). Second, practitioners and theorists have made recurring efforts during the twentieth century to improve decision making, both in the private and public sectors, by implementing variations of quantitative performance measurement (Wholey, 1997; Plantz, Greenway, & Hendricks, 1997). Third, many evaluators and audiences for evaluation have increasingly recognized the ways that descriptive methods can contribute to social betterment.

In this chapter we discuss how to design descriptive inquiry. We emphasize that both qualitative and quantitative approaches to description represent traditions of assisted sensemaking and so face similar challenges. Having established this broad view of the central role of description, whether qualitative or quantitative, we discuss the types of data that can be used for description and consider a variety of decisions that need to be made in designing descriptive inquiry. Key choices for evaluators involve the focus of inquiry, the level of analysis (individuals, programs, or systems), the timing of measurement, and the choice of comparison standards. Finally, we address some important challenges evaluators face in the proper use of descriptive methods in evaluation.

Descriptive inquiry encompasses a broad array of methods. To gain some focus in this discussion, we give most attention to the current emphasis in government and elsewhere on performance measurement. We choose this emphasis for three reasons. First, the qualitative approaches to description in evaluation are well developed, and a variety of good sources on these methods already exist (see, for example, Coffey & Atkinson, 1996; Miles & Huberman, 1994; Rossman & Rallis, 1998). Second, performance measurement is increasingly promoted as a primary foundation for evaluation in support of more effective decision making, as illustrated by the Government Performance and Results Act, which mandates that federal agencies have systems in place for performance measurement

(Wholey, 1997). And finally, we believe that some of the controversy surrounding the role of performance measurement in evaluation might be resolved in light of the commonsense realist conceptions of assisted sensemaking and the role of descriptive methodologies in supporting this sensemaking (also see Perrin, 1998, who makes similar points from the perspective of his practical experience, experience we believe is consistent with commonsense realism).

As we begin addressing the role of description in evaluation, we first consider just what it is that description typically focuses on in evaluation, then we address the ways that description can contribute to the four purposes of evaluation.

The Focus of Description

In laying out the logic of qualitative evaluation, Patton (1987) notes several things that an evaluation report should include: "detailed description of program implementation . . . analysis of major program processes . . . description of different types of participants and different kinds of participation . . . [and] descriptions of how the program has affected participants" (p. 7). Part of what is noteworthy in Patton's account is the variety of evaluation tasks that involve description. This emphasis on description is standard in the qualitative tradition, in large part because good description appears to be central to the performance of subsequent evaluative tasks. Looking again at Patton's statement, we can characterize his comments as highlighting the importance of describing these program domains: *program resources* (equipment, staff, funding, space, materials, and so on) as they relate to implementation; *program services*, comprising both internal processes (*throughputs* in the systems paradigm) and outputs (akin to McDonald's reports of how many millions of hamburgers it has served); *participants* (both who participates, and how they participate); and *program outcomes*. In addition, our realist foundations lead us to add *context* (aspects of the setting, physical, social, and cultural) to the list of domains that may be the focus of description.

This set of domains is not novel nor is it the only way to categorize the things that might be described in an evaluation. For example, Stufflebeam et al. (1971) developed a similar, frequently cited framework that distinguishes four domains that can be the focus of description in evaluation: context, inputs, process, and products (CIPP). The point of such distinctions is to help evaluators attend to the full range of issues and dynamics that are of interest. We chose the set we have delineated here because of the different roles that description of resources, of services, of participants, of contexts, and of outcomes can play in evaluation.

Thus description is applied to a wide range of domains in evaluation. We return later in this chapter to the question of the relative importance in a particular evaluation of descriptive information on each of these domains.

Description in Support of Evaluation Purposes

Before considering the various choices to be made about descriptive inquiry, it is useful to review the ways that description can contribute to each of the evaluation purposes. As we discussed earlier, description can contribute to each evaluation purposes in varying degrees, depending on the context and information needs. It can also be a vital partner with other inquiry modes.

Assessment of Merit and Worth

The role of description in assessing merit and worth varies considerably, depending on contextual issues. Descriptive methods are often an important part of the assessment of merit and worth, especially to the extent that attributes of program process are themselves highly valued. For instance, in the case of the Georgia Pre-K Program, stakeholders, including the public, care a great deal about whether program sites are safe, health standards are met, and the children receive nutritious foods. For assessing process variables such as these, descriptive methods are the tool of choice. However, many of the things that people value about a program require causal analysis rather than description. For example, it is difficult with descriptive methods alone to tell whether a pre-K program increases subsequent academic performance. (See the discussion in Chapter Four of the role of both causal analysis and description in the assessment of merit and worth, including the level of confidence required for causal questions.)

Program and Organizational Improvement

Description plays a key role in many efforts to promote program improvement through evaluation. Observation of program resources, processes, and contexts is central to several threads of evaluation practice, including process evaluation (Scheirer, 1994), evaluability assessment (for example, Rutman, 1980), and the development of program theory (Bickman, 1990). Observation of program resources and program processes is also a vital and often sampled item on the menu from which utilization-focused evaluators select (Patton, 1997). In these and closely related threads in the complex fabric of evaluation practice, descriptive methods are used to guide program improvement. Observation and interview may lead, for example, to inferences that some organizational structures are better suited than others for high-quality service delivery. Rog (1999) describes such a case in the context of a multisite pilot program for homeless families. In that evaluation, descriptive methods suggested that services were not delivered as well when the linkages between the program and the actual service deliverers were comparatively decentralized.

Descriptive methods are also central to the approach Wholey has long advocated, in which information about program services, clients, and outcomes are fed back to program managers and staff for use in identifying and making needed adjustments. Descriptive methods in an evaluation can also serve as a form of needs assessment, highlighting the need for additional or strengthened service components. In Rog's Homeless Families Program evaluation

(1999), for example, descriptive methods revealed that clients suffered very high rates of physical abuse and violence. Such a finding can serve the purpose of program improvement, suggesting such changes as adding new services to the intervention.

Oversight and Compliance

Description is central to the oversight and compliance purpose. Many legislative bodies have support agencies with an oversight and compliance function. These agencies often find description of program services and clients the preferred method when assessing a program's fidelity to its legislated responsibilities.

In some cases, programs also have stated goals or mandated outcomes to achieve. For example, as a result of the high stakes testing movement, schools are sometimes mandated to have a certain percentage of students achieving a given level of performance on standardized tests. Failure to achieve the required success rates can result in loss of funding or in state takeover of local control. In cases such as this, descriptive outcome measures can be collected and compared with the mandated standards. (There are also some shortcomings here that we discuss at the end of the chapter.) Of course, unless they are linked with methods of causal analysis, descriptive methods do not do a good job of addressing the question of whether the outcomes achieved are attributable to the program. As we have also discussed at several points, however, causal questions do not always have to be answered directly for social betterment to be enhanced.

Description is sometimes paired with classification to fulfill the oversight and compliance function. This linking, with descriptive data, say, from a performance measurement system becoming the input for classification, is most appropriate when legislation or some other directive mandates that programs be of a particular *type*. Conrad and Buelow (1990), for instance, discuss how Medicaid reimbursement for adult day-care centers was dependent on the centers' being classified as providing the necessary services to maintain clients' health.

Knowledge Development

Description can play a central role in knowledge development, especially knowledge about the nature, scope, and other parameters of a social problem. In debates about welfare, for example, it is useful to know what the typical patterns of welfare use are. Similarly, Rog's evaluation (1999) of a program for homeless families served a knowledge development function by adding to the then very limited evidence about the level of violence that accompanied homelessness for many families.

As we discussed in earlier chapters, description may be able to contribute to each of the four evaluation purposes. On the whole, description may be most important for oversight and compliance, for program improvement, and for the process aspects of merit and worth. But it will serve evaluators well to remain mindful of the varied contributions that description can make—and of its limits. Of course, the stars are not likely to be aligned so that description will contribute substantially to all four purposes in single evaluation. And description will sometimes not by itself suffice even for a single purpose, as in those cases when description needs to be wedded with causal analysis to assess merit and worth.

Data Sources for Description

We now turn to an in-depth examination of the methods involved in using description as an assisted sensemaking tool in support of social betterment. In this section we begin by addressing the types of data that evaluators use for description. In the section that follows we then consider some of the decisions that evaluators need to make in designing descriptive inquiry.

We describe four basic sources of data for description: verbal data, survey data, observational data, and archival data. Determining which data types to use, singly or, preferably, in combination, is one of the key choices for descriptive inquiry.

Verbal Data

Qualitative evaluators have emphasized the value of verbal data gathered in interpersonal interactions. Semistructured interviews with a single individual are frequently used, as they allow the interviewer to probe areas of interest in detail. Alternatively, a variety of group procedures, such as focus groups, group interviews, or joint narratives, provide a social dimension to the generation of verbal data (Flick, 1998; Krueger, 1994). Verbal data are important in the quantitative tradition as well as the qualitative. For example, even before the widespread advocacy of mixed-method evaluation, evaluators of all stripes spent considerable time talking with people associated with the programs being evaluated (Mark, Feller, & Button, 1997). In addition, even quantitatively trained evaluators have long included open-ended questions on surveys, to extend and help interpret the meaning of the close-ended questions.

Alternative explanations often exist for any item of verbal data. People's responses may reflect self-presentation or social desirability, that is, respondents' desire to look good or to give socially acceptable answers. People may respond to a question even when they do not know the answer. Careful attention to possible bias in verbal reports is therefore important, with one of the most important strategies being the search for convergence across different information sources.

Survey Data

Interpreted broadly, survey data are a type of verbal data, but the tradition is sufficiently distinct to be considered separately. Surveys can be conducted with a variety of respondent groups and can focus

on anything from resources to outcomes. In the context of performance measurement, three types of surveys dominate: citizen surveys, customer satisfaction surveys, and outcomes surveys. Citizen
surveys are often general population surveys of the residents of a
particular jurisdiction. They are designed to obtain information on
citizens' expectations for services, their use of services, and their ratings of service quality, including overall satisfaction. Customer satisfaction surveys solicit similar information but are often special
population surveys, focusing exclusively on the perceptions of those
who have received program services or benefits. Outcomes surveys
also target clients, attempting to obtain data on the behaviors,
beliefs, and conditions that the program may have changed. Of
course, variations on these three themes may occur, as when parents complete surveys for school or day-care programs in which the
clients are children too young to respond to surveys for themselves
or when a survey of former welfare clients addresses barriers to
employment and reasons for recidivism.

For all three types of surveys (and their variants), in some cases
a haphazard or convenience (that is, nonsystematic) approach is
used to select respondents from the target population. At other
times a probability sample is used to minimize bias and enable an
estimate of the precision of the statistical estimates (Henry, 1990).
The representativeness of a probability sample will often justify its
use, although cost and the requisite level of confidence need to be
considered. Like other verbal data, survey data are susceptible to
self-presentation and other sorts of bias. A number of controls for
these biases are presented in the literature on surveys (for example,
Henry, 1990; Sudman, Bradburn, & Schwarz, 1996).

Observational Data

Observation, the collection primarily of visual data, has a long history in the qualitative evaluation tradition. These qualitative
methods range from somewhat informal observation while "walk-
ing around" (Weiss, 1998), to the more systematic approaches of

participant observation and ethnography (Flick, 1998). In addition to the open-ended approach associated with the qualitative tradition, observation can be conducted with structured quantitative instruments. The more structured approach has often been used in so-called process evaluations, with observers assessing service delivery against a checklist or detailed rating instrument. Some assessments of merit and worth use structured observational methods to measure valued outcomes and processes. For example, structured instruments such as the Early Childhood Environmental Rating Scale (ECERS) (Harms & Clifford, 1980) are sometimes used in evaluations of preschool programs (see also, Henry, 1999). Measures such as the ECERS tap issues of service delivery, such as equipment, supplies, and teacher-child interactions in the case of preschool programs. A more comprehensive assessment of merit and worth would also use instruments to observe social, educational, and cognitive outcomes.

Observation can be useful but costly, particularly when it employs the structured observational methods that might be part of a performance measurement system. Travel to sites and observer time, including time for training and reliability checks, add heavily to the cost. Observations that provide information on trends across time or differences across sites can be quite expensive. Rigorous techniques are required to reduce the possibility that differences among observers or other extraneous variables are responsible for any observed differences. Although sampling rather than visiting all sites can reduce the cost, sampling errors will then contribute to fluctuations across time. Thus smaller samples conserve resources but reduce the likelihood that small but meaningful trends will be detected. In addition, observation by videocamera or other technology is sometimes possible. This may reduce initial data-collection costs somewhat and may allow for coding of more variables than would be possible for an on-site observer. However, coding from videotape or other technology can be costly and cumbersome.

When observational methods are used, especially structured observation for performance measurement, the evaluator has to

(1) find or design reliable instruments for structuring observations that cover important aspects of practice, (2) develop observation protocols that reduce procedural differences, (3) obtain the consent of those to be observed, (4) train observers, and (5) avoid conflicts between giving feedback to sites, especially those that register major deficiencies, and maintaining the integrity of the protocol.

Archival Data

A final source of raw material for description is extant files. These archival data might take the form of files, such as mission statements, policy manuals, legal contracts, and even correspondence. They might also take the form of administrative databases, which have become more available in recent years and which contain information collected by the agency or organization that administers the program. Administrative data systems can often provide measures of client characteristics and some resource and service information. Historically, they have not provided many measures of outcomes. Some databases are used to track clients, monitor service use, and audit for possible abuses of the service system. However, these are usually designed to aid in the delivery of the correct services or payments to eligible individuals. Emphasis is thus typically placed on client eligibility characteristics that condition the services or payments, fees (when relevant), and information that determines the services for which an individual is eligible. The actual resources used or services received will often not be recorded at the individual client level in administrative databases, unless they have been designed with evaluation use in mind.

In addition, it is common to find data on resources such as caseworker time, client referrals, and client attendance in counseling sessions recorded on entirely different administrative data systems that may not contain specific client information. In such cases, the information on resources cannot be linked to specific service recipients. Data on resources available or aggregate resources are more commonplace in administrative databases than is information evaluators could use about resources delivered at the individual level. In terms of outcomes, the ones most likely to be recorded are those directly related to transitions or transactions into or out of the service delivery system. For example, state mental health systems may include measures of functioning and symptoms as clients' cases are closed or when clients are dismissed from a hospital. But measures of post-treatment functioning are less likely because these are not consistently related to the administrative purposes for maintaining the archival database.

Administrative data are often collected by service workers or intake staff who have no reason to actually use the data. For them, data collection is paperwork, a burden that slows service delivery. When the data system produces reports or assignments to services that support the decisions of the personnel entering data, then data collection may be viewed more positively and data may be recorded more accurately. However, when the data are used to directly monitor the performance of the individuals who enter it, incentives may exist to *enhance* data, for example, by filling in items even though the information for them is missing. Before using administrative data, evaluators should thoroughly understand the process by which the data are collected and should analyze possible problems in the recorded responses.

Special challenges may exist in selecting the unit of analysis, because different administrative data systems in an organization may record data in terms of different units of measurement. In some cases linkages can be achieved between client databases and databases organized by transactions, transitions, service worker, or service, and such matching usually brings up another set of technical issues to be resolved (discussed later in this section). In addition, missing data and incomplete records should be examined before plans to use the data are finalized. Missing data cannot be assumed to be missing at random.

Finally, when using administrative data sets, evaluators must be careful to avoid the *bean counters' trap*. This problem, also captured by the phrase "the tail wags the dog," occurs when the measurement agenda comes to reflect whatever information already happens to be measured. Administrative data systems are unlikely to contain all the items important for monitoring program performance. In extreme cases they may be useful only for obtaining client lists for surveys or field visits. In no case, then, should existing administrative systems constrain evaluators' consideration of what variables should be measured. Instead, as suggested in previous chapters, values inquiry should occur before the administrative data system is examined for possible indicators. Values inquiry will often press the evaluator to incorporate other types of data or other archival data, including extant data that are not part of administrative systems.

Some existing databases are collected for purposes other than program operation, such as administration of other programs or as part of routine measurement processes, such as the Department of Labor's wage and employment data. In many cases these data are useful as indicators of progress on reducing or eliminating the social conditions that gave rise to the policy or program. In other cases they represent outcomes that could potentially be observed for the particular clients served by a program. Though these extant data are usually more readily available in a relatively aggregated form, in recent years several states have linked service recipient data to employment and wage data. Florida, for example, is able to produce information by high school on the earnings of graduates who have gone straight from high school to the workforce. Similar data are being sought for the monitoring of welfare reform efforts in many states. Because they may play an increasingly large role in evaluations, we discuss here two issues of special relevance in such data sets.

Privacy Rights of Individuals. Extant data should not be used in such a way that the identity of service recipients is revealed. Privacy issues are highly important to many people, such as members of HIV prevention programs and victims or juveniles who could be harmed by being identified with certain programs. Federal and state regulations such as the Federal Education Rights Privacy Act often set restrictions on the use of data. Evaluators must be equally concerned that their evaluations do no harm to the clients of the services they are examining. In addition, provisions that guarantee privacy must often be put in place before obtaining individual-level data. Rules should be specified in advance about who has access to data that contain individual identifiers and how data from which these identifiers have been stripped can be reported. For example, evaluators may agree that aggregated information in reports must contain at least ten cases to ensure that individuals cannot be identified. Evaluators are becoming increasingly sensitive to issues such as ensuring security of files, encrypting identifiers, and limiting access of secondary users to aggregate data. Some state statutes give special access to databases to evaluators, especially those conducting oversight and compliance work for state legislatures (Jonas, 1999).

Biases from Extant Data.   The issue of nonsampling bias (Henry, 1990) looms large with extant data. Extant data sets often omit some of the clients who received services or were affected by the policy or program and include others who were not. In some cases, extant data systems will measure the entire population in an area (in terms of crime rates, for instance), and it will be impossible to link these data with the individual cases in a program (such as participants in a parole experiment). Even when it is possible to link cases, bias remains likely. Consider, for instance, the Florida reports of the earnings of high school graduates. Individuals who leave the state or who are employed in jobs not covered in wage and employment data are excluded from the data set. In the case of mental health consumers, a single individual might be released from hospital care several times in a reporting period. Such duplications and omissions can significantly bias extant data and make them less accurate for use as performance indicators.

Technical issues also arise in matching, merging, analyzing, and storing data identified with specific individuals. When databases are merged, unmatched cases often result. Evaluators may have to make judgments about the accuracy of matches in order to merge data that appear to pertain to the same case but that contain some discrepant information. In addition, an evaluator often must estimate an indicator for a subgroup at a particular site. Reliability may jeopardized by the small numbers of cases when subpopulations are analyzed. Estimates may be biased by relatively few unmatched cases.

In short, when an administrative database is supplemented with another extant data set, some biases are likely to arise from mismatches in coverage. Technical and privacy issues constrain description in additional ways. Such issues should be explored collaboratively by the keepers of the data and the evaluators, preferably with consultation by representatives of those whose data are to be examined.

Conceptual and Design Issues

We have made the argument that description plays an important role in supporting evaluations. We have summarized the data sources available for description. We now turn to four strategic issues evaluators must address when using descriptive methods in an evaluation: (1) the phenomena to focus on, (2) the level(s) (individual, program, system) of embedded phenomena to describe, (3) the timing of the measurement, and (4) the comparative referents to use in interpretation. Moreover, many additional specific questions arise involving the details of precisely what measures are to be made of which variables. We can address these questions only indirectly. Evaluators must deal with them in the contexts of specific evaluations. They are, however, quite important because, as Behn (1997) has noted, "slightly different measures can motivate significantly different behavior" (p. 46).

Deciding What to Describe

Social programs and policies are complex, and those who wish to make sense of them need to balance comprehensiveness and selectivity in attending to their critical aspects. As a result most theories of evaluation have included some guidance about what it is that needs to be understood in an effective evaluation. In this section we return in more detail to the framework of program resources, services, participants, contexts, and outcomes. Such frameworks remind users of the range of phenomena that is important to address and why. We begin with a general statement about the preferred approach to description that we believe follows from the concepts of commonsense realism and evaluation as assisted sensemaking. We then discuss each of these five possible foci of description, including the relative importance of focusing on each depending on which evaluation purpose is primary.

Commonsense Realism and Assisted Sensemaking as Guides to Description. Basic to any evaluation theory is a set of beliefs about what things are most important in making sense of programs and policies. The realist grounding of our approach argues, consistent with the insights of other evaluation scholars, that description is best served when it is guided by consideration of (1) valued outcomes; (2) the mechanisms believed responsible for those outcomes, that is, the mediators that link program services and outcomes; and (3) moderating influences, including program, participant, and contextual factors.

First, if description is to serve social betterment, evaluators must usually, at a minimum, attempt to describe the various outcomes that are valued (positively or negatively) by the stakeholders and by the public. For this reason, *values inquiry should often precede other efforts at description to offer principled guidance in identifying the relevant outcomes.* For example, focus groups with stakeholders (providers, clients, families of clients) might result in priorities specifying that an educational after-school program for disadvantaged children should contribute to academic achievement, enhanced academic self-efficacy, and decreased delinquent behavior. Having identified these valued outcomes, the evaluator would try to conduct descriptive inquiry that measured them.

Second, beyond simply describing valued outcomes, realism suggests that is valuable to identify the mechanisms by which a program produces its effects. Mechanisms responsible for outcomes are, however, difficult to observe directly. Descriptive inquiry methods can reveal what level clients have achieved on an outcome measure, but they do not in and of themselves allow one to say that these outcomes have occurred because of the program. Confident answers require bridging description with the causal methods examined in Chapter Nine. One potential bridge to causal analysis is to measure the presumed mechanisms in the causal chain that yields the identified outcomes. For instance, if one is evaluating a substance abuse prevention program and the relevant program theory indicates that clients' treatment should be mediated by improved "refusal skills," then it would be important to describe the clients' refusal skills in the chain of short- and long-term outcomes.

Another way to clarify mechanisms is to identify the characteristics of participants, services, and contexts that appear to moderate the degree to which the program yields particular outcomes (Mark, 1990). This emphasis on moderating influences can also contribute to assessments of generalizability by allowing results to specify more clearly where the program does and doesn't work, and it can support efforts at program improvement by indicating where more effort is needed. So if program theory suggests that a prevention program works by increasing children's refusal skills, one might hypothesize that the program would be more effective with children who have initially low refusal skills. Description then will fit with the realist view better if it focuses not just on the desired outcome but also on depicting those relevant characteristics of the clients, services, or context that might be expected to moderate program effectiveness.

In sum, the realist view as we have discussed it (Chapter Six) suggests that to the extent possible description should focus on valued outcomes, on possible mechanisms in the causal chain that links services with outcomes, and on possible moderators, whether they are client, contextual, resource, or service characteristics. This is an ideal approach that would provide much information useful for multiple evaluation purposes. It is also an ideal that would supply a rich data set that would probably integrate well with the inquiry modes of classification and causal analysis. But it is also an ideal that an evaluation does not always need to fully meet in order to contribute to social betterment.

This ideal echoes our earlier suggestion that description in evaluation could focus on several domains, specifically, program resources, services, participants, context, and outcomes. We now return to these domains, discussing each in somewhat more detail, including the most prominent linkages between each domain and the evaluation purposes. In the context of this discussion, we suggest ways that description that falls short of the comprehensive ideal just described can nonetheless support steps toward betterment.

Program Resources. Resources are the financial, human, and physical goods that are brought to bear to address an identified social problem. Process evaluations attend to the use of these resources, and evaluation theories often classify these resources as inputs in the program system. In this view, measures of resources can be used in quantitative analyses as the denominators of measures of efficiency or productivity. In addition, both quantitative and qualitative evaluations sometimes describe resources in order to assess *quality*. An evaluation might for example try using whether or not early childhood teachers meet certification requirements an indicator of quality of the instructional program in preschool sites (although some research shows no relationship with measures of service quality; Frede & Barnett, 1992). Measures of resources can be an important part of fulfilling the oversight and compliance purpose of evaluation.

Resource measures are sometimes used to indicate merit and worth. This is appropriate when the resource itself is a valued program characteristic, as fire safety equipment might be in a preschool program. However, sometimes resource measures are used as indirect proxies for anticipated outcomes, as when measures of child-care workers' credentials are used in place of outcome measures. In general, this use of resource measures is not appropriate for assessing merit and worth; at a minimum, the desired outcomes themselves should be measured.

Resource measures can sometimes represent mediators of program effectiveness. When combined with measures of valued outcomes, these resource measures can contribute to the assessment of merit and worth. Finally, resource measures can often be considered manipulable program attributes, and may be very important when one is looking for possible program improvements.

Resource measures can come from a variety of sources. Aspects of a preschool program environment might be measured through direct observation, using formal, structured ratings of the physical environment, such as the availability of materials for creative play or space for quiet individual activities (as is recorded by the Early Childhood Environmental Rating Scale, Harms & Clifford, 1980). Alternatively, observations can be made through simpler checklists or can be less formal, as when judgments of a preschool's safety are made by program compliance personnel. Surveys can be a less costly method for collecting resource data but their accuracy will often be more suspect than that of direct observations. Information on resources can also come from administrative and financial databases, such as budget allocations or personnel files, but these sources may be limited by missing observations and may not include some important variables.

Program Services. Services are the actual interventions provided by a program. Evaluators have a variety of ways to describe services. The way chosen generally depends on the type of intervention, the nature of theory in the area, and the decision context. To take one relatively simple example, in HIV prevention activities funded through the U.S. Centers for Disease Control and Prevention, services are categorized into three types: (1) health education and risk reduction; (2) health communication and public information; and

(3) counseling, testing, referral, and partner notification (Holt-grave, 1998). For the first of these categories, the number of pre-vention materials distributed could be one service measure. A measure for the second category could be the number of times an HIV prevention message aired on TV. When describing services, evaluators should distinguish between *services delivered* and *services received*. Services delivered might be measured by the number of brochures distributed. Service received might be measured by the number of individuals in target groups who received the brochures.

Service measures are often used to provide basic informational support for oversight and compliance, to assure Congress, for exam-ple, that services provided for by law are actually delivered. Although service measures can answer this question, they are dis-astrously incomplete measures of program performance. In what might be called the *McDonald's fallacy*, the number of hamburgers served does not tell us whether human needs for nutrition or social contact have been met. Similarly, in the process of developing pro-gram standards, service indicators are sometimes used as numerators in conjunction with resources variables that serve as denominators (for example, client contacts per case worker). Such indices mea-sure performance but likely do not represent actual outcomes. That is, they do not capture the extent to which the social problem is being reduced, if at all. Thus, such indices measure productivity but not effectiveness.

In other words, service measures are seriously limited as indica-tors of merit and worth. Still, they may contribute to the assessment of merit and worth in one very important way. As noted earlier, some aspects of service delivery may be socially valued, positively or negatively, independently of their relationship to outcomes. Some delivery practices may be viewed as violating the rights of ser-vice recipients or may indicate inequities in service patterns.

In addition, service measures are often very important in pro-gram improvement efforts. In some cases, simply seeing the record of service deliveries provides ideas for program improvement. For example, information on service delivery, organized by service provider, can identify agencies, sites, or even individual staff members that have failed to provide the required services (Affholter, 1994). If some component of service is being delivered at lower levels than expected, this may stimulate a search for obstacles in the environment. Evaluators also require service measures when they want to try to trace the linkages between services and outcomes, as is sometimes done in an effort to find possible avenues to program improvement.

In using measures of services, evaluators may need to use special care. Service data are usually retrieved from administrative reporting systems, and the potential problems of such systems can apply. Direct observations in the field can be used to provide independent corroboration of the administrative service measures.

Program Participants. Participants are described in many evaluations with regard to individual characteristics such as beliefs, attitudes, or demographic attributes. Many times client characteristics are collected to generate profiles of those who have received services. Data on client characteristics may be used for a number of evaluation purposes. As just noted, they may be combined with data on service delivery to monitor the fairness of service distribution. More generally, they will often be important for the purpose of oversight and compliance, allowing evaluators to check the match between intended and actual clients. Information about client characteristics may also be useful for program improvement, for example, by pointing out a disconnect between service characteristics and client characteristics, such as would occur when a program that supplies complex written materials to clients even though the typical client's educational level is low.

In the context of merit and worth, it may be important to use client characteristics in conjunction with other inquiry modes. As realism reminds us (Pawson & Tilley, 1997; Mark, Henry, & Julnes, 1998), unless they are particularly robust (Mark & Henry, 1998), programs are not likely to be equally effective with different groups. Evaluators often use ready categories such as socioeconomic status, race, or gender to investigate the robustness of program interventions, treating these characteristics as moderating variables that act as surrogates for underlying causes that we do not yet understand or cannot readily measure. But these same characteristics can also be of direct interest, addressing common concerns about program outcomes for traditionally underserved populations. Thus the assessment of merit and worth will often be facilitated by blending descriptive inquiry about client characteristics with the methods of causal analysis in order to generate relatively confident conclusions about the effect of a program on different client subgroups.

Even when causal analysis cannot be used, client characteristics can have important implications for interpreting descriptive information about outcomes. For example, if outcomes are better for some client groups than others, this may indicate that greater barriers confront some groups. Or it may suggest a moderated relationship, such that some groups benefit more from a given program. In addition, information on the mix of clients that is being served can be important when looking at outcomes across sites or over time. For instance, when different sites (or different reporting units, such as states) have varying mixes of clients, between-site differences cannot reasonably be attributed to the services provided in each site. In these instances, performance might be reported for each client subgroup separately, or each subgroup might be weighted so that *risk-adjusted* statistics could be reported. Such procedures can lead to an interpretation dramatically different from the interpretation suggested by the unadjusted rankings, as illustrated by the changes in states' ranks after the averages for the National Assessment of Educational Progress have been risk-adjusted (Glymph & Henry, 1997). The District of Columbia, for instance, goes from the bottom to the top in these rankings once the averages are adjusted for racial composition. Still, such adjustments may remove one source of bias but retain (and in special cases even accentuate) others. For example, the comparative socioeconomic levels of whites and African Americans in the aggregate may differ from one state to another, making the adjustments less than accurate.

When the clients are in some manner selected by program staff or administrators to receive services, evaluators may need to use yet another approach. When services are not available to all the members of the target population, some mechanism must be used to determine who actually receives services. If program effectiveness carries high stakes, pressure may exist to *cream* clients, selecting those most likely to succeed rather than those most in need of services. To assess this possibility, the evaluation must compare the characteristics of the actual clients, applicants, and target population.

In short, describing client characteristics is important for several reasons, not the least of which is the possible role of client characteristics in moderating program effects.

Program Context.   Context has long been emphasized in evaluation (Stufflebeam et al., 1971). As we use it, context refers to the physical, organizational, cultural, and political settings in which programs and clients are embedded and in particular those setting aspects that influence program success (Mark & Henry, 1998; Pawson & Tilley, 1997). Telfair and Leviton (1999), for example, report that a community organizer and advocate, long active in social and health initiatives for poor and rural populations, listed ten types of community information necessary for evaluating programs in community settings, including demographics, land usage patterns, traffic patterns, market patterns, and even information about local taxes. Evaluators might collect information about context from any of the data sources discussed in this chapter (Stufflebeam & Shinkfield, 1985). St. Pierre, Kaltreider, Mark, and Aikin (1992), for example, surveyed clients in a multisite drug prevention program to assess the prevalence of crime and drug use in their communities.

Context information can add meaning to oversight and compliance measures. Evaluators might compute risk-adjusted statistics based on information about community characteristics (though in doing so they must also attend to some nontrivial statistical issues regarding the use of individual-level information with community-level information). More generally, it is important to use information about contexts when making appropriate comparisons across performance measurement systems (Glymph & Henry, 1997).

In the pursuit of program improvement, information about context can be used in several ways. It may reveal solvable impediments to service delivery, as when Hudson (1969) detected fixable client transportation problems. It may be critical in many efforts to assess program merit and worth, as when Mark, Feller, and Button (1997) used the results of project staff interviews to highlight economic conditions as a possible moderator of the effectiveness of a change to a hiring system. Without this information, a possible limit on the generalizability of the treatment effect would have been ignored. This type of analysis is consistent with the work of Pawson and Tilley (1997) that highlights the moderating effect of contextual factors on program mechanisms. Rather than assume that programs have similar worth in all contexts, evaluations can analyze moderating contextual variables to produce more nuanced conclusions about merit and worth.

Program Outcomes. No potential focus of description has received as much attention in recent years as outcomes, especially in the literature on performance measurement. This literature calls for using outcome information from management information systems to guide policy. Although some critics regard the systematic description of outcomes as called for by the performance measurement movement as only the latest fad in management, we expect to see widespread interest in the development and use of outcome indicators for some time. Indeed, the Governmental Performance and Results Act of 1993 virtually guarantees this continued interest. Evaluators must recognize, however, that in the development of a performance measurement system, outcomes are usually the most difficult type of measure to conceptualize and most difficult to actually measure.

What are outcomes? Outcomes include both intended and unintended consequences of a program or a policy. Educational performance measurement, for instance, uses average test scores, drop-out rates, and absenteeism as typical outcome indicators. Although performance measurement systems usually measure outcomes as attributes of the individuals served by a program, such as "knowl-edge, attitudes, values, skills, behavior, condition, or status" (Plantz, Greenway, & Hendricks, 1997, p. 17), complexities of interpreta-tion involving individual-level versus aggregate measures can arise, as discussed in the next section.

These complexities overlap with the complexities of selecting outcome indicators. Evaluations commonly have an interest both in short-term outcomes, such as postprogram levels of knowledge, and in long-term outcomes, such as successful employment in the field of study. Most often, short-term outcomes are measured at the individual level, although there appears to be a trend toward col-lecting population-level statistics to monitor changes at the societal level. However, the further downstream from the direct program activities and the further removed from direct client services the measurements are, the less clear it will be that the program had any-thing to do with producing them.

In selecting outcome indicators, many of the techniques of val-ues inquiry (described in detail in Chapter Ten) may brought to bear. In addition, the desirability of an indicator must be weighed against cost, feasibility, and other technical attributes. Almost any valued outcome *can* be measured. However, the expense of obtaining accu-rate data and the consequences of the data collection burden must be considered. In the past, availability often predominated other con-siderations. Performance measurement systems were often developed from existing administrative systems and contained a mixture of resource, service, and client characteristic indicators but gave short shrift to outcomes. But outcomes are essential for performance mea-surement systems to realize their potential as evaluative tools. An *optimal* performance measurement system is designed and imple-mented to maximize its potential for serving multiple evaluation purposes. Optimal performance measurement takes indicators at regular intervals from all five program categories: resources, services, participants, context, and outcomes. In designing an optimal system, other measurement considerations, such as the level of analysis and the periods when measurement takes place, are also important.

Choosing Appropriate Levels for Description

Although generally measured at the individual level (Newcomer, 1997), performance indicators are also sometimes measured at or aggregated to other levels, and this aggregation of indicators can result in complications. When indicators record incidents or transactions, for instance, a single individual can contribute more than one incident per measurement period. Thus rates of incidents involving students with firearms or injuries to students or staff per thousand students could be increased substantially by a single student who precipitates several incidents. Another option is to compile data on a student-by-student basis, but this approach too has limitations. Perhaps the most important considerations for evaluators are to match information to the needs of prospective users and to achieve comparability across units.

Similar problems arise when client transactions or transitions serve as the unit of analysis and clients are counted several times because, for example, they rotate in and out and in and out of a treatment program. This may create a misleading picture of program completion and success. Mean rates per client day or year may provide more stable and reliable measures, because the base is larger and more stable.

Another problem can occur when indicators are measured at an aggregate unit of analysis. Often service measures are taken at the level of service delivery units. Thus, when school performance measurement systems record absenteeism as the ratio of total days that enrolled students actually attended class to total days they could attend, it masks variation across schools and is hard to interpret, in part because some reasons for absenteeism are more legitimate than others. Some states instead report problem absenteeism. In Georgia, for instance, problem absenteeism is defined as the percentage of students missing ten or more school days for which they were enrolled. With absenteeism measures at the student rather than the school level and with a standard set for problem absenteeism, attention has been drawn to absentee problems that relate significantly to performance on standardized tests and to drop-out rates (Henry & Brackett, 2000).

A related problem with aggregate units of measurement is illustrated by customer satisfaction surveys, which have assumed increasing importance in performance measurement efforts, including those of cities and other local governments (Hatry, 1997). Often these surveys are intended to provide managers with information to support program improvement decisions. However, evaluators must make trade-offs between taking the larger samples that would allow reliable estimates of satisfaction in each of a number of subpopulations (sections of a city, for example) and taking the smaller and less costly sample that would provide adequate information about citizen satisfaction in the city as a whole. Average satisfaction rates may mask pockets of problems. They are useful for such tasks as highlighting overall satisfaction differences between one service and another but not for focusing service improvements on problem locations.

In short, choosing a level for descriptive inquiry involves choosing an appropriate unit of measurement for a performance indicator. This requires considered judgment about what information will inform the public, the policymakers charged with oversight, and the managers and staff who seek to realize public and policymaker expectations. At the same time, the costs of obtaining different kinds of information must always be considered. Similar issues arise when evaluators are selecting the period for measurement, to which we now turn.

Organizing the Timing of Descriptive Inquiry

Description has often been approached as a one-shot effort, in the belief that description at one point in time is sufficient for the task at hand. And indeed, for some purposes one-shot description, quan-titative or qualitative, can be meaningful and cost effective. How-ever, description may also often be associated with recurring events. Educational indicators, for example, often have an annual cycle. The school year is a natural reporting time frame for standardized test scores, drop-out rates, problem absenteeism figures, and school safety violation rates. And the annual cycle for most educational statistics matches well with key uses of the indicators. Those charged with realizing community goals for schooling, the teachers, principals, and others, usually maintain a curriculum, plan lessons and instructional activities, and organize their efforts around a school year.

Other services areas often require different cycles. Local gov-ernment services such as garbage pickup and park maintenance, for instance, can be changed more rapidly than annually in response to performance information. It is best if the period for reporting can be tied to the time frame in which changes can be made. As Hatry (1997) puts it, "For managers to make full use of outcome informa-tion, they need to receive feedback on outcomes relatively fre-quently so that they can make early adjustments and, in later reports, determine whether those adjustments have been accompa-nied by outcome improvements" (p. 40).

Some actors in a single system may need performance measure-ment feedback more often than others in the same system. One response in such cases is to provide information regularly at the shortest measurement period. But this may create other problems. Information must be novel and dramatic to receive attention on the public agenda (Hilgartner & Bosk, 1988). The relative infre-quency of annual school monitoring reports makes them more newsworthy, thus enhancing the likelihood that the public will be informed about them by the media and attend to them. Weekly or monthly school reports would have little novelty and drama. But school personnel may feel that annual information about some issues is not timely enough. Students whose absences are piling up, for example, require more frequent interventions. Therefore evaluators may need to add options such as a focused *exception* reporting system for school administrators to the annual reporting system designed for school boards and the public.

In sum, evaluators must fit the period for measurement to the purposes of the descriptive inquiry. In addition, they must strike a balance based on the various purposes for which the data will be used, all the while ensuring that actions are not based on data too imprecise for the purpose at hand and that costs do not become prohibitive.

Selecting Comparison Standards

Making sense of descriptive information generally requires some sort of comparison, even if it is only implicit. Knowing, for example, that an educational program devotes a certain percentage of instructional time to unstructured activities often means more if we also know that less time was spent that way in the past or that other programs spend far less time on unstructured activities. An additional decision evaluators and others must make, therefore, when designing descriptive inquiry is whether and how to select such comparisons. We address three general types of comparison standards available for making sense of descriptive findings: (1) established standards, or benchmarks, (2) findings from other programs or units, and (3) findings from prior periods (Henry & Dickey, 1993; Henry, McTaggart, & McMillan, 1992).

Comparisons with a Standard or Benchmark. When used with quantitative process or outcome variables, the process of comparison to a standard is relatively simple. Of course issues of bias and sampling errors can enter into the judgments, but it is relatively straightforward to determine whether performance reached some preset standard on a specific criterion. The difficulty is in setting the standard.

Consider the controversy that arises when standards are set in education. Presumably, no one would disagree that all children entering school should be ready to learn. Nevertheless this educational goal, proposed for the Goals 2000 legislation, has gone by the wayside as a nationwide standard for accountability. Why? Goals that specify that "all shall do X" or "none shall suffer Y" are impossible to achieve. When standards are structured in this way for important and meaningful indicators, failure is virtually guaranteed. Such absolute standards create more losers than winners and soon lose their motivational impact (Behn, 1997). Conversely, more realistic standards, such as "the drop-out rate will be reduced to 5 percent," suffer from a different fatal flaw. In the world of *realpolitik*, we cannot give up on anyone (or at least, we cannot admit that we have). To say that it is fine for five percent of students not to graduate from high school suggests that we are willing to give up on educating those children.

Such problems notwithstanding, comparisons to standards are common. And values inquiry, although useful, will often not provide specific enough results to set precise, absolute standards.

Comparisons with Other Programs or Units. Comparisons with other programs or units are very informative for those attempting to motivate or engage in program improvement as well as for those interested in holding a program accountable through oversight. The major difficulty with this approach is determining whether the comparisons are fair. Several complications can work against fair comparisons.

Differences between organizational units can make comparisons less reasonable. Schools with students from privileged families are advantaged on most measures in comparison to schools with students from families living in poverty. Highway maintenance districts with fewer freeze-thaw cycles are advantaged over those with more of these cycles, which cause cracking and potholes. Creating fair comparisons with descriptive data has been explored by many (for example, Henry, Dickey, & Areson, 1991; Wohlstetter, 1991). Results of comparisons across units have been found to vary considerably depending on the method used (Henry et al., 1993). Methods evaluators might employ to control for differences between units include grouping or clustering units, making risk adjustments (National Association of State Mental Health Program Directors Research Institute, 1996), and using regression-based adjustments (Powell & Steelman, 1996). It is, however, also difficult to be sure that adjustments have been properly made. This suggests that evaluators should always exercise caution in interpreting comparisons across units on the basis of descriptive data.

Comparisons with Prior Data. Comparing unit performance indicators across time to establish trends is a common approach to making sense of descriptive information. Most audiences for policy evaluation, for instance, want to know if the policy is moving the community in the right direction, whether that means higher reading scores or a fewer low-birthweight babies. Behn (1997) argues that setting target performance levels that are individually defined for every organizational unit and tracking their achievement is the best way to motivate performance improvements. Using trends as the principal analytical device often produces comparisons that avoid many of the concerns about fairness. For example, when school performance in one period is compared to performance in a previous period, the comparison is fair, assuming that resources and client characteristics have remained relatively stable. Although the first few years of data collection will not produce meaningful trends for lack of earlier data, measuring progress on important performance indicators is considered by some to be the most crucial comparison for monitoring.

Criticism of Description

Description has many important uses in evaluation but it has also been the object of criticism focused on the use of performance measurement in particular and the validity of description more broadly. In this final section, we address several of these criticisms.

Coping with Goal Displacement and
Other Challenges for Performance Measurement

Perhaps the most serious potential problem for performance measurement and other uses of description in decision making is the possibility of *goal displacement* (Perrin, 1998). Once people understand what aspects of their performance are being measured, it is natural that they will orient their behavior in that direction, especially when performance has consequences that matter. When teachers are rewarded based on their students' performance on a standardized test, is it surprising that they begin to teach to the test? Not only does goal displacement result in neglect of other important though not measured activities, it also tends to degrade the value of the measure over time. A test intended to sample the broader domain of what students know may come to represent *all* they know. High stakes performance measurement systems can be expected to increase the pressures for goal displacement. As Campbell (1975a) noted, "The more any quantitative social indicator is used for social decision making, the more subject it will be to corruption pressures and the more apt it will be to distort and corrupt the social processes it is intended to monitor" (p. 36; original italicized).

Evaluators can take several steps to reduce the likelihood of goal displacement. They might use a broad array of performance indicators so that people would be unlikely to tilt their behavior toward a single indicator. As long as performance measures represent the desired valued outcomes well and widely, then it is not a problem if they motivate people to try to increase their performance. Evaluators may rotate indicators in and out of the performance measurement system, again forestalling people from skewing performance toward one indicator. This has disadvantages for tracking trends over time, however. Evaluators might also recall Mawhood's observation (1997) that "judgment can be informed by indicators, but cannot be determined by them"

(p. 142). As a general rule, information from performance indicators should be an input to judgment, not a substitute for it. When evaluators and program personnel see performance indicators as contributions to informed judgment, rather than as criteria for automatic rewards and punishment, pressure toward goal displacement may be reduced.

In his detailed critique of performance measurement, Perrin (1998) notes the problem of goal displacement and also that there is little consensus on what constitutes a performance indicator, that performance measurement fails to take contextual factors into account, and that it glosses over subgroup analyses. We believe the perspective presented in this chapter, especially when used in conjunction with the methods of values inquiry described in Chapter Ten, can help evaluators avoid these potential problems.

Understanding the Crisis of Representation

The qualitative tradition has been experiencing a challenge regarding the meaning of description. Denzin and Lincoln (1994) identify five *moments*, or phases, in qualitative inquiry, beginning with the belief that good description yields an accurate representation, and moving to the belief that the product of description is always a constructed interpretation. The first phase is the *traditional period*, during which the ethnographic interests in the early decades of the twentieth century of groups such as the Chicago School of sociology predominated. Their concern was with methods that supported objective description and subsequent interpretation of different cultures. The *modernist phase*, ranging from the middle of the twentieth century to the 1970s, is characterized by the work of Glaser and Strauss (1967), built on the traditional foundation by attempting to formalize the methods that would support proper description. From the 1970s to the 1980s, the *blurred genres* phase saw the recognition of diversity of perspectives, ethnomethodology, symbolic interactionism, and feminist critique, with these views promoted both as competing and as complementary perspectives, and as foundations for qualitative inquiry.

This diversity presaged the next period, the *crisis of representation*, when the question arose whether the description that resulted from any method whatsoever had any special claim to being a meaningful representation of some phenomenon of interest. The critical observation was that different people using different qualitative methods arrive at different descriptions of what might be thought of as the same phenomenon. The conclusion drawn was that there is no one correct description and so it is not clear how one can assess the quality of one representation over another. In the most recent phase, characterized by a focus on *narratives*, description is viewed as part of the development of narratives by a particular researcher operating in a specific historical context. In this view, representation has meaning only as a subjective act that involves the politics of interpretation.

Thus description does not seem as straightforward as earlier evaluators had hoped it would prove. Moreover, some in the field use this acknowledgment of complexity to argue against the value of careful description. We think it is fortunate that not all qualitative evaluators claim to be "fifth momentists." At the same time, most do recognize the tension implied by the crisis of representation and most, therefore, try to characterize their evaluation work as involving a balance of representation and interpretation. As realists, we take the view that the tendency to define description as a narrative is a movement in the wrong direction, unless it also comes with explicit acknowledgment that some narratives are better than others and that better narratives are the ones that better match the world out there. The recognition that each observer may obtain a somewhat different description is not, we believe, fundamentally troubling. As we discussed in Chapter Six (and look at again in the context of classification in Chapter Eight), realism does not assume that there is a single right framing to bring to a given situation. Different observers may describe different aspects of what is occurring, or they may describe the same aspects from the vantage points of different theories. Even so, some descriptions are more accurate than others, and some are more likely to contribute to social betterment than others.

We believe evaluators will benefit from striving to understand the limits of descriptive inquiry without limiting their appreciation of what it can accomplish.

Conclusion

Description is a major inquiry mode for evaluations. It involves the representation and interpretation of program resources, services, participants, context, and outcomes. When translated into the quantitative framework of performance measurement, description involves repeated measurement of valued characteristics or outcomes of a policy or program. A wide range of choices must be made in developing a performance measurement system or in conducting any other form of description. These choices determine the indicators the evaluation will measure—of what type, with what data sources, at what unit of analysis and measurement period, and with what comparison standard. Ideally, evaluators make all these choices in light of the evaluation purpose. The purposes most likely to use description alone are program improvement and oversight and compliance. In addition, description may sometimes suffice for a rough assessment of merit and worth and will often be an important component of an evaluation where the primary purpose is assessment of merit, being used to establish such things as whether program activities violate participants' rights.

However, by itself, description does not empirically identify categories of program or client types or allow confident conclusions about the effect of a program or policy on valued outcomes. For these tasks, we must turn to methods for classification and for causal inquiry.

8

Classification

In the previous chapter, we pointed out that descriptive methods leave several important questions unanswered. One of these questions concerns the existence of underlying structures: Do the sites in a large, multisite program cluster into meaningfully different categories or types? Is there some common component to one set of outcome measures that causes them to hang together and differ distinctly from other sets? Of the many communities in which clients live, are some subsets fundamentally similar and also fundamentally distinct from other clusters of communities? Classification helps evaluators answer such questions by applying systematic, assisted sensemaking techniques for discovering or confirming underlying structures (which we also refer to as *categories* or *types*) and for identifying the category into which a specific case falls.

Realism posits that the observed patterns in people's everyday observations result from underlying mechanisms acting on deep structures. Classification aims to go beneath the surface of observed differences and to reveal the structural differences that give rise to important regularities. In a program designed for homeless individuals, for example, staff might naturally observe that the clients seem to differ from one another in somewhat regular ways, and they might even speculate that some client *types* are influenced more by the program than others. Classification techniques can be used to assess whether different types of homeless persons can be more formally identified and, if this is the case, classification methods can also be used to describe the attributes of each type. This information could then be combined with the inquiry mode of causal analysis to see whether the intervention is indeed more effective for one homeless type than another. If evaluators and others are to understand the underlying structures of our social world in such ways, and if they are to try to use the resulting groupings to assist sensemaking about policies and programs, they need techniques that help them accurately represent the underlying structures. We refer to these methods designed to probe underlying structures as classification methods.

One definition of classification is the "ordering of entities into groups or classes on the basis of their similarity" (Bailey, 1994, p. 1). Echoing Plato, advocates of classification often refer to "carving nature at its joints," that is, to finding distinctions that are nonarbitrary, meaningful, and real in terms of underlying structures (for example, Waller & Meehl, 1998). Many realists use the term *natural kinds* to represent the underlying structures that separate things into meaningful groups in the way that joints mark the separation between bones. According to Boyd (1991), natural kinds are "defined by a set or cluster of properties whose membership is determined by the causal structure of the world" (p. 129). Aronson, Harré, & Way (1995) define a natural kind as "a set of entities which have a certain cluster of properties in common, [with] that cluster being fixed by the natural laws appropriate to the case" (p. 39).

Classification procedures, like other methods, have their flaws and limitations. Perhaps the most fundamental criticism of classification is that differences really exist on a continuum rather than in distinct groups. This concern has been raised eloquently by Flew: "God makes the spectrum, man makes the pigeonholes" (cited in Bhaskar, 1978, p. 213). Later in the chapter, we address this and other important criticisms of classification. First, we present the case that humans use categories naturally to help organize observations about the world around them. We then consider how social researchers in general and evaluators specifically have applied the assisted sensemaking techniques of classification to achieve better understanding of social programs and their improvement.

Natural Categorization

Teachers of introductory psychology sometimes begin their initial lecture on personality by observing that "there are two kinds of people: those who divide other people into types, and those who don't." But in fact, when it comes to categorizing things, there seems to be only one type of person. The human tendency to put people and other things into groups is powerful and pervasive. Psychologists who have studied this tendency refer to it as *categorization*. We follow this practice, using the term categorization to refer to the natural, *un*assisted, everyday act of grouping things. We use *classification* to refer to assisted sensemaking techniques in which tools of systematic research are applied to develop, test, and use a system that sorts persons or other entities into groups.

Recent research on natural category formation and use, fascinating in its own right, also has some lessons for how commonsense realists should think about classification. Numerous studies have demonstrated that the way people categorize depends on the existing cognitive framework and motivation that they bring to the situation. Novices and experts differ in the way they categorize (Medin & Aguilar, 1999), presumably because experts bring more detailed knowledge to the situation. And experts may differ among themselves. For example, different types of tree experts (taxonomists, landscape architects, and maintenance workers) were found to classify tree species somewhat differently (Medin, Lynch, Coley, & Atran, 1997), presumably because different types of experts have somewhat different knowledge and different motivations. The landscape architect, for instance, often has to think about which trees are interchangeable in terms of height, so that the same visual profile can be maintained if one type of tree is unavailable or undesirable to the client. The same attribute, height, is probably less central for taxonomists. Cross-cultural studies similarly show the influence of cultural background on categorization (Martinez & Shatz, 1996). Laboratory studies have shown that even short-term shifts in knowledge and motivation can influence categorization. For example, subjects who had been exposed to specific adjectives about people in a prior (and supposedly irrelevant) task showed greater access to conceptually related attitudes in their subsequent categorization of a target person (Smith, Fazio, & Cejka, 1996). Similarly, subjects who had been given background knowledge about a particular category were faster in using that category (Lin & Murphy, 1997). Three lessons of such research for commonsense realist classification are (1) that different classification schemes may be appropriate for different purposes; (2) that classification systems should be thought of as evolving, as gaining accuracy as individuals' understanding of the relevant structures increases, but still useful even if imperfect; and (3) that the idiosyncratic tendencies in individuals' natural categorization make assisted sensemaking in the form of systematic classification methods a valuable support to natural sensemaking.

Even though the outcomes of natural categorization depend on prior knowledge and motivations, some aspects of natural categorization do seem fundamental. There is, for example, evidence that humans, regardless of level of expertise in the substantive area, do have a basic level of preferred categorization (Johnson & Mervis, 1997). And many studies have shown that there are predictable progressions in how infants develop their facility for categorization (Greco-Vigorito, 1996; Kotovsky & Gentner, 1996). The view of categorization that emerges from recent research is strikingly consistent with the sensemaking perspective. Initial templates guide an individual's classification process. The individual may then develop new, more refined categories to better reflect his or her experience. Iteration, a central theme of sensemaking, then occurs, as the person iterates between explanatory accounts (in this case involving underlying structures) and observations (Weick, 1995).

This process is highly congruent with an evolutionary view of human sensemaking. Although people's view of the world is constructed based on their available templates (their cognitive structures for viewing the world), the constructions are not arbitrary. The templates that people use are not randomly or even haphazardly selected. They are likely to be ones that have previously been effective and that have been modified further by subsequent experience (Campbell, 1988). Indeed, some templates that have proven particularly effective during human evolution are likely hard-wired in our brains—perhaps including a higher order template that leads us to categorize!

Thus the categories that people use do generally seem to be effective as templates for making sense of the world, yet the particular categorization system used need not be seen as the only way of understanding the phenomena at hand. Different purposes and different background knowledge result in the application of different categorization schemes. For categorization to be adaptive as a sensemaking approach, all that is required is that it be sensitive to some of the more relevant aspects of underlying structure. "Our only hope as competent knowers is that we be the heirs of a substantial set of well-winnowed presuppositions . . . that we might come from a highly selected ancestry of organisms" (Campbell, 1988, p. 444). We will return to the notion of applying different categorization systems to the same objects later in this chapter. Before dealing with such complexities, we turn to the ways that classification may serve evaluation.

Classification in Support of Evaluation Purposes

In previous chapters, we made the case that classification could, under the right conditions, serve any of the four evaluation purposes. In this section, we expand on these ideas and provide some examples of how systematic inquiry on classification has been used effectively to promote each purpose.

Assessment of Merit and Worth

The assessment of merit and worth is concerned with understanding the effects and other important characteristics of a policy or program. Classification can satisfy this purpose *if* so much is already known that simply knowing a program's type is sufficient to assert its value—just as being able to classify a metal as platinum is enough to establish its value for a number of functions. Similarly, if one type of preschool curriculum, say a Montessori or High/Scope curriculum, always or at least most of the time provides real value (to all children, in all settings, and so on), then simple classification of a preschool program's curriculum as a Montessori or High/Scope curriculum would be enough to justify a claim of its overall worth (for an illustration of this strategy, see Brett, 1996).

Our view is that at least for the foreseeable future, the level of understanding about how program effects are produced will rarely be sufficient to justify using classification as a proxy for more comprehensive and more demanding evidence of merit and worth. Even when prior evidence exists about a program type's general effectiveness, there will often be uncertainty whether the same impact will occur in a new context and with new clients (Pawson & Tilley, 1997). At this point in the history of evaluation, classification is most likely to aid the assessment of merit and worth when it is combined with other inquiry modes, especially causal analysis. When combined in this way, classification can be essential in identifying the critical client and condition characteristics under which specific types of programs are more (or less) effective.

Program and Organizational Improvement

Perhaps the most common way evaluators use classification in the service of program improvement is in the best practices or program quality tradition (Bickman, 1985, Bickman & Peterson, 1990). In this approach, ostensibly successful programs are identified (often by expert nomination) and then analyzed to reveal common features or characteristics. This analysis, if done well, involves classification. The initial goal is to identify and define the characteristics that the effective programs have in common *and* that differentiate them from less successful programs (see, for example, Harkreader & Weathersby, 1998). These are the characteristics frequently called best practices. Other programs' practices can then be compared with these best practices—in essence, a program is classified relative to the category "best practice program." "Addressing the question, *To what extent does the program design and operation reflect best practice?* helps program developers and managers identify specific components of their programs that could be improved" (Loucks-Horsley, 1996, p. 6). A promising related technique for guiding the classification of program components uses *program templates* (Scheirer, 1996) to compare the program as designed with the program as implemented. The crucial issue for evaluators using either program templates or best practices is whether the practices identified as the best are actually the best ones to use or, at worst, just the ones that sound good (Bickman & Peterson, 1990).

Classification need not be limited to entire sites or programs. A more molecular level of analysis can also be adopted, with program components, or *elements* (Cook, Leviton, & Shadish, 1985), classified in terms of identified variations. Sometimes this narrower focus on specific elements is more appropriate for program improvement efforts, and the evidence identifying best practices may be stronger.

Classification can also involve groupings of program participants or clients, settings, or even outcomes. Using classification for program improvement purposes, Kuhn and Culhane (1998) identified three distinct clusters of homeless individuals—transitional, episodic, and chronic—and concluded that "efforts designed to reduce homelessness would be more efficient and potentially more effective if they were tailored and targeted by cluster" (p. 228). More generally, systematic classification will sometimes be enough by itself to spark program improvement, by leading program designers and staff to a more accurate and perhaps more nuanced view of the complexities they face.

When the best practices correspond to program mandates, both program improvement and oversight can be facilitated with the same evaluation (see, for example, Loucks-Horsley, 1996). Similarly, the evaluation of the Georgia Pre-K Program contributed to program improvement by identifying areas where improvement was needed, although also serving oversight and compliance.

Oversight and Compliance

The simplest and probably most common way that classification can serve oversight and compliance is by identifying whether a program or program site belongs to an approved or mandated program type. Roberts and Wasik (1994) describe the difficulties that ensue when local projects in a multisite evaluation differ in population targeted, services offered, and other aspects of overall service strategy. One way to address this, especially when program funders have mandated implementation of some model program, is by classifying the program sites and seeing how many fall into the prescribed category. In practice this might require a combination of inquiry modes, with the classification itself based on data derived from descriptive methods such as performance measurement.

Classification for oversight and compliance occurred in an evaluation of Georgia Pre-K Program sites (Byron & Henry, 1998). Rather than mandating a specific curriculum, the state required that program operators provide a "high-quality" program of services that would encourage the social and emotional growth of four-year-olds and readiness for kindergarten. Prior to the evaluation, a values inquiry had shown that high-quality services were highly valued by parents, teachers, program staff, and the public in Georgia (Henry, 1999). To conduct the classification of sites by quality of services, the evaluators used the Early Childhood Environmental Rating Scale (Harms & Clifford, 1980), an observational instrument based on expert opinion about quality preschool programs (Bredekamp, 1986; Bredekamp & Copple, 1997) and validated in several studies of the effects of preschool on young children (for example, Peisner-Feinberg & Burchinal, 1997). This instrument was used to structure observations at a sample of one hundred sites. Based on qualitative information on thirty-two discrete characteristics, each site was characterized as *minimal, adequate, good,* or *excellent.* A rating of good or excellent was required for classification of services as high quality.

This example illustrates the criticism by Flew and others that classification imposes categories on what are really continuous dimensions. We return to this issue later in the chapter. For now, we point out that categorical thinking was almost required by the state's mandate of high-quality services. In addition, as many of the subsequent examples will show, in many cases the existence of categories is more real than imposed. The Georgia Pre-K example also illustrates that classification can contribute to more than one purpose. Although only a quarter of the sites were rated as high quality, the data for each site revealed which characteristics needed most improvement and which were closest to meeting the high-quality standard (Byron & Henry, 1998). Although compliance with mandates for high quality was the principle purpose of the evaluation, these data also helped administrators focus efforts for program improvement.

Knowledge Development

As we noted in Chapter Five, we believe that knowledge development should not be the primary purpose for most evaluations. At the same time, when carried out in conjunction with other evaluation purposes, knowledge development may result in more effective interventions. Indeed, many of the examples offered already in this chapter might also be considered examples of classification in service of knowledge development. For example, establishing that there are three basic clusters, or types, of homeless individuals

(Kuhn & Culhane, 1998) advances the state of knowledge about this important social condition. And such an increase in understanding could lead to a variety of program improvements as well as to assessments of merit and worth that could estimate program effects separately for each client type. Knowledge development through classification will often be relatively more important in the periods when a policy or program is relatively stable and a long-term view can be taken, with incremental refinements accumulating about the way the policy or program is understood.

Conceptual and Design Issues

Evaluators need to consider several important ways in which *systematic* classification techniques can differ. First, classification methods differ in the extent to which they rely, initially at least, on categories developed prior to the current inquiry or during the current investigation. This difference corresponds loosely to the inductive-deductive distinction or, perhaps more accurately, to the distinction between emergent and a priori approaches to the development of categorical structures. Second, classification methods also differ in terms of the conventional quantitative and qualitative approaches, although we will argue that this distinction in classification is not as meaningful as many believe. Finally, different types of things can be classified, including programs, individuals, environments, occasions, and measures of outcomes.

Inductive (Emergent) Versus Deductive (A Priori) Approaches

One of the first things to think about in using classification in evaluation is the broad choice of either a priori categories as the point of departure for the inquiry or working more inductively first to identify patterns from the data that are collected. In other words, evaluators may decide to begin either with the conceptual categories of interest and then search for cases that fall within those categories or with the evidence from which they can empirically develop the relevant categories. As the sensemaking model suggests, these are not pure alternatives. An evaluator always begins classification with some a priori templates that help reveal the structure of what is experienced; these empirically derived categories then influence the conceptual categories subsequently available. Iteration between conceptual categories and empirical evidence is more the rule than the exception, but it is instructive to address these two approaches as if they were distinct. And it is pragmatically important, too, in that in any given investigation one *begins* with either a more deductive or more inductive approach.

Deductive Approaches: Beginning with a Conceptual Typology. Traditional classification schemes begin with a priori conceptual categories that are then used to explain and account for other aspects of the domain of interest. The a priori scheme may have been derived from prior inductive research, from theory, or from some other source such as program documents or subject matter experts. For instance, previously developed program templates (Scheirer, 1996) could serve as an a priori classification scheme, or typology, and individual program sites could be classified into one or another of the categories defined by the templates. Henderson, Basile, and Henry (1999) took as a starting point the classification system developed by Marcon (1992, 1994a, 1999), which specifies that preschool and elementary school teachers fall into one of three groups: teacher directed, child centered, or middle of the road. Using this a priori classification system, Henderson, Basile, and Henry surveyed individual teachers, and classified the teachers into one of these three categories.

Inductive Approaches: Empirically Driven Creation of a Taxonomy. In contrast, inductive classification methods begin with data and induce the categories. Thus evaluators might collect data on homeless individuals and derive categories that account for observed patterns of similarities and differences, as Kuhn and

Culhane (1998) did. Or they might use cluster analysis to delineate four categories of high-risk youths—a taxonomy that has important implications for more effective treatment of such youths (Dembo et al., 1996).

Although the distinction between inductive and deductive classification methods is useful, it applies primarily to the starting point for an investigation. Most classification partakes of both deduction and induction, both a priori and emergent. The classification system developed by Marcon (1992, 1994a, 1999) began, like many classifications of preschool instructional methods, with a two-category system of child-centered (or developmentally appropriate) and teacher-directed instructional models. However, in examining data on teachers' beliefs and practices, Marcon found evidence that three rather than two groups of teachers existed. Accordingly, a middle-of-the-road classification was added to more accurately represent the teaching models actually employed. Thus the three-category system was inductively derived, from the desire to develop models of instruction that represent actual practice.

Qualitative Versus Quantitative Versus Mixed Methods

Some students of classification suggest that an alignment can be made between the inductive-deductive dimension of classification and the qualitative-quantitative distinction. Bailey (1994) illustrates the tradition that associates the inductive, empirical development of taxonomies with quantitative methods: "The construction of empirical taxonomies is generally accomplished through cluster analysis, or various methods of numerical taxonomy" (p. 34). But both qualitative and quantitative methods exist for deductive, a priori classification, and inductive methods are also drawn from both the qualitative and quantitative traditions (see Table 8.1). Indeed, even more possibilities exist than are illustrated in Table 8.1, because evaluators may mix qualitative and quantitative methods (Greene & Caracelli, 1997). Qualitative inductive methods of classification are, we believe, more widespread than Bailey's remarks suggest.

Indeed, others have suggested that an important strength of qualitative methods is that their open-endedness allows patterns to emerge (Smith, 1992). Even the qualitative-quantitative distinction itself should be taken with a grain of salt in that in practice it can be difficult to classify methods as either quantitative or qualitative (Caracelli & Greene, 1997, p. 20). Still, the distinction is a long-standing one and often appears in discussions of classification.

Recognition of the various alternatives suggested in Table 8.1 should broaden the array of possibilities that evaluators consider as they begin to consider specific methods appropriate for the classification at hand. Whatever specific method is chosen, evaluators (and other) will have to decide what it is that they want to classify.

Choosing from a Typology of Things to Be Considered

Before carrying out classification, an evaluator must decide what is to be classified, with an understanding that the choice of classification methods depends in part on the type of thing being classified. Following Cattell (1952), it is often said that three basic *dimensions* can be the subject of classification efforts. *Entities* are what people typically think of as discrete physical objects or things. Individuals, programs, machines, and communities are all examples of entities. Most often, classification in evaluation will focus on particular entities. Perhaps the most common entities to be classified are clients. Programs or program sites, service deliverers, and program settings, as physical places, can also be seen as entities.

TABLE 8.1. Four Approaches to Classification.

Tradition	Deduction from A Priori Categories	Induction from Empirical Analysis
Qualitative	Conceptual typologies	Qualitative taxonomies
Quantitative	Confirmatory quantitative analysis	Empirical (quantitative) taxonomies

Attributes can alternatively be the focus of classification. Attributes are the characteristics of entities or of occasions, usually represented as variables in quantitative research. An individual has the attributes of age, height, occupation, income, political affiliation, religiosity, and gender, for example. Mowbray and Bybee (1998), in identifying the core dimensions of program contexts that need to be understood for program planning and implementation, emphasize the importance of classifying attributes. In the quantitative tradition, the classification of attributes is often carried out through factor analysis.

Occasions are an element of longitudinal analyses, in which data are collected repeatedly over time, and the dimension of *occasions* refers to time periods. In principle, occasions can be the subject of classification. One might, for instance, identify clusters of time periods, such as liberal eras or economic recessions, based on many variables (or on many entities, such as countries). Our sense is that in evaluation practice, classification of occasions has and will continue to be rare. In most cases, as we said, the evaluator's focus is likely to be on entities, either clients, programs or sites, service providers, or settings, though in some instances attributes may be the focus of classification.

Specific Methods for Classification

It is not possible or probably desirable to provide a complete and detailed review of all of the procedures that can be used for classification. Blashfield and Aldenderfer (1988) estimated that for the cluster analysis approach to classification alone, there were over three hundred varieties! Instead, we offer a selective review, beginning with one frequently used approach to classification and then describing recent developments in another approach that may sometimes prove useful for evaluators. We end with a summary of several other methods of interest to evaluators.

Waller and Meehl (1998) point out that those with different kinds of disciplinary training seem to prefer different approaches to classification. Applied psychologists generally rely on cluster analysis (Blashfield & Aldenderfer, 1988; Everitt, 1993), sociologists and psychometricians tend to favor latent class models, such as latent profile analysis (Clogg & Shockey, 1988; Molenaar & von Eye, 1994), and statisticians have recently seemed to prefer fixed or parametric mixture models (Aitken & Rubin, 1985; Lindsay & Basak, 1993). Waller and Meehl themselves advocate an approach increasingly used by some individual difference psychologists, called *taxometrics* (Meehl, 1995). In evaluation, our unsystematic review suggests, the most common quantitative classification method may be cluster analysis.

Quantitative Analysis of Categorical Structures: Cluster Analysis

In many research areas, arguably including evaluation (for example, Conrad & Buelow, 1990; Trochim, 1985), the primary tradition for developing quantitative taxonomies calls for the set of techniques known as *cluster analysis*. The goal of cluster analysis is to develop a taxonomy in which those things most similar in terms of some set of measured characteristics are grouped together. In general this involves identifying "clusters of objects that display small within-cluster variation relative to the between-cluster variation" (Dillon & Goldstein, 1984, pp. 157–158). The many variants of cluster analysis employ somewhat differing ways of measuring similarity and of defining groups based on degree of similarity. Broadly speaking, in all variants one calculates the distances between all pairwise comparisons of entities (say, clients), and the entities with the least distance between them are defined as being the most similar. Once similarity scores are calculated for all objects being considered, these scores form the basis for defining clusters (see Hartigan, 1975, on whether to standardize variables, as is the usual practice). Cluster analysis is primarily used for classifying objects (entities), such as types of homeless individuals or types of local projects in a multisite program. Cluster analysis can also be employed to classify variables (attributes) or even time periods (occasions), although this use is far less common. When used to cluster entities, cluster analysis requires many variables per case (Bailey, 1994), a requirement that those new to cluster analysis often find surprising.

Some versions of cluster analysis search for hierarchical classification schemes. These versions derive largely from biology, where classification is concerned with such things as grouping individual animals into species, species into families, and families into taxa. Although there are some fairly different approaches to carrying out hierarchical classification (Milligan, 1981; Rapkin & Luke, 1993), the general goal is to derive clusters that can be organized into a hierarchy of sets and subsets.

Another popular approach to cluster analysis simply assigns entities to groups within one level of clusters. These nonhierarchical methods, often referred to as *k-means clustering methods*, employ an iterative approach to partitioning. The logic is to begin with an initial set of clusters that by some criterion or another seems reasonable. The center of each initial cluster is calculated, and individuals are assigned to the cluster with the closest center. And after this round of assignment, cluster centers are recalculated (the centers will have changed with the introduction of the new members). Then all individuals can be considered for regrouping based on their similarity to the new cluster centers.

One of the problems in selecting among clustering techniques is that there does not as yet appear to be a single best approach, or even a convincing roadmap for selecting the right approach for given conditions. As Milligan (1981) concludes, "None of the clustering methods currently in use offer any theoretical proof which ensures that the algorithm will recover the correct structure" (p. 380). Prior conceptualizations may guide some choices (such as whether a hierarchical solution is desirable), and simulations provide some guidance about which variants to choose (Milligan, 1981; Blashfield & Aldenderfer, 1988). Nevertheless, the choice of the right cluster method requires, we believe, a bit of luck, or an exploratory tactic of trying out more than one approach and then selecting the best solution based on interpretability of results and consistency with other evidence.

A single clustering method may provide multiple solutions, such as two, three, and four cluster solutions. So evaluators must also decide which of these possible solutions to use as the basis for interpretation. One criterion for making this decision is the *inverse scree test*, which examines the relative amount of variance accounted for by the classification of entities into clusters (Lathrop & Williams, 1990). Another criterion is to use analysis of variance (or some other between-group test) to assess whether cluster membership as an independent variable entails significant differences on other selected variables. If cluster means are not sufficiently different to yield significance, a solution with more clusters might be preferred (Rapkin & Luke, 1993). Beyond these and other purely empirical criteria for choosing the number of clusters, however, is the larger issue for the evaluator of deriving a classification scheme that is consistent with his or her conceptual understanding. The sensemaking view suggests that exploratory work is always guided by some prior conceptual framework, and therefore evaluators should seek a derived cluster structure that corresponds in some ways to the understanding developed independently through practice.

Taxometrics

Taxometrics is a recent approach to classification developed by Paul Meehl and his associates (Meehl, 1995; Meehl & Younce, 1994; Waller & Meehl, 1998). To date, taxonometric procedures have been primarily used by individual difference psychologists, especially in the study of psychopathology. A question that frequently arises among those who study personality disorders is whether people diagnosed with some disorder are different in kind from others or different only in degree along some continuum. For example, are psychopaths categorically different from nonpsychopaths, or are they simply at the low end of an empathy and responsibility continuum? Meehl developed taxometrics to address such questions. In some instances these methods may be useful for evaluation. They also reveal some interesting things about categories.

One of the things Meehl emphasizes, in keeping with realism, is that you cannot tell from most descriptive data whether or not categories exist. Intuitively, one might think that when there are distinct groups, it would be possible to see them on variables related to group membership. But, as shown in Figure 8.1, this is not the case. The two dashed lines represent two separate categories, each with a normal distribution of scores. The solid line gives the composite distribution (that is, the combination of the two categories). The composite distribution looks normal. Even though it is created by the mixture of two underlying groups, there is no bimodality or any other sign that underlying categories are involved. As we have suggested, it is generally necessary to look beneath the surface to discover categories. Figure 8.1 also illustrates another important point. Sometimes people speak as though there are either categories *or* dimensions. But as Waller and Meehl (1998) state, the existence of distinct categories "does not preclude dimensionality" (p. 9). As an illustration, they cite the existence of PKU, a genetic disorder in which an enzyme deficiency causes impaired brain cell function, resulting in lower IQ. PKU is a distinct category, but it is an overlay on the normal distribution of intelligence scores.

Telling whether categories exist can be difficult even when evaluators have multiple variables to examine rather than just one (as in Figure 8.1). Figure 8.2 illustrates how the existence of distinct groups can create artificial correlations among variables. The F's stand for the individual members of one group and the M's stand for the members of a second group. Within each group, there is no correlation between the two variables Y and Z. But because one group (the M's) is lower on both variables, the two variables are positively correlated in the mixed sample. If the evaluator did not know about the underlying categorical structure, the composite relationship between the two variables would probably seem to suggest that the variables were continuous and correlated, not categorical.

FIGURE 8.1. Normal Compound Distribution Based on Two Distinct Underlying Groups.

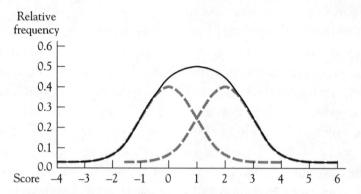

Source: Waller, N. G., & Meehl, P. E., *Multivariate Taxometric Procedures,* p. 8, copyright © 1998 by Sage Publications, Inc.

Meehl (1995; Waller & Meehl, 1998) has developed a number of procedures for discerning categories. For example, assume, as is usually the case, that an evaluator has only a rough idea about the fundamental attributes of the categories to be used, and that category membership is represented by a set of fallible, imperfect measures, with the imperfections especially strong at the earliest stages of classification efforts. Imagine also that as in Waller and Meehl's example (1998), the evaluator is a visiting alien researcher, from a planet whose inhabitants have very different methods of reproduction than earth people do. Having heard that there might be two categories of people, males and females, the alien sets out to determine in an adolescent sample whether this is really so. To the alien researcher all earthlings look alike, but the researcher finds in an old epic poem three possible indicators of sex: hair length, hip-to-waist ratio, and ability to identify types of flowers.

Also assume that the indicators are related to each other much as the indicators are in Figure 8.2. Within each sex, for example, assume that hair length and knowledge of flowers is not correlated but that the average difference between men and women on both variables creates a correlation in the mixed sample. If this is the case, what happens when the researcher arrays the adolescents

FIGURE 8.2. Correlation Between Two Variables Created by Two Partially Overlapping, Distinct Groups.

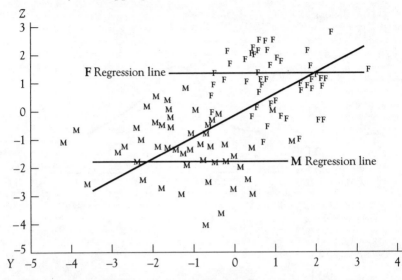

Source: Waller, N. G., & Meehl, P. E., *Multivariate Taxometric Procedures*, p. 13, copyright © 1998 by Sage Publications, Inc.

in terms of hip-to-waist ratio? At each extreme end of this dimension should be people primarily (or exclusively) of one sex. For this reason, on the one hand, at either end of the hip-to-waist ratio dimension the correlation between hair length and knowledge of flowers should be near zero. (Note that on the left-hand side of Figure 8.2, where there are only M's, and on the right-hand side, where there are only F's, the correlation is zero.) On the other hand, in the middle of the hip-to-waist ratio dimension, where there is a mixture of males and females, hair length and knowledge of flowers should be correlated. (Note that, in the middle of Figure 8.2, where there are both F's and M's, there appears to be a correlation). Figure 8.3 illustrates the product of such an analysis. If, as in the boy-girl example, there are distinct groups (or *taxonicity*, as Meehl, 1995, calls it), the interrelationship between the two variables will show a peak when plotted against the third variable, as in the top graph. If there are no distinct underlying groups, the plot will be flat, as in the bottom graph.

FIGURE 8.3. Pattern of Covariance with and Without Categorical Groups.

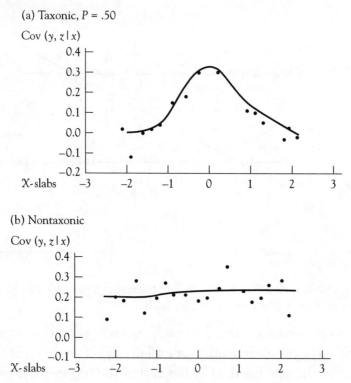

(a) Taxonic, $P = .50$

Cov $(y, z \,|\, x)$

(b) Nontaxonic

Cov $(y, z \,|\, x)$

Source: Waller, N. G., & Meehl, P. E., *Multivariate Taxometric Procedures,* p. 21, copyright © 1998 by Sage Publications, Inc.

Waller and Meehl present many such tests and argue that a conclusion that distinct groups exist should be based on consistency across several tests. For evaluators, the taxometric approach may be most important when it is not adequate to act *as if* categories are meaningful; or to put it another way, when more confidence is required that distinctions are real (we discuss this issue further later). This approach often requires a relatively large number of cases, however, and so may not be appropriate for smaller evaluations. Nevertheless, even evaluators who do not use taxometrics may find that a basic understanding of the approach will enhance their thinking about classification. It indicates, for example, how difficult it can be with simple descriptive data to assess whether there are different categories.

Other Approaches

As noted earlier, a variety of approaches can be used for classification. Some statisticians apply what are called *mixture models* (for example, Aitken & Rubin, 1985; Lindsay & Basak, 1993). In essence, these are statistical models that can assess whether some set of scores is likely to have resulted from the combination of distinct but overlapping underlying groups. As we mentioned at the outset, it is infeasible to review all possible systematic methods for classification in detail here. We focus instead in the following sections on an overview of the use of exploratory factor analysis and of confirmatory factor analysis for classification, and we offer some thoughts about classification in qualitative methods.

Exploratory Factor Analysis. *Factor analysis* is a family of techniques for grouping attributes or characteristics that have a common underlying component (Q factor analysis, in contrast, is used to group entities). Exploratory factor analysis is used inductively to obtain a model of the structure presumed to underlie observed scores. Confirmatory factor analysis, in contrast, provides a more deductive test of the extent to which the data are consistent with some a priori model of the underlying structure.

Factor analysis was developed, first by Spearman (1904) and then by Thurstone (1935), to identify sources of variation that are common to a variety of measurements. "Factor analysis is based on the fundamental assumption that some underlying factors, which are smaller in number than the number of observed variables, are responsible for the covariation among the observed variables" (Kim & Mueller, 1978a, p. 12). Thus the basic logic of factor analysis is consistent with the realist notion of underlying structures. For example, imagine that some children do well on a variety of tests requiring mathematical reasoning, whereas other children do poorly.

This pattern might suggest that there is an underlying factor, call it *quantitative reasoning ability*, that is responsible for the observed scores. This underlying factor could account for the overall differences across children (why John did better than James, for instance) and for a pattern of similar performance levels from a given child across tests (why John did well on all the tests).

Given a set of data with numerous variables measured on each person, factor analysis can probe underlying structure in the sense of the factors that apparently give rise to the scores. Looking at children's results on a battery of tests, does there appear to be only one factor, reflecting general intelligence? Or are there two factors, reflecting a quantitative reasoning factor and a language proficiency factor? Or are there many more specific factors? As this example suggests, exploratory factor analysis may be thought of as a quantitative, inductive method for classifying attributes. That is, this method moves from the observed data to a taxonomy of measures. Do the measures appear to arise from one, or two, or three underlying factors, or more? And if more than one factor emerges, which measures fall together on each factor?

In general, the first derived factor is selected to account for the most covariance, with the second and subsequent dimensions chosen to be those that, given the constraint (usually) of being orthogonal to prior dimensions, account for the greatest amount of the remaining covariance. There is a long list of decisions to be made in choosing the proper methods for factor analysis in a particular context. Among the main decisions are choosing an extraction method for constructing the factors (such as the principal factor method or the maximum likelihood approach); determining whether and how to rotate the initial factors in order to enhance their interpretation (with orthogonal rotations, such as varimax or quartimax, retaining the initial orthogonal characteristic of the factors, whereas oblique rotations, such as promax, allow the factors to become correlated); and selecting the number of factors to retain (determined by such criteria as the scree test, the size of the eigenvalues, and interpretability). Various sources address these and related issues involved in factor analysis in greater depth (Mulaik, 1972; Kim & Meuller, 1978a, 1978b; Gorsuch, 1983; Julnes, 1999).

Confirmatory Factor Analysis. In the traditional, exploratory variant of factor analysis, structure is induced from the data. Confirmatory factor analysis, or CFA, is a more deductive procedure, starting with specific hypotheses about the underlying structure responsible for the observed indicators. In the language of structural equation modeling, CFA represents the measurement model for the full-blown latent structural model. The important contrast to exploratory factor analysis is that CFA involves developing a priori hypotheses and testing them. The logic of factor analysis still applies in the presumption of underlying structure, but now the methodology allows the researcher to place constraints on the connections between the observed variables and underlying factors and then to see how those constraints affect the fit of the a priori model with the data. This is an simplified description, and the practice of CFA is typically more iterative. The evaluator often makes some revisions to the initially hypothesized model and then assesses the fit of the actual data to the revised model.

Evaluators face several decisions in implementing CFA. Perhaps most noteworthy are the need to make decisions among competing models, including new models that incorporate inductively driven revisions to one's a priori model, and the associated need to select one or more goodness-of-fit measures. Goodness-of-fit indices are used to represent how closely a given model corresponds to the actual data. There are many alternative goodness-of-fit criteria, and currently no consensus on which is best. Common practice is to use several (see Bentler & Bonnet, 1990, for details). Despite these and other complications and limitations, CFA can be a useful tool in probing the soundness of prior hypotheses about the underlying structures that cause measures to hang together. That is, like its more exploratory cousin, CFA is usually used to classify attributes (with the resultant latent factors then used for other purposes, such as causal analysis). More complex variations can also be used to assess hypotheses about group membership for participants or other entities (Clogg & Shockey, 1988; Molenaar & von Eye, 1994).

Classification in Qualitative Methods

Although this chapter has emphasized quantitative methods for classification, investigators using qualitative methods also commonly identify different groups and assign people (or other entities) into groups. That is, qualitative researchers often carry out classification. For example, in a text on qualitative methods Berg (1998) discusses categorization in the context of case studies, ethnography, interviews, and content analysis. One could just as easily discuss categorization in the context of focus groups, participant and nonparticipant observation, and virtually any other qualitative method. Indeed, the frequent use of classification in qualitative research is one reason that we have focused more on quantitative approaches to classification, for it is among the adherents of the quantitative tradition in evaluation that change is more needed.

More generally, some of the points in this book can be seen as bringing lessons from qualitative methods to quantitative methods. For example, the focus on iteration, embodied most strongly in the discussion of principled discovery and competitive elaboration in the next chapter, brings a routine aspect of qualitative inquiry into quantitative research. But lessons can go in both directions. Take the case of "negative case analysis," one of the criteria sometimes used by qualitative researchers for assessing the adequacy of an account, including classification systems. This approach can benefit from some modifications borrowing from the quantitative tradition. According to Kidder and Fine (1987), "the process of negative case analysis . . . requires . . . that there be no disconfirming evidence. Any instances that contradict the emerging hypotheses are used to revise the hypothesis until it incorporates all evidence. No incident or informant is discounted as 'random error' or 'an outlier'" (pp. 63–64). But measurements are not perfect, and some observations are appropriately considered as the result of random error.

Relationships in a complex world are in a sense probabilistic. To construct a classification system that provides a perfect fit to all cases (or to construct any kind of explanatory system that perfectly accounts for all cases) is overly ambitious, and probably treats noise as something meaningful. Fortunately, qualitative research does not generally rely on negative case analysis, strictly applied, but instead on "the researcher's reasoned and disciplined weighting of [confirming versus disconfirming] evidence" (Smith, 1997, p. 82).

Classification in Combination with Other Inquiry Modes

As some of our examples have suggested, classification may often be combined with other inquiry modes in an evaluation or series of evaluations. These combinations will often contribute more to social betterment than will evaluations lacking classification methods. In addition, the data necessary for quantitative classification will often be at hand, and the only resource cost will be some additional time for analysis and reporting. It is perhaps unnecessary to say that qualitative methods of classification should often be integrated with other inquiry modes, because qualitative evaluators generally do this as standard practice (see Smith, 1997, for an example). As in the first part of this chapter, we again focus more on quantitative methods, because it is in this tradition that linking of classification to other inquiry modes needs to occur more frequently.

Perhaps the most obvious linkages between classification and another inquiry mode involve causal analysis. As noted in Chapter Four, causal analysis often may be carried out for the assessment of merit and worth, and sometimes (usually in a less rigorous fashion) for program improvement. Adding classification to causal analysis will usually lead to more refined and therefore often more useful understanding. This is true whether the classification focuses on program services, on clients, on settings, or even on the way outcome measures should be grouped. For example, once alternative interventions or sites within a single program are classified, causal analysis can then examine differences between the program types in terms of differences in the outcomes they produce. To know that one type of treatment is more powerful than another is generally useful information. Once clients have been grouped into different types on the basis of preexisting attributes, it is possible to specify how much benefit an intervention brings to each client type, and a more refined assessment of merit and worth is possible. Clients might also be classified based on the pattern of change they experience over time. For example, Rapkin and Luke (1993) describe using cluster analysis to differentiate the *trajectories* that clients follow as a result of participating in a program. That is, by measuring some outcome variable(s) of interest at regular intervals during a program and a follow-up period, an evaluation could distinguish several categories of clients: those who respond to treatment and retain gains, those who initially respond to treatment but lose gains afterward, and those who do not respond to treatment. Several quantitative methods allow evaluators to identify different patterns of response to a treatment. One approach has come to be called *latent growth curve modeling* in the structural equation modeling literature (for example, Muthen & Curran, 1997). Alternatively, patterns of response can be estimated through multilevel modeling (for example, Bryk & Raudenbush, 1992). Once subgroups of clients with different types of growth curves are identified, the evaluation could proceed to causal analysis to identify the reasons for the different trajectories.

Although this is less common in practice, program settings may also be classified, and the results used to assess whether the intervention is more effective in some types of sites or communities than others. Such analyses can be important for realist evaluators who recognize the possible moderating effects of context (Pawson & Tilley, 1997).

The classification of outcomes or other measures can also facilitate causal inquiry. Although the notion of classifying measures may at first sound foreign to some researchers, this is of course just what evaluators do when they systematically create scales and sub-scales. Indeed, the very notion of construct validity has classification at its heart. Briefly, *construct validity* refers to the extent to which some procedure (in given circumstances) actually measures the underlying construct it is intended to measure (Cronbach & Meehl, 1955; Cronbach, 1995). Campbell and Fiske's fundamental insight (1959) about construct validity was that measures directed at one construct should fall together and that measures employing similar methods to measure another construct should not fall together with the first set of measures. Although construct validity is usually not talked about with the language of classification, that language is in fact appropriate. The realist language of underlying structures also fits well, in that the idea of construct validity is premised on the assumption that there are phenomena (attitudes, abilities, or what-ever) that are not directly observed but that give rise to patterns of interrelations across measures. The use of *latent factor models* (for example, Jöreskog & Sörbom, 1993) to test hypotheses about which items will covary is a prominent contemporary method by which quantitative researchers attempt to classify measures. Clas-sification of measures in this and related ways can enhance causal analysis by increasing confidence that one has properly identified the relevant cause and effect variables (Cook & Campbell, 1979).

In similar fashion, classification can fruitfully be linked with the inquiry modes of description and with values inquiry. A few examples will suggest the process. In the case of description, sup-pose that the evaluator has constructed a performance measure-ment system for a social service program. At some point the client data in the measurement system could be used to assess whether the clients fall into different groups. If they do, this information might call for subsequent modifications in the performance mea-surement process. For example, findings might subsequently be reported separately for each subgroup. Likewise, descriptive data on the pattern of services offered at different program sites could be used to classify sites. Again, if different types of sites exist, sub-sequent reports might provide outcome levels by site type. In the case of values inquiry, instead of relying on prior notions about stakeholder groups, evaluators might employ empirical classification methods to identify types of respondents according to the values they hold. And classification of measures might simplify reporting of value positions.

Criticism of Classification

Despite the potential benefits of classification, this inquiry mode has its skeptics. As we mentioned in the introduction to this chapter, some people criticize the notion of natural kinds and, more generally, classification. In this section, we consider and respond to some of the more important criticisms.

Nature Has No Joints (No Wonder It Seems Inflexible)

One of the critics' main arguments is that nature does not have the so-called joints that classifiers are seeking to find. Their position is that categories are constructions imposed by people on the continuous variations that exist in nature. We may call some people tall and others short, but the critics point out, height is found along a continuum.

Some of the distinctions in which evaluators and others are interested almost certainly are carved out of continua. We believe that others, however, are clearly categorical. As Meehl (1994) points out, "There are gophers, there are chipmunks, but there are no gophmunks" (cited in Waller & Meehl, 1994, p. 11). To Flew's "God makes the spectrum, man makes the pigeonholes," Bhaskar (1978) responded, "I can find no possible warrant for such an assumption [that all differences in nature are continuous, not discrete]. Taken literally, it would imply that a chromosome count is irrelevant in determining the biological sex of an individual, that the class of the living is only conventionally divided from the class of the dead" (p. 213). We too are willing to believe that the living and the dead are (for the time being) real, distinct categories and, more generally, that at least some other categories really exist in the world for people to find.

The Social World Has No Joints

A related but narrower criticism is that although real categories may apply in the domains of the natural sciences, they do not exist in the social world. Even some prominent realists appear to be taking this position at least some of the time (for example, Bhaskar, 1979). This stance allows the skeptic to acknowledge that there are natural kinds in the world of chemistry (carbon versus helium) and biology (the living versus the dead) but still deny the utility of classification in evaluation and the social and behavioral sciences. There are in fact divergent practices in the use of the term natural kinds, with some authors restricting it to fundamental hard science categories such as carbon atoms versus oxygen atoms; others including more complex categories such as oak trees versus elm trees and male versus female; and still others including constructed products such as chairs versus shoes or even leaders versus followers (Pepper, 1942; Quine, 1969; Putnam, 1975).

We acknowledge that like natural phenomena, some social phenomena are almost certainly represented better as continuous dimensions than as categories. For example, in thinking about the clients in a welfare-to-work initiative, it may well be more accurate to identify an underlying dimension of past welfare dependence, measured by such variables as a client's total length of time on public assistance and percentage of life on public assistance, rather than attempt to pigeonhole clients into more distinct categories. There may be many such situations, yet categorical and continuous dimension representations should be viewed as complementary alternatives rather than as somehow competitive. In addition, often the only way to accept a dimensional model with confidence is to fit and reject a categorical model.

Although some aspects of the social world may be best represented as continua, we are convinced that others are best represented as categories. The fact that they result from social processes does not make them less real or less categorical. For example, Waller, Putnam, and Carlson (1996) argue that childhood sexual abuse—a social rather than a hard science cause—often results in a specific psychopathology, dissociative identity disorder. And they offer evidence that this disorder is a distinct category, not just the extreme on a continuum. Are we all to believe that atoms, viruses, and genes can cause real categorical differences but that political ideologies, economic conditions, long-standing traditions, human inventions, and intense interpersonal interactions cannot? No. We believe that truly categorical distinctions can result from social causes. If the term natural kinds is still a barrier, these categories could be called *real kinds*. Even in a category such as shoes, although the category members are not identical and although they share characteristics only because people have made them with those characteristics, they are similar in some important, fundamental way that transcends a merely convenient human construction. So too social programs.

Perhaps There Are Some Real Joints, but Can One Ever Find Them?

Even accepting that there are real categorical distinctions in the world, it is possible to ask whether classification methods identify these real distinctions or instead find arbitrary ones. Recall that cognitive research on categorization indicates that the categories individuals use to order the world are influenced by their background knowledge and motivation. This raises the question whether the categories people use are at all related to real underlying distinctions or are instead convenient groupings of the moment. Fortunately, despite the findings that variations can occur in the categories individuals use, there is also evidence from cognitive research that individuals generally tend to be attuned to the important differences facing them. A clever example comes from research on perceived similarity, a topic closely linked to categorization. Medin and Shoben (1988) showed that although white hair and gray hair are judged as more similar than gray and black hair, white clouds and gray clouds are judged as less similar than gray clouds and black clouds. The perceived similarity of colors is contextual and depends on underlying structural forces that make a difference in the world. "In other words, psychological similarity is tuned to those superficial properties that are likely to be causally linked to a deeper level. This is particularly likely to be true with respect to natural kinds" (Medin & Ortony, 1989, p. 186). When real, meaningful structural differences exist, somehow ordinary perceivers are surprisingly good at noting them. Perhaps, what Campbell suggested is true, perhaps we have "come from a highly selected ancestry of organisms."

Still, for any systematic classification an evaluator might carry out, the question can be asked, How close did you come to carving nature at its joints? One response is that it is usually not necessary to carve perfectly in order to assist sensemaking. To see why this is true, imagine a graphical rendering of the clients (or other entities) being classified. Further imagine what it would look like if one knew and measured all the attributes relevant for the underlying categories at hand and then displayed each client's values in a multidimensional space. "If we plot the locations of individuals of one natural kind in such an n-space, they cluster tightly together. In contrast, the space between any two natural kinds is vast" (Campbell, 1988, p. 457). In practice, classification efforts may fall short of this ideal if evaluators fail to measure (and to measure well) one or more of the dimensions critical to the groupings or if they include many measures that tap something other than the underlying categories of interest. But if they nevertheless correctly classify *most* of the clients, they may still be able to discern, even if imperfectly, how category membership relates to other things of interest such as program effects. And they may learn enough to do even better the next time.

Another response to the question of how close one has come to carving nature at its joints may seem somewhat remarkable.

Sometimes it is pragmatically justifiable to carve arbitrarily. Even when the underlying structure appears to be a continuous dimension, it may often be useful to act *as if* there are categories. Thus program developers and staff might find it reasonable to develop treatment alternatives in response to a report that describes specific needs of two or three types of clients, whereas they might throw up their hands in frustration in response to a report that identifies how a client dimension measured as a continuous variable relates to client outcomes. Statisticians correctly point out that classifying a continuous variable will usually result in a loss of information, but we suggest this loss will often be outweighed by an increase in commonsense usefulness, especially when decisions must be made because there is a fork in the policy road.

Cronbach (1989) argues that in applied social research, a researcher "may adopt a construct he or she finds useful without asking that it cut Nature at a joint God put there." And he adds, "Philosophers, I think, can accept our position because even the realists expect truthlike, close-to-the joint constructs only in a 'mature' science, not in a field whose constructions are mostly in flux" (p. 161). Though we in evaluation can rarely claim to cut nature cleanly at its joints, commonsense realist classification affirms that we often come close enough and that it is often appropriate to act as if there are natural kinds even when there are not.

Different Classification Schemes Apply to Different Entities

Some critics of natural kinds and of classification more generally have noted that as we discussed earlier, different classification systems may be applied to the same entities. They have used this observation to argue that classification must be arbitrary and must not get at real underlying structures.

The notion of embedded levels, a prominent theme for many realists (see Chapter Six), provides one of the reasons that the application of different classification systems to the same entities is not a problem. According to this notion, underlying structures can be analyzed at any number of more molar or more molecular levels. Indeed, because any particular effort to understand underlying structure can always be followed by a more molecular analysis, in theory there is no endpoint in looking for underlying structures. The early chemists, who thought they would understand the makeup of the physical world once they completed the periodic table, would marvel at contemporary research on subatomic particles. Similarly, once evaluators identify groups of clients, it would almost always be possible to go further and identify subgroups within any of these groups.

Hierarchical classification systems reflect this sort of embedded organization. That is, the more molecular subcategories are subsets, with each one falling completely within a single larger, more molar category, just as humans, chimpanzees, and cattle all fall as subsets within the more molar category of mammals. Cognitive researchers have studied the natural human tendency to engage in hierarchical classification. For example, Behl-Chadha (1996) demonstrated that even very young infants (three to four months old) were able to form superordinate (more molar) classifications when confronted with instances of furniture and mammals. Johnson and Mervis (1997) studied the use of subordinate (more molecular) and sub-subordinate categories in classifying songbirds and found that increased knowledge about songbirds led to increased use of more molecular categories. The fact that classification hierarchies have more and less molecular levels clearly does not invalidate classification—though in practice it may raise questions about the appropriate level for classification in any given evaluation.

Seemingly more vexing is the idea that there can be different nonhierarchical classifications for the same set of things, with different classification systems appropriate for different purposes (Aronson, Harré, & Way, 1995). In Chapter Six, we used the example of different systems for classifying grandfather clocks, in terms of pendulum attributes, maker and age, or size and color, depending on the purpose for which the classification was made.

Sometimes people are interested in the joints in nature's skeleton, and sometimes they are interested in the structure of nature's endocrine system. As numerous realists have recently noted, commitment to realism and to the idea of natural kinds does not require a belief that there is "a unique best taxonomy in terms of natural kinds" (Hacking, 1991, p. 111; also see Aronson, Harré, & Way, 1995; for an empirical example related to evaluation, see Buckner, 1991).

The details and purpose of an evaluation as well as the current state of knowledge are likely to determine the choice of classification systems when alternative systems are available. The ideal of course is to employ different systems, for example, to use both molar and molecular frameworks. At the same time, the details of an evaluation and the potential pathway to social betterment will often suggest one system over others. For instance, for interventions targeted at individuals, individual-level classifications are more likely to be employed.

Conclusion

Gaining confidence about a taxonomy takes time, replication, and the convergence of evidence from several types of sources. In evaluation, a lengthy program of classification studies is unlikely to be feasible. Instead, evaluators may have to be satisfied with a set of classifications that although imperfect, although probably not carving nature at its joints, approximates real underlying groups closely enough to aid the natural sensemaking of those who must make decisions about social policies and programs.

Despite the criticisms of classification, we believe it is reasonable to adopt a pragmatic and nuanced perspective. This view says that real and useful categories may result from people's social actions. Entities and the attributes of those entities can be classified in more than one way, and no classification system can claim to be definitive. Evaluators, we believe, are charged with bringing their view of the world and ultimately the view of all those who fill roles in a democracy more closely in alignment with the way the world actually operates. By using classification for assisted sensemaking about policies and programs, evaluators can often identify and discuss categories of programs, individuals, environments, occasions, and measures of outcomes in ways that will bring greater precision to efforts to improve the lives of those in need of services and, in turn, social conditions. Although the categories used may be imperfect and may be open to refinement as more classification work is done, using them *as if* they were accurate depictions may help speed the improvement of social conditions.

9

Causal Analysis

Causal questions abound in the evaluation of social programs and policies. What is the effect of welfare reform on the well-being of poor children? Does drug abuse resistance training actually reduce drug use among adolescents? Are needle exchange programs effective in reducing the spread of HIV? Does smaller class size in early grades increase student achievement and reduce the achievement gap between minority and nonminority students? In a statewide prekindergarten program, are children better served on average by one of the several approved curricula? How do preschool programs achieve positive effects on social outcomes? Does one type of juvenile offender obtain better social outcomes from counseling and does another type achieve better outcomes from more structured programs?

Causal Analysis in Support of Evaluation Purposes

Causal questions seem to predominate when the evaluation purpose is assessment of merit and worth. Whether a welfare reform policy is viewed as having merit depends, for example, on whether it improves or harms the well-being of poor children. When decisions are made about substance abuse interventions in schools, the decision makers are poorly served if no one can tell them whether a popular drug abuse resistance training program is effective. In short, the merit and worth of a program primarily depends on the program's effects—a causal question.

Of course, as we have discussed, causal analysis is not always necessary for the assessment of merit and worth. In some domains other than policies and programs, causal analyses for this purpose are far less common. In product evaluations, such as the assessments of new cars in *Consumer Reports* or *Car and Driver*, the methods of causal analysis are not generally used. Instead, evaluators assesses the extent to which the car has certain (presumably) valued attributes, such as ample leg room, good gas mileage, and a smooth, quiet ride. Causal analysis recedes in importance when the characteristics people value can be assessed through simpler means of description, as is common with consumer products. For cars, for example, acceleration rate can be observed descriptively with limited ambiguity. For social programs and policies, however, the key issues—the things that people value and that make a program or policy worthwhile or not—are causal, as illustrated in the set of questions at the beginning of this chapter. Of course causal analysis cannot answer all the questions involved in assessing the merit and worth of a policy or program. As noted previously, issues of clients' rights and dignity and issues of fiscal propriety often need to be addressed to assess merit and worth but do not require causal analysis. But overall, it is causal analysis that is often central to assisted sense-making about the merit and worth of a policy or program.

Causal analysis can also play a major role when program improvement is the primary evaluation purpose, although less compelling causal evidence may be required (as discussed in Chapter Four). Program improvement often involves making choices among methods of delivering services. For example, each year in a pre-K program, local staff may select professional development activities they think will improve instruction. Causal evidence about the consequences of participating in each type of activity could inform these selections. In addition, program improvement can result from knowledge about underlying mechanisms. If it is shown that preschools have a positive effect on children's academic achievement because preschools increase parents' expectations, then they could expend more direct efforts to enhance parental expectations, potentially increasing their positive effects.

Causal analysis can also contribute to the purpose of knowledge development. One major contribution is the identification and testing of mechanisms that lead to more positive outcomes. Theories large and small have been based on causal analysis in evaluation. For instance, Lipsey (1997) has sought to develop a general framework of the types of interventions that are most effective for different types of juvenile offenders. This knowledge development work has been based on a large number of evaluations that study the effects of interventions for juvenile offenders.

In short, methods for causal analysis are a vital part of the evaluator's toolkit. However, attributing an effect to a program is usually not a simple matter. The literature on causation is voluminous, with countless books, chapters, and articles on the philosophy of causation, on research methods for inferring causation, on the psychology of causal inference, and on more specialized topics such as the meaning of causation in the law. In this chapter, we discuss causal analysis methods, but given the wide array of existing writings, we do not attempt a comprehensive review. Rather, we present an integrative view of the concept of cause, discuss the logic of causal inference, and then address selected methods for causal analysis in evaluation.

Conceptual and Design Issues

In this section, we address two general questions. First, what is meant by *causation* and by the oft-used terms *cause* and *effect*? Second, what is the general process through which people make causal inferences? The answers to these two questions frame the subsequent review of specific methods for causal analysis.

The Concept of Cause

The nature of causation is an enduring question. Hume, Mills, Popper, and a galaxy of philosophers and scientist-philosophers, major and minor, have wrestled with it. Our view is that causation can best be understood through the integration of three perspectives from the philosophy of science: a counterfactualist definition of cause and effect, a realist view of underlying generative mechanisms, and an understanding of the contingent and elliptical nature of causal relations.

The Counterfactualist Definition of Cause and Effect. Imagine that an evaluator wants to know the effect of a needle exchange program on the HIV status of an individual heroin addict, named James. Her question is: Did participation in the needle exchange program cause James to remain HIV free? What would it take to gain a confident answer to this question? A number of philosophers (for example, Mackie, 1974) and methodologists (for example, Mohr, 1995; Reichardt & Mark, 1998) take a *counterfactualist* perspective in answering this question and, more generally, in defining causation. According to this perspective, the evaluator would first need to know, factually, that James participated in the program and that at some subsequent time of interest, he remained uninfected by HIV. She would also need to know, counterfactually, whether, *if James had not participated* in the program but everything else had been just the same, James would have contracted the virus by that later time.

Or, to state the counterfactualist perspective more generally, evaluators can define an effect and by implication a cause as follows: the effect of causal state A (for example, participating in the program) as compared to the effect of causal state B (not participating) is the difference between (1) the outcome that arose at time 2 after A had been administered at time 1 and (2) the outcome that *would have arisen* at time 2 if B had been administered at time 1 but everything else at time 1 had been the same. This comparison is called the *ideal comparison*.

More accurately, we might call this the *ideal but unattainable comparison*, because the ideal comparison cannot be achieved in practice. It is impossible for *everything else* to be the same when a program is administered in one condition and not administered in the other (or when program A is administered in one condition and program B in the other). For example, an evaluator might compare the HIV status of James, who participated in a needle exchange program, with the HIV status of Tom, a heroin addict who did not participate in a needle exchange program. The intervention, or treatment, would differ in the two conditions, but that is not all—the individuals receiving the treatments would also differ. Therefore any observed difference in James's and Tom's HIV status might be the result of differences between these two individuals rather than the result of the needle exchange program.

To obtain the ideal comparison, the evaluator would have to travel back in time and arrange things so that James participated in the needle exchange in one sequence but not in another sequence. The difference between the outcomes would then exactly equal the effect of the needle exchange program. Any difference in an outcome variable at time 2 would be due *only* to the treatment differences that were introduced at time 1, because everything else would have been the same. But lacking the ability to travel back in time, evaluators cannot have everything else be the same in real-life comparisons. As a result, incorrect conclusions may be drawn about causal relations. Scientists have developed a repertoire of assisted sensemaking techniques to minimize the likely errors. One important step in the evolution of these techniques has been the identification of several categories of factors other than the program of interest that can vary across the treatment conditions in real-life comparisons. These factors are commonly called *threats to internal validity*, and we describe several of them later in the context of specific research designs.

The counterfactualist perspective on cause offers several advantages. It provides a clear, useful definition of a cause and an effect (Reichardt & Mark, 1998). In addition, by comparing actual research designs to the ideal but unattainable comparison, evaluators can see strengths and weaknesses of alternative designs more clearly (Mohr, 1995), as we illustrate later. The counterfactualist framing of causality also reveals that one can talk meaningfully about causality for single cases in a particular context. But the strongest methods for causal analysis ask not about the effect for a single case but about *average effects* over some population or subgroup of individuals (Rubin, 1974). Fortunately, judgments about programs and policies are not usually based on individual clients, and policy and program evaluation generally focuses on average effects. Thus methods that reasonably approximate the ideal but unattainable counterfactual comparison can serve social betterment by providing warranted assessment of the average merits of a social program or policy, averaging across groupings that are meaningful for achieving social betterment.

The Realist View of Underlying Generative Mechanisms.
Although the counterfactualist conception of cause has several advantages, it also has important limits that lead us to combine it with two other views of causality. One shortcoming is an insufficient emphasis on addressing *why* effects have occurred, that is, on the mechanisms through which a cause influences an effect, or to put it yet another way, on the processes that connect causes and effects.

In contrast, as noted in Chapter Six, the approach to causation taken by most contemporary realists emphasizes underlying generative mechanisms. Thus a search for underlying generative mechanisms would go beyond finding that a particular preschool program produced increased success in school. One would also identify possible mechanisms such as heightened social and educational expectations for the children held by their teachers and parents, with these expectations in turn internalized by the children; avoidance of negative tracking in school; and an increase in readiness for kindergarten and first grade (Entwhisle, 1995). A simple counterfactualist view of cause often ignores these or other underlying mechanisms. Admittedly, knowledge of cause-effect relations without an understanding of underlying mechanisms can be useful (Cook & Campbell, 1979; Julnes & Mark, 1998). Nevertheless, an understanding of mechanisms will typically enhance usefulness, contributing in several ways to the cause of social betterment (Cronbach, 1982; Mark, Henry, & Julnes, 1998). Moreover, we believe that a view of causation that does not emphasize underlying generative mechanisms is simply deficient as a representation of causal forces in the world.

Although our emphasis on underlying generative mechanisms is grounded in realism, many others—whom we believe are realists even if they are unaware of it—also emphasize mechanisms. Bunge (1997) goes so far as to posit that all empirical theories are really about mechanisms. For example, the emphasis on underlying generative mechanisms is shared by many seasoned researchers and evaluators, including those who have little use for philosophy of science. Many methodologists have given considerable attention to the study of *mediation*, that is, to the causal chains that connect a cause and an effect. This has been a major focus in work on causal modeling, structural equation modeling, and similar methods (for example, Baron & Kenny, 1986; Jöreskog & Sörbom, 1993). Underlying generative mechanisms are also the focus of most theory testing research, even in research that is strictly experimental. For example, following Festinger (1957), much research examined the attitude change that occurred after an individual behaved in a way that ran counter to an existing attitude. A primary focus of this research was to determine whether the attitude change was attributable to the uncomfortable internal state called dissonance or to some other mechanism.

In short, our conception of causality begins with the counterfactualist view and then adds to it by including an emphasis on the mechanisms that underlie cause and effect relations. One can define cause and effect counterfactually, but a complete view of causation requires attention to underlying generative mechanisms as well.

The Contingent and Elliptical Nature of Causal Knowledge. In what remains one of the most useful reviews of concepts of causation for social scientists, Cook and Campbell (1979, chap. 1) indicate that causation is *probabilistic*. An earlier, more elaborate conceptualization of the contingent nature of causation is provided by Mackie (1965, 1974), whose work has been imported into the evaluation literature by Cronbach (1982), House (1991), and others. Mackie suggests that what we think of as causes are, more specifically, *INUS conditions:* an Insufficient but Necessary part of a condition that is itself Unnecessary but Sufficient to cause the result. For example, a dropped cigarette may be identified as the cause of a house fire. The cigarette alone was *insufficient* as a cause in that other conditions had to occur, such as the presence of combustible material and the absence of a sprinkler system. But the cigarette was a *necessary* component of the causal package that actually caused the fire (the fire would not have started spontaneously). Nevertheless, the causal package that included the dropped cigarette was *unnecessary* in that several other causal packages could have led to a fire (such as packages involving an electrical short circuit, lightning, or arson). But the package of conditions including the cigarette was *sufficient* to cause the house fire.

The counterfactualist approach emphasizes one cause as the manipulable focus of interest and this may lead evaluators to miss the other conditions that must be present for this cause to produce the effect. Some realists group all these other conditions (which might, for instance, be present in some program sites but not others) together as *context* (Pawson & Tilley, 1997). Mackie's approach highlights these conditions, or forces, as well as the alternative causal mechanisms that may be triggered by other forces in a causally complex world.

The logic of INUS causes can be readily applied to social programs and policies. For example, consider again the question of whether a needle exchange program is effective in preventing a heroin addict such as James from contracting HIV. Perhaps the needle exchange program is effective for him because James and his environment include the other needed components of the relevant causal package. These additional components might involve a heroin addict with the intelligence, self-control, and self-efficacy to use clean needles if they are available; a local culture of heroin use that does not stigmatize those who use clean needles; and a low level of exposure to HIV from other sources, particularly unsafe sex practices. Thus the needle exchange program may generally be effective when the rest of the relevant causal package is present and, conversely, less likely to work when one or more critical components of the causal package are not there. Thus the needle exchange program may be effective for James but would not be effective for another heroin addict with less self-control or in a different environment. In addition, another causal package, lacking a needle exchange program, might exist that would prevent another heroin addict from contracting HIV. Generalizing this logic beyond dichotomous judgments about whether the program works or not: sometimes the program will have a powerful effect and sometimes it will have a weak one, depending on which ingredients from the causal package are present. Furthermore, sometimes outcomes will be good in the absence of the program because another causal package is present. It is because of such alternatives, we believe, that Cook and Campbell (1979) referred to causes as probabilistic.

In addition to the implications it holds for evaluation theory and practice, the INUS perspective has important implications for evaluators' view of causation. Given that one never sees *causation* directly, positivists, inspired by Hume, have insisted that inferring cause requires observing a constant conjunction between presumed cause and effect (that is, the effect is observed whenever and only when the cause is observed), contiguity between the cause and the effect, and temporal precedence of the cause. One benefit of Mackie's INUS model is that it demonstrates why constant conjunction should not be expected for the causes and effects of interest in the social world. Some philosophers, dissatisfied with the idea of causes as contingent, or probabilistic, have argued that the term cause should be limited to those conditions or packages of conditions that are both necessary and sufficient. This seems to us to be inconsistent with natural sensemaking, and also impractical for people living in a real world in which they seek to achieve social betterment in the face of incomplete knowledge.

By highlighting the contingencies on which program effectiveness depends, the INUS approach reminds evaluators that a program may be effective in some contexts with some clients and not be effective elsewhere. The INUS approach also suggests modesty in one's aspirations, in that evaluators can usually hope to achieve only incomplete knowledge about the program and policy effectiveness. This incompleteness has been captured in the phrase *elliptical knowledge* (House, 1991). *Elliptical* derives from the ancient Greek *elleipein*, meaning to leave out or fall short, and the word *ellipsis* refers to the three periods (...) used to show that some portion of a quote or a mathematical equation is missing. Knowledge of causes is elliptical in the sense that evaluators and others generally do not know all the ingredients in the causal package or packages relevant to a program or policy of interest. So if an evaluator knows some but not all of the conditions needed for a needle exchange program to operate, he could symbolize this using an ellipsis, specifying that the causal package includes factors (A, B, C, D, E, ... N), where A, B, C, D, and E are known, but an uncertain number of additional factors are not known. The commonsense realist, sensemaking perspective strongly suggests that even elliptical knowledge of a program's effects is better than no knowledge and that although it is worthwhile to try to fill in ellipses over time, it is usually not feasible to delay action in the meantime.

The INUS formulation also suggests what type of theories evaluators should look for to guide an evaluation and the type of theories they should attempt to contribute to. From the INUS perspective a good theory identifies the components of the causal package, in addition to the program or policy, that are required for the intervention to be effective. Completion of this task is facilitated by the use of data intensive techniques for identifying moderators of program impact (Julnes, 1995; Mark, Hofmann, & Reichardt, 1992), which we describe below in the context of principled discovery.

In sum, a useful and meaningful perspective on causation can be achieved by integrating the counterfactualist definition of cause with the realist emphasis on underlying generative mechanisms and with Mackie's model of the contingent and elliptical nature of causal relations.

The Nature of Causal Inference

In addition to an understanding of what causality is, evaluators must also have a sense of how to achieve warranted causal inferences. How is it that people in general and evaluators more specifically can go about making warranted causal inferences? We address this question at a general, conceptual level in the remainder of this section, discussing pattern matching, competitive elaboration, and principled discovery.

Pattern Matching as the Underlying Logic. It can be argued that pattern matching is a general logic that underlies all causal analyses (Campbell, 1966; Trochim, 1985; Mark, 1990). The researcher first specifies possible observable implications of a causal hypothesis and then compares the observed pattern of actual observations with the pattern predicted by the causal hypothesis and with the patterns predicted by competing hypotheses. The importance of pattern matching in causal analysis has been observed by many statisticians and methodologists. For example, Cochran (1965) reported that when asked, "What can be done in observational [that is, nonexperimental] studies to clarify the step from association to causation, Sir Ronald Fisher replied, 'Make your theories elaborate.'" As Cochran explains, Fisher meant that "when constructing a causal hypothesis one should envisage as many *different* consequences of the truth as possible, and plan observational studies to discover whether each of these consequences is found to hold" (p. 252). In other words, Fisher, one of the founding fathers of modern statistics and research design, argued that to test a causal hypothesis, at least when strict experimental methods are not available, one should derive a complex pattern of predictions from the hypothesis and then assess the extent to which this pattern holds in reality.

Donald Campbell, the primary theorist of quasi-experimental design and a major contributor to the logic of experimental validity, also emphasized the general importance of pattern matching (for example, Campbell, 1966, 1975). For instance, in revising his earlier dismissal of case studies, Campbell (1975) noted that

> In a case study done by an alert social scientist who has
> thorough local acquaintance, the theory he uses to explain
> the focal difference also generates predictions or expectations
> on dozens of other aspects of the culture, and he does not
> retain the theory unless most of these are also confirmed. In
> some sense, he has tested the theory with degrees of freedom
> coming from the multiple implications of any one theory.
> The process is a kind of pattern matching (Campbell, 1966;
> Raser, 1969) in which there are many aspects of the pattern
> demanded by theory that are available for matching with
> his observations on the local setting [pp. 182–183].

In this observation Campbell indicates that even without a strong quasi-experimental design, causal inference can be achieved by developing and testing a complex pattern of predictions derived from a causal hypothesis. Yin (1993) makes a similar point in the context of the logic of case studies. In addition, Campbell (1966), Rosenbaum (1984), Platt (1964), Trochim (1985), and Mark (1990) make statements describing the role of pattern matching in causal inference.

Competitive Elaboration and Principled Discovery. Although they share the same underlying pattern matching logic and are best combined in practice, we find it heuristically useful to distinguish between two general approaches to estimating effects and studying underlying mechanisms: *competitive elaboration*, applied when alternative explanations or alternative generative mechanisms can be articulated a priori, and *principled discovery*, applied when generative mechanisms are not adequately specified a priori.

Competitive Elaboration. Competitive elaboration refers to the process by which alternative explanations (mechanisms)—whether alternative program theories or validity threats—are ruled out (Reichardt & Mark, 1998). Competitive elaboration involves specifying the implications of a possible mechanism so as to discover the implications that conflict with the implications of alternative mechanisms, and then obtaining data to see whether the implications of the mechanism or those of its competitor(s) hold true. In other words, when an explanatory account is susceptible to alternative explanations, the plausibility of the alternatives and of the original can be put to the test by adding a comparison that puts the two accounts into competition.

Evaluators may make comparisons with respect to any of the elements of a causal relationship—cause, recipients, setting, time, and outcome variables (Reichardt & Mark, 1998)—and with respect to any indicators of the hypothesized mediating process. Recall the example we have been using concerning the long-term effects of preschool programs. Entwhisle (1995) has articulated three potential generative mechanisms for the long-term effects that have been observed. (For descriptions of the effects, see Barnett, 1995; Consortium for Longitudinal Studies, 1983; McKey et al., 1985.) The first possible mechanism is that temporary IQ score increases allow preschoolers to avoid negative tracking assignments, and these assignments to higher level reading groups and the like then stimulate better outcomes. A second potential mechanism is that preschool participation causes parents, teachers, and others in the children's social world to raise their social and educational expectations for the children, and the children then internalize these higher expectations for their own futures. According to the third possible generative mechanism, the preschool serves directly as a means of preparing children for the social behaviors and communication skills expected in kindergarten and first grade.

Each mechanism specifies some short-term changes in mediators that can be measured and tested. For example, the second mechanism specifies that changes in parents' or teachers' expectations will mediate the program's effect on children's outcomes. Thus if changes in expectations appear to occur *in between* program activities and program outcomes, that pattern would support the expectations explanation. In addition, each mechanism might work differently with children from different family and social environments. For example, the second mechanism might suggest larger effects for children whose parents initially hold low but malleable expectations, as might be the case for children whose parents have lower educational attainment. If only one mechanism leads to this particular prediction, then testing that prediction would help identify the actual underlying mechanism. (Other examples are discussed later, and also see Mark, 1990; Mark, Hoffman, & Reichardt, 1992; Reichardt & Mark, 1998.)

Competitive elaboration may also be viewed in terms of our earlier three-perspective view of causation. When competitive elaboration is well done (that is, when the empirical comparisons sort out the mechanism of interest from its competitors), then the evaluator has achieved a reasonably good approximation of the ideal but unattainable counterfactual comparison. This is accomplished in practice by filling in the details of the causal package (for example, by specifying that the expectation mechanism but not its competitors would lead to larger effects for a particular subset of students) and by probing underlying mechanisms (for example, by seeing if parental expectations change in the way specified by the expectations hypothesis).

Competitive elaboration can be accomplished through a variety of research designs (Mark, Henry, & Julnes, 1998), some of which are discussed later in this chapter. We discuss for example, the well-known time series quasi-experiment in which Ross, Campbell, and Glass (1970) found that a crackdown on drunken driving in Britain was followed by reduced traffic fatalities during the hours pubs were open and that no such decline occurred during the hours pubs were closed. This pattern helped demonstrate that the crackdown did reduce drunk driving, and helped rule out such alternative explanations for the decline as a change in the weather, road conditions, or some other safety feature. That is, the hypothesis that the crackdown would be effective also implies that its effects would be small or nonexistent in the nonpub hours whereas the other possible explanations did not seem to lead to this prediction. The same form of reasoning can be extended to evaluations that involve vastly different data collection frameworks.

Principled Discovery. In carrying out competitive elaboration, the evaluator begins with a potential explanation involving an underlying mechanism, perhaps derived from a program theory. At a minimum, the evaluator begins with a hypothesis about a cause and effect relationship and possible alternative explanations. But in many cases, theories about the mechanisms underlying program effects may be nonexistent or woefully inadequate. Further, if there are a large number of equally speculative theories, competitive elaboration may be no easier than if there were no theory. Even when there is a reasonable initial hypothesis, it may be more molar than desired, and it may not be adequate for the complexities of an open system world of INUS causes. So how does one apply pattern matching when lacking a sufficiently good and specific hypothesis about the underlying mechanism? Bhaskar (1989b), in considering the implications of theory tests that did not involve traditional, a priori, theory-derived predictions, commented that "[p]articularly important here will be the capacity of a theory to be developed in a non–ad hoc way so as to situate, and preferably explain [a finding] . . . when it could never, given the openness of the social world, have predicted it" (p. 83). To put the dilemma another way, evaluators may require a methodology that is appropriate for the complexities of open systems yet still provides a means by which they can discipline the conclusions that result from their efforts at interpretation. This methodology is principled discovery. Its function is to do warranted pattern matching in the absence of strong initial theory. The name suggests methods that can allow discovery via induction within the complexities of an open system but that are principled in that the discoveries are subsequently disciplined by data and are not simply post hoc explanations that exploit chance variation in a particular sample. Put differently, the function of "principled discovery" is to do warranted pattern matching in the absence of strong initial theory.

Attention to principled discovery is especially important for evaluators who have been trained predominantly in quantitative methods. Standard statistical models emphasize confirmation of a priori hypotheses and understate the importance of discovery. As Tukey put it, "Exploration has been rather neglected; confirmation has been rather sanctified. Neither action is justifiable" (1980; cited in Tukey, 1986, p. 822). Others have cast the issue not simply in terms of what is justifiable but in terms of what is ethical: "Many of us have been taught that it is technically improper and perhaps even immoral to analyze and reanalyze our data in many ways (that is, to snoop around in the data). We were taught to test the prediction with one particular preplanned test . . . and definitely not look further at our data. . . . [This] makes for bad science and for bad ethics" (Rosenthal, 1994, p. 130). Evaluators trained in more qualitative traditions have generally been quite open and attuned to discovery. For these researchers, if there is a need it is for greater attention to principling discoveries through additional tests.

Principled discovery has two main steps. First, the researcher carries out some exploratory analyses that may demonstrate the contingent limits of a causal relationship (that is, the moderators of the effect) or suggest an underlying mechanism or do both. Second, the researcher replicates the initial finding or, as is perhaps more likely in evaluation, conducts a pattern matching test of a theoretical implication of the new finding or does both.

There are several possible approaches to the first step, the exploratory analyses through which discovery occurs (Mark, Henry, & Julnes, 1998). Consider but three mostly quantitative examples. First, the exploratory data analyses of Tukey (1977; also see Behrens, 1997) and other graphical methods (Henry, 1995) can be used to discover possible moderators of program effects and to guide informed speculation about underlying mechanisms. Even when not predicted, an observation that larger effects cluster in one subgroup or in one setting should set off additional investigation and the search for the underlying mechanism. Second, as Tukey (1977) advocates, techniques such as regression and analysis of covariance can be used in an exploratory fashion to search for variations in treatment effectiveness across subgroups and settings. One specific approach, analogous to the extreme case analysis employed by some qualitative researchers, is to use residuals to identify sites or cases that have larger or smaller outcomes than would be expected from standard predictors. These extreme cases can be contrasted, relying perhaps on qualitative data from interviews or observations, to see whether the variations in outcome appear to be associated with differences in types of participants or in treatment implementation. Third, classification techniques can be applied. If distinct groups of program clients or program subtypes emerge, this will generally lead to questions about whether there are differential effects, which may in turn lead to new hypotheses about causal mechanisms.

In these and other ways evaluators can discover possible variations in treatment effectiveness and also identify possible underlying mechanisms (see Mark, Henry, & Julnes, 1998, for more specific methods for discovery). In competitive elaboration, one begins with an initially hypothesized mechanism and then derives predictions about an elaborate pattern of findings. In principled discovery, one begins with the actual pattern of results and derives from that a hypothesis about a possible underlying mechanism.

Principled discovery thus corresponds to what some philosophers call *retroduction*.

The second step of principled discovery is what makes it principled. Discovery of, say, an interaction does not imply confirmation of a hypothesized mechanism. Rather, such a discovery should be subjected to replication or one or more other tests. This is important because chance generally exists as one plausible alternative explanation for the discovery, and other plausible explanations may exist as well. *Multiplicity*, the problem of multiple tests' leading to chance findings "is one of the most prominent difficulties with data-analytic procedures. Roughly speaking, if enough different statistics are computed, some of them will be sure to show structure" (Diaconis, 1985, p. 9). Or as Stigler (1987) put it, more metaphorically, "Beware the problem of testing too many hypotheses; the more you torture the data, the more likely they are to confess, but confessions obtained under duress may not be admissible in the court of scientific opinion" (p. 148), and, we add, may not convince the "juries" in democratic institutions.

Replication is widely recommended as the ideal way to *discipline* discoveries. And replication can be an ideal way to ensure that a discovery is real and not due to chance or some other artifact. But replication, especially with adequate statistical power and integrity, is not feasible most of the time in evaluation, or at least is not likely to be accomplished before decisions must be made. And costs will generally preclude replication via cross-validation with a split sample (in which discoveries are searched for in half the sample and then verified in the other half). Even when replication is possible in a particular case, ambiguities in causal inference can exist if the replication and original evaluation both include the same unrecognized validity threat responsible for the original discovery.

In the absence of replication the second step of principled discovery will generally require that other tests be carried out in the same data set. This strategy is illustrated well by the *context-confirmatory approach* (Julnes, 1995). In brief, an empirical discovery (such as differential effects across subgroups on a key outcome) is used to infer a mechanism. This newly induced mechanism is then used to generate a prediction (perhaps about the pattern of differences on some other outcomes) that should prove true if the mechanism is operating. This new prediction is subsequently tested in the same context as that which suggested the mechanism. Julnes (1995) illustrated the context-confirmatory approach in an evaluation of a resource mother program, in which staff provided support to new single mothers. An a priori planned test that compared program client outcomes with those of a comparison group found that the program was effective on average. In the discovery phase of the inquiry, further inquiry revealed that the effects were larger for older than for younger mothers. Julnes then posited that younger mothers' needs were more tangible and task oriented and not necessarily met by the resource mothers, who were often providing emotional support. To further test this new account, Julnes differentiated the resource mothers on the basis of the extent to which they provided tangible support versus emotional support. As expected, the program was especially ineffective for younger mothers when the support mothers emphasized emotional support. As this example illustrates, in carrying out principled discovery the evaluator ideally iterates between the initial exploratory investigation and the subsequent competitive elaboration that it instigates in order to test the newly hypothesized underlying mechanism. (For an additional example, see Mark, Henry, and Julnes's 1998 discussion of a boot camp program, p. 15.)

Although we advocate the use of principled discovery, it is not a panacea. Practical limits will often apply. Existing data may not be adequate to provide a strong test of a new explanatory account. If Julnes had not had information on service providers, for example, he could not have tested to see whether treatment was especially ineffective when younger clients received services from resource mothers who emphasized emotional support. In addition, statistical power to detect moderator effects may sometime be lacking (Cohen, 1988). Along with practical and methodological limits, the potentially complex nature of causality can make the relevant patterns difficult to detect. Mackie's INUS notion tells evaluators that more than one mechanism may be operating simultaneously. Different mechanisms may be operating for different subgroups of clients or in different circumstances, a condition Baron and Kenny (1986) call *moderated mediation*. Although such complexities do not render principled discovery invalid or useless, they may make it more difficult. Moreover, some aspects of principled discovery as a research strategy are not yet well developed. For instance, it would be useful to have procedures for specifying the degree to which a new test is independent of the original discovery. Despite these limitations, we believe principled discovery is a valuable approach for evaluation.

Sequencing and Integrating Competitive Elaboration and Principled Discovery. Consistent with the concept of sensemaking, the combined workings of competitive elaboration and principled discovery suggest the ongoing nature of the interplay between findings and explanation. At some junctures, one begins with data and searches for explanations for the observed patterns; at others, one starts with competing a priori explanations that guide the design of a more elaborated inquiry to assess which account provides the best fit to the data. But when should one initially adopt the more confirmatory approach of competitive elaboration, and when should one begin with the more exploratory steps of principled discovery?

The primary determinant should be the state of existing knowledge. The less that is known about possible underlying generative mechanisms the more likely it is that the evaluator will need to initially employ principled discovery. Conversely, when possible mechanisms can be identified in advance, the evaluator would start with competitive elaboration and work to collect those observations that will best indicate what mechanism is in operation. Even when competitive elaboration is feasible from the beginning, however, one should still engage in principled discovery. This more exploratory work may lead to a refined theory of the mechanism (suggesting that the relationships predicted by the mechanism hold in some conditions but not others, for instance) or to exploring a possible mechanism that was not identified in advance. As suggested by the context-confirmatory approach, the thoughtful evaluator will probably use both principled discovery and competitive elaboration, sometimes in an overlapping fashion and sometimes iterating between the two. This overlapping and iterative process is in keeping with the notion that sensemaking "is a continuous alternation between particulars and explanations, with each cycle giving added form and substance to the other" (Weick, 1995, p. 133). According to Julnes and Mark (1998), "The rallying cry for the context-confirmatory approach is, One never knows so little that competitive elaboration should not be initiated; one never knows so much that principled discovery is redundant" (p. 49).

The addition of principled discovery to the more traditional confirmatory methods used by quantitative researchers can also help evaluators avoid some of the potential negative side effects of being theory driven. Although many evaluation scholars have emphasized the advantages of using theory to guide evaluation design (for example, Bickman, 1987; Chen, 1990), theory can also have some undesirable consequences (for example, Greenwald, Pratkanis, Leippe, & Baumgardner, 1986). Because theories are at best only partially correct, any theory used in a theory-driven evaluation may fail to specify important outcome measures, possible mediators, and significant moderators of the program's success. Strong adherence to a program theory can even lead an evaluator to misinterpret results or overgeneralize conclusions (Greenwald, Pratkanis, Leippe, & Baumgardner, 1986). The spirit of principled discovery should reduce the occurrence of these and other negative consequences of *confirmation bias*.

In sum, causal inference is based on pattern matching. Competitive elaboration and principled discovery are two general strategies that can be applied and fruitfully integrated for causal analysis in program and policy evaluation. In the section that follows, we describe a number of specific research methods for causal analysis, from which evaluators may select to conduct causal analysis in service of social betterment.

Specific Methods for Causal Analysis

In this section, we describe and illustrate many of the research methods that can be used to estimate the effects of programs and policies and to test underlying generative mechanisms. In particular, we discuss quasi-experiments and natural experiments, randomized experiments, and qualitative methods for causal analysis. There are several useful guides to methods for causal analysis (for example, Boruch, 1997; Cook & Campbell, 1979; Mohr, 1995; Reichardt & Mark, 1998; Yin, 1994) and we do not attempt to summarize all the relevant points here. Instead, we selectively review some causal methods, illustrating how they relate to the conception of cause described in the first half of this chapter.

Quasi-Experiments and Natural Experiments

The term *quasi-experiment* has been popularized by Campbell (1957, 1969b) and his associates (Campbell & Stanley, 1966; Cook & Campbell, 1979). It refers to approximations of experiments, to studies that have several but not all the characteristics of full-scale controlled experiments. The term *natural experiment* has a less clear origin and more variability in meaning. Generally, it refers to cases in which program variants (or other treatments of interest) are not experimentally controlled but vary in the natural environment and in which causal inference is still desired. Many so-called natural experiments involve simple quasi-experimental designs, and the same pattern matching logic can be applied to natural and to quasi-experiments, so we treat the two together here.

Simple Pretest-Posttest One-Group Designs

In a classic quasi-experimental study known as the British Breathalyzer study, Ross, Campbell, and Glass (1970) examined the effect of a crackdown on drunk driving in Great Britain. As outlined earlier, Ross, Campbell, and Glass actually used a complex design that cleverly implemented competitive elaboration. However, for illustrative purposes, let us pretend for the moment that Ross, Campbell, and Glass simply observed the number of automobile casualties (fatalities and serious injuries) in the month before the Breathalyzer crackdown and in the month after. Such a simple pretest-posttest comparison would have revealed a drop of about eight hundred casualties, roughly a 10 percent drop.

One might apply counterfactual thinking to the simple pretest-posttest design as follows. The posttest observation, obviously, shows what really happened after the intervention. If the pretest observation shows what would have happened at the time of the posttest if the intervention had not occurred, then one could estimate the treatment effect as the difference between the pretest and the posttest—or a reduction of about eight hundred casualties. The problem, of course, is that the pretest observation may *not* well represent what would have happened at the posttest if the intervention had not taken place. The pretest may be a very poor and biased approximation of the ideal but unattainable comparison. Several generic alternative mechanisms exist that can lead to changes over time in traffic casualties and, more generally, in the kind of outcomes measured by evaluators and others interested in human behavior. These generic mechanisms, or forces, have come to be called *internal validity threats*, and we examine two of them in the context of this partial version of the British Breathalyzer study.

History is a threat to validity. It refers to the possibility that a specific event other than the intended treatment could also have occurred between the pretest and posttest observations and could have caused a change in the outcome of interest. Consider, for example, the possibility that at about the same time as the Breathalyzer crackdown, there had also been a reduction in the speed limit or a new seat belt law or an increase in gas prices that reduced driving. Any of these historical events might be responsible for some or all of the drop in automobile casualties between the pretest and the posttest.

Or perhaps the decline in traffic fatalities actually occurred because the average driver was older at the time of the posttest than at the time of the pretest. This would be a case of *maturation* as a threat to internal validity. Maturation refers to the processes that occur over time in research participants, such as growing older, hungrier, more fatigued, wiser, and the like. Although maturation does not appear plausible in the British Breathalyzer example, where the pretest and posttest are only a month apart, it is a plausible threat to the validity of many simple pretest-posttest designs. For example, maturation would be quite plausible as an explanation in a simple pretest-posttest evaluation of a yearlong preschool program, for children at that age tend to change a good deal with the passage of a year.

The simple pretest-posttest design is subject to several internal validity threats in addition to history and maturation. These include instrumentation, regression to the mean, testing, and attrition (Cook & Campbell, 1979; Reichardt & Mark, 1998). These internal validity threats do not automatically apply whenever this design is used. Still, in most instances of policy and program evaluation, at least some of the threats applicable to the simple pretest-posttest design will be sufficiently plausible that the potential users of evaluation results would be well served if a more complex design were implemented instead.

It would be better, however, for evaluators not to think about more complex designs simply as though there were a menu of design alternatives, with the evaluator's task being to select from the preset menu (as we believe many readers have concluded from most writings about designs for causal analysis). Instead, evaluators should be thinking in terms of the kind of pattern matching logic that underlies competitive elaboration. They should attempt to specify what kinds of implications the preferred hypothesis has; identify implications of the preferred hypothesis that differ from those of competing hypotheses, including validity threats; and see which of the predictions hold true in the actual data. For example, if faced with conducting a pretest-posttest evaluation of the Breathalyzer experiment, an evaluator might conclude that the hypothesis of a treatment effect would predict a drop only in alcohol-related fatalities, whereas the validity threat of history would instead predict a drop in fatalities whether alcohol related or not. The move to a more elaborate design will be more sensible if motivated by the pattern matching logic of competitive elaboration.

Interrupted Time Series Designs

The notion of competitive elaboration also applies to interrupted time series (ITS) designs, which are generally regarded as strong quasi-experimental designs (Campbell & Stanley, 1966; Cook & Campbell, 1979; Marcantonio & Cook, 1994; Reichardt & Mark, 1998). ITS designs use *time series data,* that is, the repeated measurement of an outcome variable at (approximately) equally spaced intervals, such as months, quarters, or years, to estimate the effect of a treatment. In a simple interrupted time series design, observations are collected over a period of time, a treatment is introduced, and the series of observations continues. In effect, the trend in the pretreatment observations is estimated and projected forward in time to provide the counterfactual estimate of how the posttreatment data would have appeared if there had been no treatment. The treatment effect is then derived from the difference, if any, between the projected and the actual posttreatment trend. For example, in their study of the British Breathalyzer crackdown, Ross, Campbell, and Glass actually examined time series data. Although their complete design was even more complex, the simple ITS component is summarized with the dashed line in Figure 9.1, which reports a subset of monthly automobile casualties both before and after the crackdown. (The nature of the subset is explained momentarily.) The abrupt, downward *interruption* that occurs at the time the treatment was introduced suggests that the crackdown was effective, at least initially.

Interrupted time series designs have an advantage over other quasi-experimental designs: the serial observations allow the researcher to observe the temporal pattern of the effect. Does the intervention cause a shift in the level of the outcome variable (such as an abrupt drop) or in its slope (such as a new upward trend leveling out) or both? Is the effect permanent, continuing for as long as the time series has been collected, or temporary, dying out after a short while? Time series data make it possible to answer these and related questions about the temporal pattern of a policy or program's effects.

Even more important, the simple ITS design has benefits for causal inference. In our simple pretest-posttest version of the British Breathalyzer study, one might argue that the decline in traffic fatalities actually occurred because the average driver was older at the time of the posttest than at the pretest. The ITS design can render such a maturation threat implausible. It allows the researcher to estimate the pattern of maturation from the trend in the pretreatment observations. To the extent that the pretreatment trend allows the researcher to correctly model and project the maturational trend into the posttreatment time period, maturation may be removed as a threat to internal validity in the ITS design. In Figure 9.1, there appears to perhaps be a slight downward trend in the pretreatment observations in the dashed line, possibly corresponding to a slow, steady maturation effect. But the drop in casualties at the time of the crackdown appears to be far greater than would be predicted from the pretreatment trend. Thus, maturation does not appear to be capable of accounting for all of the interruption in the time series. (For further discussion, including the possibility of nonlinear maturation, see Cook & Campbell, 1979; Mark, Reichardt, & Sanna, 2000.)

Although the simple ITS design allows evaluators to rule out some threats to valid causal inference through competitive elaboration, it does not rule out all internal validity threats. The threat

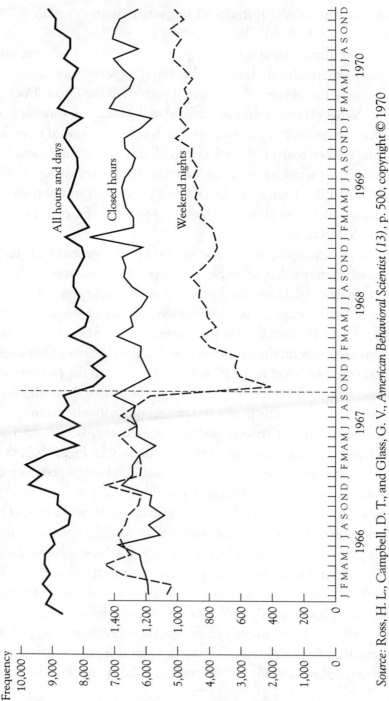

FIGURE 9.1. Traffic Casualties Before and After a Breathalyzer Crackdown.

Source: Ross, H. L., Campbell, D. T., and Glass, G. V., *American Behavioral Scientist (13)*, p. 500, copyright © 1970 by Sage Publications, Inc.

of history is equally as plausible in the simple ITS time series design as in a pretest-posttest design, assuming the interval between observations is the same. That is, the addition of earlier pretest and later posttest observations will not reduce the possibility that some other historical event occurred at the same time as the treatment of interest. However, it is also true that the shorter the time interval between observations, the less plausible history will generally be as a threat, and time series designs often use a shorter interval than other causal analysis designs do. For example, Ross, Campbell, and Glass examined monthly casualties in their ITS design, but it seems likely they would have examined quarterly or annual data in a simple pretest-posttest design. Annual data are more likely to allow historical events to be confounded with the treatment.

In short, expanding a simple pretest-posttest design into a simple ITS design allows the use of competitive elaboration to reduce the plausibility of several threats to internal validity. Validity threats such as history may remain plausible, but they too can be reduced by the use of more complex ITS designs (see Cook & Campbell, 1979, chap. 5; Marcantonio & Cook, 1994; Mark, Reichardt, & Sanna, 2000). For example, an evaluator might extend the simple ITS design by adding a *nonequivalent dependent variable*. That is, in addition to the examining the dependent variable that should be affected by the treatment, the evaluator examines another time series variable that should not be affected by the treatment but that should be affected by competing mechanisms, particularly those that are plausible threats to internal validity. This design feature was used in the British Breathalyzer study, which we have examined only in part up to this point. In their examination of the effect of the crackdown on drunk driving, Ross, Campbell, and Glass capitalized on the facts that drinking and driving in Britain was largely associated with going out to pubs and that pubs at that time had very specific and limited hours of operation. On the one hand, Ross, Campbell, and Glass reasoned, if the Breathalyzer crackdown were effective, a drop in automobile casualties should occur during busy pub times, such as weekend nights, but not during those times when pubs were closed. On the other hand, most other factors, such as a widespread change in automotive safety resulting from some other historical event, could be expected to effect both time series. As shown in Figure 9.1, the pattern of results corresponded precisely to the pattern expected if the crackdown had an effect. There was a dramatic decline in weekend night casualties at the time of the crackdown. The number of casualties during the hours pubs were closed, however, went virtually unchanged. In many cases, such a more elaborate pattern of data can be alternatively achieved by adding a control group to the simple ITS design. For example, one might study the effect of a crackdown on drunk driving in one state, and use neighboring states for a control time series comparison.

In short, the simple ITS design is a great improvement over a simple pretest-posttest design, and more complex ITS designs are even stronger for achieving warranted causal inferences. The advantages of ITS designs can be viewed from the perspective of competitive elaboration in that the ITS designs allow the researcher to put into competition the pattern of predictions derived from a treatment effect causal hypothesis and the pattern of predictions derived from various validity threats. Although ITS designs will be infeasible for some evaluations because of the need for repeated pretest and posttest measurements, in other cases measures of interest will already exist (as traffic casualty data did for the British Breathalyzer study). In still other instances the evaluator will be able to implement repeated measurement of important outcome variables (for example, Kazi, 1997). Even if available for only one of several outcome variables, an ITS design included as part of an evaluation can contribute considerably to overall validity by providing a more competitive form of elaboration. Evaluators should recognize, however, that time series data in existing archives are not likely to include measures of underlying processes (Mark, Sanna, & Shotland, 1992) and that they need to be inspected carefully for possible instrumentation problems.

Another issue of special note for time series investigations is statistical analysis. The analysis of ITS designs is more complex than that of many other forms of causal analysis. (For descriptions of key issues in the statistical analysis of ITS studies see Box, Jenkins, & Reinsel, 1994; Kendall & Ord, 1990; Mark, Reichardt, & Sanna, 2000; McCain & McCleary, 1979; McCleary, Hay, Meidinger, & McDowall, 1980; Orwin, 1997.) Although the statistical analysis of ITS has received considerable attention, we find more of interest in the *reasoning* behind ITS designs.

Nonequivalent Groups Designs

In both the simple pretest-posttest and the simple interrupted time series designs, in place of the ideal but unattainable comparison, a comparison is made of the same individual or aggregate unit at different points in time, that is, before the treatment and after. The other major way that researchers find an approximation of the ideal comparison is by comparing different individuals at the same time. In a set of quasi-experimental designs known as *nonequivalent groups designs*, individuals or other units self-select into the different groups (for example, they choose to participate in a needle exchange program or not), are assigned in some nonrandom fashion into groups by others such as program administrators, have their group assignment determined by their geographical location, or are assigned to different treatment groups in some other nonrandom fashion. Such nonrandom assignments also characterize many of the cases that are called natural experiments.

The simplest between-group design is the *posttest-only nonequivalent groups design*. In this design, individuals or other units, such as schools or communities, fall into two groups: the treatment group, which receives the program (or policy), and the control, or comparison, group, which does not receive the program or which experiences some alternative program. At some later time, presumably long enough for the treatment to work, the members of both groups are measured on one or more outcome variables of interest, with the control group substituting for the ideal but unattainable comparison. The difference between the two groups on the out-come measure is used as the estimate of the program's effect.

The fundamental shortcoming of this design is the validity threat known as *selection*. Selection refers to the possibility that the difference between the treatment group and the control group on an outcome measure results from preexisting differences between the groups and not from the program. That is, the groups may have initial differences that cause subsequent differences on the outcome variable. In most evaluations the threat of initial selection differ-ences will create great uncertainty about program effect in the posttest-only nonequivalent groups design. Without information to the contrary, it is typically quite plausible that the groups would have differed to the same extent even in the absence of treatment. Again, through the logic of competitive elaboration the evaluator may be led to make other comparisons that allow more confident causal inference. Before we consider any additional examples apply-ing this logic, we look at another common design that is a some-what more complex nonequivalent groups design.

In this frequently used design the nonequivalent groups are observed on both a pretest and a posttest. The evaluator reasons that the treatment effect should be estimated not by the difference between treatment and control groups at the posttest but by the dif-ference between the two groups in the amount of change on the average between pretest and posttest. That is, the treatment effect is estimated by how much more or less the treatment group gained on average relative to the control group. This reasoning involves what is called *change score*, or *gain score*, or in the language of some economists, *first difference* analysis. Consider the reasoning under-lying the gain score approach from the perspective of a counter-factual comparison. Gain score analysis is predicated on the assumption that if there were no treatment effect, the treatment group would change the same amount as the control group over the same time. When this assumption is correct, gain score analysis works well (in more technical language, it controls well for simple main effects of initial selection differences).

Suppose, for example, that in an evaluation in an elementary school, the students in the treatment group score on average ten points higher than those in the control group at the pretest and would remain ten points ahead at the posttest unless there is some effect of the treatment. In this instance, gain score analysis would adjust perfectly for the effect of the initial selection difference. The problem, perhaps obviously, is that the assumption underlying the gain score approach may not be true. Perhaps the treatment group starts out ten points ahead at the pretest, but would be fifteen points ahead at the posttest even if there were no treatment effect. As the old saying goes, sometimes "the rich get richer." Many differences increase with time: the difference in running speed between the fastest and slowest eighth-grader is much greater than the difference between the fastest and slowest preschooler. Such possibilities led Campbell and Stanley (1966) to describe *selection by maturation interaction* as a threat to the internal validity of the pretest-posttest nonequivalent groups design. This threat refers to the possibility that one of the groups will change at a different rate than the other group even in when there is no treatment effect.

Another possible approach to the analysis of data from the pretest-posttest nonequivalent groups design is the analysis of covariance, or ANCOVA (for example, Reichardt, 1979). Other, more recent approaches include structural equation modeling (for example, Bentler, 1992), selection modeling (for example, Rindskopf, 1986), and propensity scoring (for example, Rosenbaum & Rubin, 1983; Rosenbaum, 1995). Each of these involves a different approach toward controlling statistically for initial selection differences. In essence, each also involves a different way of substituting for the ideal but unattainable counterfactual comparison. Each approach will give unbiased estimates of the treatment effect if the assumptions underlying the approach hold. But it is generally not possible for an evaluator to be confident about this (Boruch, 1997; Reichardt, 1979). Consequently, multiple analyses are often recommended for the pretest-posttest nonequivalent groups design, in order to demonstrate that conclusions about the merit of a program are robust across different analytical assumptions (for example, Wortman, Reichardt, & St. Pierre, 1981; Reynolds, 1998).

Evaluators who use the pretest-posttest nonequivalent groups design also need to be concerned about other threats in the form of interactions with selection (Cook & Campbell, 1979). *Selection by history* refers to the possibility that the two groups have been subject to different historical forces and that these forces may have caused a larger effect in one than in the other. For instance, in an evaluation using two schools as the treatment and control groups to assess the effect of a policy requiring smaller class sizes in grades K–4, selection by history would operate if a new principal were installed in one school at about the same time as the class size change was introduced. Again, the concept of competitive elaboration suggests the way to address such alternative explanations: try to identify a pattern that the treatment effect hypothesis would predict but that the alternative hypothesis does not. In the class size example, a treatment effect hypothesis would predict large effects in grades K–4 but no effects for older children who did not experience smaller class sizes. In contrast, a history effect hypothesis based on the change in principals might lead to the prediction of comparable effects across all grade levels. Recall also that competitive elaboration can sometimes be carried out with indicators of the underlying generative mechanism. For example, the relevant theory might suggest that class size reductions improve student achievement because teachers in smaller classes spend more time on instruction and less time on discipline. If classroom observations confirm that this change in classroom process happened in the K–4 classrooms of the treatment school but not in higher grades in the treatment school or in any grades of the comparison school, the treatment effect hypothesis becomes more plausible relative to its competitors.

Randomized Experiments

In a randomized experiment, individuals or other units are randomly assigned to treatment conditions. One of the great benefits of random assignment is that it removes bias due to initial selection differences and thus creates a fair comparison (Boruch, 1997). Random assignment does not, however, guarantee that there will be *no* initial selection differences. Even randomly assigned treatment and control groups are still likely to differ somewhat initially. Even in the absence of a treatment effect, the mean difference between the two groups on an outcome variable is unlikely to be exactly zero. What random assignment does is to guarantee that the initial selection differences between the groups are completely random. This results in the second great benefit of random assignment: classical statistical procedures of confidence intervals and hypothesis tests take into account the random selection differences that exist and thus allow well-grounded statements about the warrant for confidence in evaluation results (Boruch, 1997).

Consider the randomized experiment from the counterfactualist perspective. The response of the people randomly assigned to the control group serves to approximate what would happen if the treatment had not been presented to those in the treatment group. Assuming that the randomized experiment is carried out well, this comparison should be a close approximation of the ideal comparison. Now consider the randomized experiment from the perspective of competitive elaboration. The treatment effect hypothesis predicts that the treatment group will outperform the comparison group. Because of random assignment to conditions, there is no systematic selection to make this prediction. Random selection differences could make this prediction, but as noted earlier, classic hypothesis testing statistics supply a technology for assessing how likely this is. Maturation does not predict a between-group difference on the outcome measures, again because the two groups should be initially comparable. And so it is with other validity threats in the well-conducted randomized experiment. Note, however, that we are focusing here on the (molar) hypothesis of a treatment effect. For (more molecular) hypotheses about the underlying mechanism, the randomized experiment is not intrinsically so strong. If, for example, parental expectations are the hypothesized underlying mechanism in a pre-K program, a randomized experiment will not necessarily rule out an alternative mechanism such as avoiding tracking in lower reading groups (compare the distinction between internal and construct validity in the Cook & Campbell, 1979, validity scheme). In addition, the randomized experiment does not necessarily assist evaluators in identifying the components of the causal package other than the treatment that are required for the effect to occur (compare here the concept of external validity).

Indeed, the randomized experiment has been criticized by some realists because it allows researchers to examine cause and effect relationships without also examining underlying mechanisms (Pawson & Tilley, 1997). Although we agree that the randomized experiment enables this, we contend it is not an inevitable by-product of randomized experiments (Julnes, Mark, & Henry, 1998; Mark, Henry, & Julnes, 1998). To the contrary the randomized experiment can be a powerful tool for studying underlying processes. Evaluators can examine groups or subgroups for patterns of differential effects that support one underlying mechanism and discount others (Mark, 1990). In addition, they can study mediation, using statistical techniques such as structural equation modeling to test for changes in a sequence of hypothesized mediating variables that occur between the intervention and outcome variables (Fiske, Kenny, & Taylor, 1982; Mark, 1990). And assuming the randomized experiment is reasonably well carried out, as they test underlying mechanisms in either of these ways, they can at be relatively confident about their estimate of the magnitude of the treatment effect.

The caveat that the randomized experiment be well carried out is important. There are several reasons a randomized experiment can fall short, including flawed methods of random assignment, whether unintentional or due to subversion of the assignment process by program staff not committed to randomization; differential refusal or attrition across conditions, so that initial randomization is not maintained among the participants who remain in the experiment at the end; failure of the treatment and comparison group to be implemented as planned; an inadequate number of cases for sufficiently powerful statistical tests, perhaps because of initial overestimates of client flow; resistance to randomization as a method for assignment to groups, for practical or ethical reasons; restriction of random assignment to unusual circumstances that may hinder generalization to settings of interest; and awareness by control group participants that they did not receive the treatment, which may lead to between-group differences erroneously attributed to the program. (For further discussion of these problems and their potential solutions, see Boruch, 1997; Boruch & Wothke, 1985; Braucht & Reichardt, 1993; Cook & Campbell, 1979; Conner, 1977.)

In short, the randomized experiment is in principle an outstanding tool for causal analysis, particularly for estimating the effects of a program or policy. Random assignment provides a close approximation of the ideal counterfactual comparison as applied to the estimate of an average treatment effect. Admittedly, random assignment is not feasible in every case in which causal analysis is important. Random assignment is not possible when a treatment is applied uniformly across some geographical area, for example. Nevertheless, there are a number of circumstances in which it is feasible (Boruch, 1997; Cook & Campbell, 1979), perhaps more than many practicing evaluators believe. At the same time, randomized experiments require considerable effort to conduct effectively and entail a number of management responsibilities (Boruch, 1997; Cook & Campbell, 1979).

Qualitative Approaches

As we have been emphasizing, as realists we do not subscribe to the position that there are incompatible paradigms necessarily associated with so-called quantitative and so-called qualitative methods. At the same time, it is clear that different inquiry traditions have emerged and that there are some historical differences of interest associated with these traditions. Most obvious, of course, is that quantitative methods tend to emphasize numbers, in the form of statistical summaries, whereas qualitative methods tend to emphasize words, in the form of narrative accounts.

Less commonly recognized but equally striking, we believe, is that quantitative methods have traditionally tended to involve competitive elaboration, whereas qualitative methods have tended to foster principled discovery. Neither set of methods consistently measures up to the ideals of either of these approaches to pattern matching. Quantitative research has not always adequately searched for competing explanations and the elaborated patterns required to differentiate between competitors. Qualitative research has not always adequately emphasized the principling of new discoveries. Nevertheless, a relationship has developed in practice between these two approaches to pattern matching and the qualitative-quantitative distinction. Quantitative methods have been associated with a priori predictions, with structured designs and analysis plans that are determined in advance, and with formal tests of hypotheses as arbitrators of the competition. In contrast, qualitative methods have been associated with allowing explanations to emerge during the process of inquiry, with flexible designs and analysis strategies that shift with new evidence, and with discovery.

We contend that this association, although historical, is not necessary. Quantitative methods can be used in service of principled discovery, as illustrated in Julnes' context-confirmatory evaluation (1995). And qualitative methods can be used to test a priori hypotheses through competitive elaboration, as in much of Yin's work (1994) with case study methods. Moreover, using either qualitative or quantitative methods or, preferably, mixing them, an evaluator can iterate between principled discovery and competitive elaboration. We hope one of the enduring messages of this chapter will be the value of combining more inductive, discovery-oriented methods with more deductive, confirmation-oriented ones.

With respect to past practice, it appears that the best approaches to qualitative inquiry implement pattern matching logic by way of principled discovery. For example, in discussing an evaluation she conducted in which her reasoning was informed by qualitative traditions, Smith (1997, pp. 80–81) describes a modified method of analytical induction conceived by Erickson (1986). Consider Smith's description of this method (shown in italics) and our "translation" of it into the terms of our discussion in this chapter.

Erickson's method is based on the researcher's repeated reading of the data as a whole and then arriving inductively and intuitively at a set of credible assertions. Assertions are statements that the researcher believes to be true based on an understanding of all the data. From a review of the available data, the researcher develops some tentative hypotheses, including, but not limited to, hypotheses about the presence or absence of treatment effects on particular outcomes. These hypotheses reflect discovery based on the researcher's comprehensive review and understanding of the evidence.

Next, the researcher goes through a process of establishing the warrant for each assertion, assembling the confirming evidence from the record of data, searching vigorously for disconfirming evidence, weighing the evidence one way or the other, and then casting out unwarranted assertions or substantially altering them so they fit with the data. The researcher carries out pattern matching to assess the fit between the implications of each hypothesis and the evidence. Depending on the degree of fit between hypothesized and observed patterns, hypotheses may be revised or rejected. The discovery of the first stage is now being principled, by applying competitive elaboration to the previously induced hypotheses. For some qualitative researchers this might involve the collection of new data to test an implication of an induced hypothesis.

Having settled on a final list of warranted assertions and any linkages between them, the researcher then builds representations of the evidence so that the reader can participate as co-analyst. The researcher must thoroughly and honestly report the inferential process and the evidence, so that the reader can assess the extent to which each hypothesis is supported and alternative explanations are plausible.

In conclusion, the use of qualitative methods and mixed methods from a traditionally qualitative perspective will be feasible in many circumstances where a randomized experiment or regression-discontinuity design would not be feasible. A classic complaint about qualitative methods is that the findings they produce may not be robust across investigators. That is, different evaluators may reach different answers. This criticism applies to traditional quantitative methods as well, which have many choice points such as the selection of outcome measures that may affect conclusions. Still, the investigator is probably more integral to the findings generated through qualitative procedures, and thus it seems plausible that reliability across investigators is a greater issue. Nevertheless, if an evaluator carefully follows pattern matching logic, is creative in collecting and critical in considering data relevant to causal and other hypotheses, and clearly reports the analytical process and findings so that the reader can assess the plausibility of the conclusions, qualitative methods for causal analysis can be valuable and influential in facilitating social betterment.

A Final Example

In this section we present a summarizing example of the approach to causal analysis described in this chapter. Imagine that an evaluator has been called in to evaluate an intervention in a large urban high school. The intervention, known as Partnership for Academic and Total Health (PATH), involves an effort to create a larger sense of community and a greater sense of responsibility, self-determination, and ownership in the long-troubled school. The theory of the program suggests that these processes will lead to less violence in the school and to fewer disciplinary problems in the classroom. This should in turn allow more attention to academic matters in the classroom and, consequently, lead to increased academic achievement. Generally speaking, the multipronged intervention involves some decentralization of authority to teacher teams and to student planning teams that are empowered to select specific programming and activities to be carried out (following a quick review) under the PATH umbrella. In the first year of PATH these teams selected a violence prevention curriculum to be implemented in health classes, obtained improved lighting in school areas they felt were especially prone to violent events, and instituted a series of professional development activities designed to alert faculty and staff to potential sources of conflicts and methods for intervening.

There are of course constraints on the evaluation. Because the program is attempting to build community in the school as a whole, the evaluation cannot, randomly or otherwise, assign students, teachers, or classrooms to a control group. The evaluator can obtain at least some data from other schools in the district not participating in the program but cannot assign schools to conditions. Indeed, the school board wants to learn how things work in the target school before approving the program elsewhere. And of course the evaluation budget does not approach infinity, though funding is available to follow the program for four years.

This hypothetical situation (based in part on real programs that other evaluators have studied) exemplifies attributes that characterize much of evaluation practice. Questions of merit and worth matter, but randomized experimentation, the gold standard of causal analysis for many, is not feasible. Moreover, the intervention itself is a something of a hodgepodge. And interestingly, the crux of the intervention is focused on the school—that is, on a higher level social organization, as increasing numbers of interventions seem to be—rather than on individual students, as most traditional interventions used to be. In addition, there are certainly other forces in the world, from new standards for teachers and students to television and the movies to the economy, that could potentially influence the outcomes of interest and obscure inferences about whether and by how much the new program made a difference.

The evaluator's hypothesized program effect predicts decreases in school violence and disciplinary problems and increases in academic achievement. The problem, from the perspective of competitive elaboration, is that history, maturation, and other validity threats could also account for these changes or could mask the real treatment effect. So let us assume that the predicted improvements occur. Data from one or more comparison schools where the program was not implemented could determine whether general historical forces and widespread maturational trends can be ruled out as causes of these improvements. For example, if violence declined because of a new school district policy requiring see-through backpacks so that guns and knives cannot be brought into school easily and if academic scores increased because of the new word-of-the-week feature on *MTV*, then these changes should be seen in the control as well as the program school. The value of the control group will be even greater if data for some outcomes are available on a time series basis, as much data often is in educational contexts.

However, control school data do not help the evaluator to differentiate between the hypothesized treatment effect and highly local historical events (such as the addition of a metal detector at the treatment school only) or highly local maturational patterns (such as ongoing shifts in the socioeconomic status [SES] of students in the program school but not the control school). In these and other instances auxiliary data sources may contribute to competitive elaboration. For example, if improved outcomes might actually be the result of local maturational patterns related to SES, then background data on SES could be examined to see if such local SES shifts are occurring. If they are not, the treatment effect hypothesis becomes more plausible by comparison. Similarly, historical records, interviews, and observations can often reveal whether some local historical event other than the treatment occurred that might account for the improved outcomes.

Recall also that in carrying out competitive elaboration the evaluator should go beyond simple treatment effect hypotheses if possible and base more elaborated patterns of predictions on the hypothesized underlying mechanisms. The expected mechanism for PATH is that the treatment will lead to an increased sense of community, ownership, and self-responsibility, which is in turn expected to result in less school violence and decreased attention to disciplinary matters in the classroom. These changes are in turn expected to lead to more attention to academic matters and thus to improved academic outcomes. Ideally, an evaluation would track the details of this sequence and show changes occurring at one level before changes occurred at the next level. The elaborate pattern of precisely sequenced change would be predicted by the program theory but presumably not by any competitors. Unfortunately, it requires a huge amount of ongoing observation to produce measures sensitive enough to observe such a precise pattern. Fortunately, even less ideal information about intervening processes can often aid in competitive elaboration. In this case the hypothesized mechanism suggests that changes will be seen on indicators of community and ownership. These indicators might include changes such as an increase the number of teachers actively participating at teacher meetings; an increase in the number of students wearing clothes with school insignias or school colors; a decrease in new graffiti or vandalism; an increase in the proportion of teachers and students who use first-person plural pronouns ("we") or other signals of community when asked about the school; and certain changes in responses to surveys administered to students and teachers. The program theory would predict these changes, whereas most if not all competing explanations would not. The program theory would also predict reduced time spent on disciplinary problems and increased time spent on academic concerns. If classroom observations bore this out, confidence in the hypothesized mechanism and treatment effect would increase unless a competing explanation made the same prediction.

The hypothesized underlying mechanism might also lead to some specific predictions about where effects should be larger and where they should be smaller. According to the hypothesized causal chain underlying the program, classrooms are expected to exhibit decreased attention to disciplinary matters, for example. But classrooms will differ in their preexisting levels of disciplinary problems. Presumably, the program will make less difference in classrooms with initially low levels of such problems. If classrooms are measured on their initial level of disciplinary problems, this implication of the program theory can be tested. Other predictions from the program theory can be devised and tested in like fashion.

Given a complex program like PATH, it is possible to assess the effect of various components as well as the overall program. One can examine the more micro-level elements of the more macro intervention. The newly empowered PATH teams had new lights installed in locations they thought were especially dangerous. Thus a more elaborated prediction could be made that larger reductions in violence should occur in these locations than in others. In addition, the decline should occur just after the new lights are installed. If the requisite data are available, this prediction could be revealing in that it is easily derived from PATH's lighting component but does not appear to be consistent with any alternative explanation. (For a similar and more extended example, see Pawson & Tilley, 1997.)

At the same time as competitive elaboration is being carried out in ways such as those just suggested, the PATH evaluator should also be engaged in principled discovery. In addition, if the findings of the evaluation appear to be positive, there may be opportunities to attempt replication when the intervention is subsequently implemented in other schools.

Conclusion

In this chapter we have considered a wide array of topics related to causal analysis. We defined causation in terms of the integration of a counterfactualist definition of cause and effect, a realist view of underlying generative mechanisms, and an understanding of the contingent and elliptical nature of causal relations. We discussed causal inference as involving the logic of pattern matching, with competitive elaboration and principled discovery being two related manifestations of that logic. We reviewed a number of specific research methods for causal analysis, including several quasi-experiments, randomized experiments, and qualitative methods. In the context of reviewing specific methods, we described a number of specific threats to the validity of a causal inference, applied the concept of the ideal but unattainable comparison to better see the relative strengths of various designs, and revisited the concepts of competitive elaboration and principled discovery, illustrating their application through some specific research designs.

In considering all these matters important to causal inference, it may be easy to fail to see the forest (social betterment) for the trees (the details of causal inference and its specific methods). Nevertheless, it is important to remember that inquiry modes and their associated research techniques should not drive evaluation choices. Instead, a thoughtful analysis of the primary and secondary purposes of an evaluation and of the evaluation's possible contribution to social betterment should drive choices about methods.

As we noted at the beginning of this chapter, causal analysis can contribute considerably when program improvement or knowledge development is the purpose of an evaluation. Most important, however, is the linkage between causal analysis and the assessment of merit and worth. Consider again the British Breathalyzer study described at some detail in this chapter. For a government considering whether to initiate (or maintain or repeat) such a crackdown on drunk driving, the question of the crackdown's effects is crucial. How much does such a crackdown reduce fatalities and serious injuries, if at all? Moreover, by itself, the answer to this question may not totally reveal merit and worth. One may also need to ask whether a crackdown of this sort violates individual freedom. Consider the PATH example as well. Causal questions again are important for a judgment of merit and worth. Does PATH lead to reduced crime and increased student achievement? But how is one to know which of the many possible effects is most important to look for in the evaluation? Further, how are results to be interpreted? Is PATH a success or a failure if teachers and students do have a stronger sense of school community but crime does not go down and achievement does not go up? For guidance on such questions, we turn to values inquiry.

10

Values Inquiry

To pursue social betterment through evaluation, evaluators must distill sometimes confusing and contradictory statements about what it means to improve social conditions. Consider for a moment a seemingly straightforward program for public schools, the implementation of computer-based instruction. When computers are integrated into instruction, should the evaluation focus on the impact on test scores or on academic self-concept? Is the most important outcome for the children the development of love of learning or the development of specific technical skills? Do evaluators need to concern themselves with teachers' satisfaction with the computer hardware, software, and technical support? Should the evaluation be concerned with whether the program reduces gender inequities in use of computers? Or with whether it compensates for the unequal distribution of computers in students' homes? As discussed in the last chapter, causal inquiry can help answer questions about program effects, but it does not indicate which effects are most important to examine. It is values inquiry that addresses the questions: What are the criteria by which the success of the policy or program should be judged? By probing the sometimes ambiguous and conflicting values that surround social policies and programs, values inquiry can inform people's judgment about what contributes to social betterment.

Values inquiry is, along with description, among the most versatile of inquiry modes, adapting easily to all purposes and linking with most other inquiry modes. This broad applicability is evident in the fact that many other evaluation theorists have also promoted values inquiry, though in different terms (and often with less systematic methods). When Patton (1997) advocates "intended use by intended users," for example, one of the things he encourages is the use of values inquiry to probe the values of the intended users. When Wholey (1994) suggests the involvement of managers in evaluability assessment, one goal is to gain managers' agreement on those outcomes that are highly enough valued to be the focus of subsequent evaluation. Similarly, Scriven's goal-free evaluation begins with a grounded discovery of desired outcomes that can be inferred from direct observations (Scriven, 1973). Guba and Lincoln's (1989) concept of *negotiation* largely involves discussion and deliberation about values issues. More recently, House and Howe (1999) have proposed deliberation as a specific method for raising and resolving values issues in an evaluation. Given that values, in some form or another, sometimes implicitly and sometimes explicitly, frequently appear in these and other evaluation theories, it seems desirable to have a systematic treatment of values inquiry in evaluation.

This chapter addresses the methods by which evaluators can learn about the values that underlie and surround policies and program and that have important implications for the choices in an evaluation. Recall that our commonsense realist approach presumes that although there are no formal solutions to determining social value, people are often capable of making appropriate value-based choices in everyday life. The goal of values inquiry, therefore, is not to *determine* value but to support natural human abilities in identifying, sorting through, and winnowing out potentially germane values. Values inquiry can reveal different individuals' view of whether a program is moving society toward social betterment. We describe several specific examples of methods that evaluators can use to enhance the natural valuation of those involved in the deliberative democratic processes. These are methods for representing the values of relevant stakeholders and the public, for simulating deliberative processes to see what valuation emerges, for applying some form of critical review to identify values that may underlie a program or policy, and for integrating values inquiry to other inquiry modes in order to better link values to findings about the processes and outcomes of social programs and policies.

Before turning to the specific methods for values inquiry, we consider the idea of natural valuation as a guiding concept. Humans have evolved sophisticated means of recognizing that they value one condition over another. The complexities of the valuation process may not be well captured through simple formal models; however, many of the preferences that follow from natural valuation have been established and codified through democratic processes. After developing this idea of natural valuation within the commonsense realist, sensemaking frame, we present the ways that values inquiry contributes to different evaluation purposes. We close with our discussion of the methods available for values inquiry in evaluation.

Natural Valuation

Most of the ethical theories offered as potential foundations for warranted value judgments in evaluation seek to ground these value judgments on some specific abstract principle, such as equity, equality, or empowerment. The idea of natural valuation does not offer such a singular grounding. We will not be offering a fixed list of values to which evaluation should attend. Instead, the concept of natural valuation suggests that evaluators and others concerned about policies and programs should develop an informed wisdom about the dynamics involved in meeting real human needs. We develop the concept of natural valuation in some detail here, because the concepts of natural and assisted sensemaking have not received much attention in the evaluation literature, especially as they apply to valuation, yet they have important implications for the methods of values inquiry. We first emphasize the primacy of practical wisdom, including the need to move beyond the fact-value dichotomy, and then we elaborate three aspects of valuation that need to be addressed if evaluation is to promote social betterment.

The Primacy of Practical Wisdom

The first step in understanding a commonsense realist, sensemaking approach to values is to recognize that people make value judgments every day in choosing some activities over others (Putnam, 1995). This experience of everyday valuing is a reminder that valuation is a natural activity, adaptive and important, despite the apparent inability of philosophers and others to capture its complexity in formal theories. To the consternation of logical empiricists, value judgments rarely seem objective. Even with the help of social philosophers, one often cannot identify universally accepted bases of value judgments. Nevertheless, we contend that valuing is not as arbitrary as some radical constructivists would have people believe. Nor is it as singularly self-interested as some economists and policy analysts presume (Aaron, Mann, & Taylor, 1994; Mansbridge, 1994; Green, 1992). Although complex, valuation is natural and ordinary, and amenable to systematic investigation.

The second step in understanding a commonsense realist, sensemaking view of natural valuation involves moving beyond artificial dichotomies. For example, one of the least recognized but most irreconcilable differences in the so-called paradigm wars has involved the ways values are treated in evaluations. In one camp, many constructivists focused primarily on studying values, often making values identification an end in itself. In the other camp, logical empiricists were known to make sweeping assumptions about values without any effort to empirically study the values held by relevant individuals (Henry & Julnes, 1999, pp. 53–54). Thompson, Ellis, and Wildavsky (1990) have remarked that "[t]oo often social scientists create needless controversies by seizing upon one side of a dualism and proclaiming it the more important" (p. 21).

Many who have tackled the issue of values in evaluation and other social processes have repeated this error of making a forced and, in our view, false choice between two extreme, polemical positions. A strict dichotomy has often been presumed between facts and values. Adherence to one arm or the other of this dualism leads some to neglect values in an effort to maintain objectivity and others to focus on values in terms of subjective differences.

The third step of understanding natural valuation involves positing a workable way out of the extremes of the fact-value dichotomy. This requires identifying something that underlies the fact-value dichotomy, something that is responsible for the dichotomy but that when understood, can resolve it. This entails pursuing an intermediate path, claiming that values (deeply held normative beliefs about how things *should* be) can be differentiated from facts (warranted representations of how things *are*), that it sometimes is pragmatically useful to make this distinction, but that the distinction is inevitably limiting because, as Thompson, Ellis, and Wildavsky (1990) put it, the "fact-value distinction, although analytically defensible, obscures the extensive interpenetration of facts and values in the real world" (p. 22; also see House & Howe, 1999). That is, it can be meaningful to distinguish facts and values for some purposes, yet one should also recognizing that supposedly objective facts are framed by subjective values and that values can be more objective than sometimes recognized. This position contrasts with the belief some seem to express, that one must either deduce value priorities from a formal theory or slide into complete relativism. Our alternative, discussed in Chapter Three, is to anchor natural valuation on the concept of human needs. As Putnam (1987) points out, need-based valuation does not presume some static conception of human nature—human needs can change over time, as can our understanding of them. Thus an emphasis on need-based valuation is not an attempt to simplify the tasks of the evaluator; instead, evaluators must attempt to balance conflicting needs. This requires attention to the role of democratic processes in maintaining a functional balance between competing needs.

Values Inquiry in Democracy

Hurley (1989) presents the argument that democracy "is a way of realizing as well as discovering what ought to be the case" (p. 349). Democratic institutions allow various opinions to arise and some of those opinions to be debunked by evidence. And democracy is more likely than any other arrangement to lead to "the truth about what should be done" (Hurley, 1989, p. 349). Putnam (1987) seems to agree. However, he adds to Hurley's emphasis on individual autonomy and on the democratic processes through which the struggle over values is carried out an inspiration for these requirements—a moral image of the world, "a picture of how our virtues and ideals hang together with one another and of what they have to do with the position we are in" (p. 51).

This moral image, however, is affected by views of human needs, and these needs are seen differently by different people. Democratic deliberations serve as a forum both for sharpening people's understanding of human needs and for resolving conflicts between needs. But simple majoritarianism will not suffice (Cohen, 1997). Minorities must be protected in terms of rights, including the right to access to and participation in democratic processes (Madison, [1783] 1953; Dahl, [1956] 1973). Without these protections, minority views (which so many currently accepted human rights once were) would never be able to extend their influence to the point of becoming majority views over time. Betterment thus requires that minority views be given voice and consideration through access and participation. Evaluations that take into account the value perspectives of both majorities and minorities can contribute to democratic institutions and to the protection of minority interests. The civic fabric and civil deliberations are more likely to be strengthened when issues of various minorities are given status in evaluation. Properly conceived, values inquiry can contribute to respect for diversity in democratic institutions. Developing this respect requires understanding some of the balances that must be maintained in addressing human needs, as discussed in the following section.

Contextual Valuation

People's natural sense of the proper balance among conflicting needs is influenced by a variety of contextual factors. The value people place on program or policy outcomes is influenced by contextual factors that are consistent with common sense but hard to specify formally with precision. We address three of these contextual factors here.

Balance Among Individuals. One of the major problems in justifying social programs is that programs that benefit some almost always entail costs to others. For example, laws that increase access to public services for an underserved group might be supported by most citizens even though such laws also result in increased taxes or decreased access for more privileged groups. And yet there is limited agreement as to just how much citizens are willing to pay to support the underprivileged.

One approach some have taken in response to this problem of contingent valuation is to ignore the distribution of benefits and costs and to estimate instead the aggregate effect, defined by subtracting the overall costs from the overall benefits. The benefit-cost analyses that follow from this solution adopt the Kaldor-Hicks criterion of program value and calculate net present value of program services (Gramlich, 1990). Another commonly used methodology, which takes the same aggregate perspective, is to calculate average net effects, as is often done in randomized experiments. A very different approach seeks to solve the problem through minimizing complexity and focusing not on the entire distribution of program effects but on the program's impact on those who are least advantaged. Taken to an the extreme, this Rawlsian position (Rawls, 1971) would conclude that an expensive program with special benefits for the disadvantaged is always preferable to an inexpensive program that provides small benefits to everyone.

But most people, regardless of political persuasion, fall somewhere between the extreme Rawlsian and the Kaldor-Hicks positions. For most people the distribution of program effects is often relevant when they judge overall value. Most observers would value a program that provided benefits to the poorest Americans differently than they would value a program that was identical except that it provided benefits to the richest Americans. But most people would also agree that the value of equality is not infinite. To say that people place some value on equality is to say that before discussing the value of a program, an evaluator needs to know something of the program context: What are some of the characteristics of the people affected by the program? Who benefits most from the program?

Consider, for example, a judgment regarding the value of a publicly funded educational television program such as *Sesame Street*. This judgment will be influenced by the value one places on giving particular help to children in families with limited resources. To the extent that one cares about helping the less advantaged, one must know the characteristics of the children reached by such a program and the characteristics of those who derive the greatest benefit in order to value it. Cook et al. (1975) provide an example of the contextual subtleties in assigning value to a program like *Sesame Street*. Although the program had a positive overall impact on the cognitive development of the children who watched, its impact was greatest for the children in higher socioeconomic groups. Thus the program increased the development gap between those with greater and lesser resources. An evaluator who focused solely on the aggregate effect, or *average net effect,* would have missed this differential impact. The lesson is that values inquiry generally should assess the importance of the distribution of outcomes and should link with methods that analyze the actual distributional consequences of a program. This allows distributional consequences to be considered in the debates of democratic institutions. We return to the issue of distributional consequences later in this chapter.

Balance Among Values. Whereas Kaldor-Hicks implicitly assigns efficiency as the primary value to be used in evaluation, a Rawlsian account places value on programs and policies based on their impact on those least advantaged. Many debates, inside and outside of the evaluation field, have addressed whether efficiency or equality is (or should be) fundamental in judgments about social programs and policies. As Berlin (1998; 1990) began describing over fifty years ago and as Okun (1975) also emphasized, many of individuals' basic values clash in that more of one leads naturally to less of another. "Both liberty and equality are among the primary goals pursued by human beings through many centuries, but total liberty for wolves is death to the lambs" (Berlin, 1990, p. 12). It is because important values clash that there is no possibility of technical solutions to values questions—there is no privileged position from which to maximize social welfare. Thus, rather than profess a principled argument for one side or the other of such a debate, we contend that the relative importance one assigns to a value such as efficiency or equality is contextual. Indeed, even the meaning of such values is contextual. As Wildavsky (1991) points out, "what is efficient for people who prefer one way of life may not be efficient for people who value a different culture" (p. 149, emphasis omitted).

To say that value is contextual, however, is not to say that all values are relative. The commonsense approach to realism endorses contextual judgments, not relativistic theories (Putnam, 1990). Culture has profound effects on the values that people promote, but that "human perception is everywhere culturally biased does not mean that people can make the world come out any way they wish" (Thompson, Ellis, & Wildavsky, 1990, p. 3). Not all value systems are equally insightful and constructive, but there is no *ideal* balance waiting to be discovered. Not only do people differ in the relative value that they place on efficiency and equity, but even the view of the majority changes with changes in contextual factors. For example, Yankelovich (1994) describes how increasing affluence has led Americans to place a greater emphasis on equity. And of course it is not unknown for evaluators, like government officials, to find themselves in situations where an action is exactly right in utilitarian terms and exactly wrong in moral terms (Tong, 1987).

We have argued that the notion of contextual complexity places on evaluators the responsibility to consider the impacts of programs and policies in terms of a balance of needs and thus of values. Admittedly, this is not the most glamorous position with which to try to inspire the field. As Berlin (1990) noted about his conclusion that the proper goal is to maintain a precarious balance of values to avoid extreme suffering, "This may seem a very flat answer, not the kind of thing that the idealistic young would wish, if need be, to fight and suffer for, in the cause of a new and nobler society" (p. 18). Recognizing that our answer also lacks the dash of the pursuit of some ideal such as equality, social justice, liberty, or human emancipation, we nonetheless offer it as a commonsense alternative to those single-minded pursuits. It is of course not the ideals themselves to which we object; we have much sympathy for these social objectives. However, the single-minded pursuit of any of these ideals seems inevitably to lead to internal contradictions or to positions that are largely at odds with one's ideals (Berlin, 1990). Efforts to attach evaluation to a specific formal set of moral principles have never withstood the dissecting scalpel wielded by social philosophers (Schwandt, 1997). This leaves evaluators without unequivocal guideposts. The extreme alternative to absolute guideposts, absolute relativism, is unsatisfying and, we believe, wrong. Instead, we argue for an intermediate position, in which evaluators let go of the dream of absolute values but continue to search in each particular case for areas of meaningful convergence on values. Berlin (1990) acknowledges this intermediate position when he comments that "[t]here are, if not universal values, at any rate a minimum without which societies could scarcely survive" (p. 18). House (1995) also argued this point for evaluators in concluding that although "philosophers, legislators, and the public disagree, they disagree within frameworks of overall agreement about fundamental values, for example that all legitimate interests should be represented in a democracy" (p. 44). This intermediate perspective has two important implications for evaluation. First, it reinforces the need to integrate evaluation with a vision of democracy, for it is in democratic debates that societies adjudicate conflicts about values. Second, it suggests that methods of values inquiry will be preferred to the extent they can reveal contextual variations—across communities, across time periods, and across socioeconomic conditions—in the values held by relevant stakeholders and by the public.

Emergent Values. Another way that values are contextual is that they emerge over time. They emerge through social evolution, and they emerge as a result of analysis and critical examination. Changes in society, such as increasing affluence (Yankelovich, 1994), can lead to changes in values, as can the transformation of previously private concerns into public issues (Habermas, 1996a). Activists and issue networks (Heclo, 1978) can focus attention on emerging values.

Evaluation itself can contribute to changes in values over time. For example, evaluations of Head Start initially focused on children's cognitive development as the criterion for merit (McKey et al., 1985). However, as findings showed that the children's cognitive gains dissipated with passing years but social benefits persisted (Barnett, 1995), the social world of children took on more importance in the way people valued Head Start. In addition, experience with a program can identify both positive and negative products or by-products that might arise. As Scriven (1993) has noted, by-products that come about from "living with the policy" can be as important to the determination of that policy's merit as success in achieving the policy's original objectives. For instance, critics contend that the structure of welfare in the United States has produced as unintended by-products an increase in out-of-wedlock births among the poor and a culture of dependency (Murray, 1984). Because of the ways that values can emerge over time, some degree of modesty is called for. Values inquiry can support natural valuation at specific moments in time, but a given values inquiry may not endure through the ages.

Stratified Valuation

Even in periods when values are relatively stable over time, there is another important dimension across which values can vary. One of the principles of realism discussed in Chapter Six is that the social world is stratified in terms of its embedded order and that it is meaningful to conduct analyses at various molecular or molar levels. There are two ways to address this stratification, in terms of hierarchical systems and in terms of the depth of values.

The hierarchical model alerts evaluators to the possibility that understanding the values of individuals, the focus of most economic research, may not be enough to understand the values of communities. In reaction to the focus in economics on individuals, some communitarians claim that community values should be given priority over individual values (Newman & De Zoysa, 1997). Our realist perspective is consistent with the communitarian view that individuals have layered values, holding some values that they recognize are in their best interest as individuals and some values that they recognize are in the best interest of their communities. Although we agree with critics who view the communitarian position as flawed when it argues against individuals making free choices (Newman & De Zoysa, 1997), we argue that it is both possible and desirable for values inquiry to focus individuals on the values that they have for their communities. When assessed, these views provide insights into what may be called public values.

Values are also stratified non-hierarchically, in terms of their depth. That is, to any individual some values appear fundamental and other values seem secondary. We follow others in referring to the secondary or more superficial values as preferences, and we distinguish them from more fundamental, core values.

In conclusion, we have presented natural valuation as something that people do every day in choosing some activities and outcomes over others. The values involved cannot be reduced to formal formulations. Instead, natural valuation is sensitive to maintaining a balance of opportunities in society as well as a balance of conflicting values. Further, values are complex in that people have layers of loyalty, to themselves, to their families, to their communities, even to their societies and beyond.

Values Inquiry in Support of Evaluation Purposes

Values inquiry, as we have discussed, fits well with any of the four evaluation purposes. In the case of the assessment of merit and worth, values inquiry can fruitfully be used to identify the values that, in turn, inform the selection of outcomes and other standards (such as those relating to the rights of clients) relevant to merit. In addition, after evidence has been obtained by a means such as causal analysis about how well the policy performs, values inquiry can support judgments about whether the policy has worth to society. For the assessment of merit and worth, values inquiry will often be conducted first in order to guide the selection of effects for other inquiries, but it also may be carried out following other modes of inquiry in order to assess how much weight should be given to the various findings from the other inquiry modes.

Values inquiry can also feed into program and organizational improvement. It can clarify which aspects of the program should be the focus of improvement efforts. It can also identify the outcomes that are most important to service recipients or to other communities, including service providers or taxpayers. These results can then guide staff members' program improvement efforts toward those activities they believe are most strongly linked to the more valued outcomes. The results of values inquiry can also guide other evaluation activities intended to assist with program improvement (perhaps through the selection of measures for descriptive monitoring methods). In addition, values inquiry can be useful in assessing the relative importance of procedural issues, such as respecting individual liberties, practicing nondiscrimination, and exercising fiduciary responsibility. Values inquiries that address both procedural and outcome issues can be useful for the selection of indicators for monitoring, which will often serve both program improvement and oversight and accountability purposes. For these purposes, values inquiry will often be used in tandem with another inquiry mode, such as the descriptive methods of performance measurement.

Values inquiry can have a special relationship to knowledge development about social problems and people's views about them. Values inquiry may be used to point up gaps or oversights in previous discussions about a public program. It can, for example, identify concerns that the public or program clients have that have not been raised in public forums. It may act as a vehicle for bringing forward the outcomes that are most important to a group that has been previously unrepresented in policy debate. It may provide more precise estimates of values and preferences that can then be used to reexamine the implications of previous evaluation results. Methods of values inquiry can also be used to examine the way that new evidence influences expressed values. For instance, one might tell respondents about recent findings regarding the mechanism that underlies a program success in order to see how this information influences which long- and short-term outcomes they value most. Values inquiry, in short, can contribute to our understanding of social problems and the way people construe them.

In these ways, values inquiry can support each of the four purposes of evaluation. In a few instances, values inquiry may stand on its own as an inquiry mode, but more often it will be conducted in conjunction with one or more other modes. The reason values inquiry should so often be joined with another inquiry mode is that it provides support to natural valuation, and natural valuation, as we have shown, is pivotal in sensemaking about social policies and programs.

Specific Methods for Values Inquiry

At this point, we turn to the methods for values inquiry, with particular attention to empirical methods for representing the values held by stakeholder groups and the public.

Representation of Stakeholder and Public Values

The first task of values inquiry is to represent the relevant values of those involved in, affected by, or concerned about a program or policy. If evaluators know the values of stakeholders and the public, these values can help guide the design of the evaluation. A variety of techniques can be used to represent values; in this section we focus on surveys, often associated with quantitative research, and focus groups, often associated with qualitative research. Surveys can tap extant value preferences, which is especially appropriate when values have had sufficient time to crystallize. The focus group method, as a group interview technique, can better assess the strength of various value positions and other subtleties difficult to capture in formal surveys.

Surveys to Assess Current Values.   Surveys, including interviews, can give evaluators access to value positions as they currently exist among the public and among stakeholder groups. Surveys that rely on probability samples of members of the groups can generate estimates of the error associated with the measured support for various value positions. In situations in which respondents, especially clients and other stakeholders, may be reluctant to reveal their actual opinions, surveys can provide some degree of confidentiality, thereby reducing one type of bias and increasing response rates. Surveys are most useful when opinion formation among the respondents has been ongoing for some time. When an issue has been salient for a time, natural valuation processes, such as seeking and retaining information and informal deliberations, will have occurred. In addition, when issues are highly salient, people engage in more thorough and more thoughtful cognitive processing, and their views are therefore less subject to change (Petty & Cacioppo, 1986). However, surveys are not limited to topics that have received intense scrutiny or debate. Research on mass opinion has shown that, although opinions are likely to fluctuate mildly over time in individuals (Converse, 1964; Alwin & Krosnick, 1991; McClendon, 1991), aggregate opinion is reasonably stable and shifts in largely predictable ways (Page & Shapiro, 1992; Carmines & Stimson, 1994; Stimson, 1998).

In considering the use of surveys for values inquiry, we deal with four issues: stakeholders as respondents, the public as respondents, the types of questions to be asked, and the method of administration. There is an extensive literature available on surveys and survey sampling; our focus here is on issues of specific relevance to the use of surveys in values inquiry.

Stakeholder Surveys. In conducting a survey of members of stakeholder groups, four issues arise related to the selection of members: How is the group defined? What list of each group's members is available (or can sampling techniques be used that do not require a list)? How can the maximum cooperation of the selected group members be obtained? Which combination of sampling design and sample size will yield acceptable levels of precision? We illustrate possible ways of answering these questions with a values inquiry from an evaluation of the Georgia Pre-K Program. In this inquiry, parents, program administrators, and classroom teachers were identified as three important stakeholder groups (Henry, 1999). The stakeholder group of teachers, for example, was defined as all teachers for any classroom currently funded by the program. A list of classes with teachers' names, addresses and telephone numbers was obtained from program administrative records. A disproportionate stratified sample of 220 teachers was selected. Interviews were sought with these teachers (Henry, 1997) and obtained with 200 of them (a 91 percent cooperation rate). In an effort to gain cooperation, evaluators had sent preliminary letters to the teachers and their program directors, or if they worked within public schools, their principals and school system superintendents. The teachers were then contacted by phone and appointments for the survey interviews were set. Teachers were offered the option of responding at the classroom site or at home.

In any sample selection process, nonsampling bias, sampling bias, and sampling error must all be concerns (see Henry, 1990). Inaccurate lists and nonresponse are the major sources of nonsampling bias. Sampling biases can occur inadvertently when the list used actually contains groups rather than individuals (for example, if it lists sites that each have multiple stakeholders) or if the selection mechanism results in unequal probabilities (for example, if a greater percentage of stakeholders is chosen from one region than from another). Sampling errors result from choosing a subset of group members to represent the entire group. The sample design ideas influence the sampling error, but increasing sample size is the most readily available means for reducing this source of error (Henry, 1990; Kalton, 1983). Even with these sources of bias and error, surveys of stakeholder groups using probability samples can produce an accurate reflection of the values held by the groups' members.

Public Surveys. In moving from stakeholder surveys to surveys of the public, evaluators move in a sense from individual valuation to social valuation. Recognizing that there are no technical solutions to determining social values (for example, Arrow, 1963), we are left with the goal of adequately representing the values of the public as a stakeholder. One important tradition in attempting to identify public values is the study of voter behavior—conducting exit polls, organizing findings, and interpreting voting patterns. To extend the examination of values to those held by citizens or the public in the practice of evaluation, we propose increasing the reach of survey methods to include public values.

The public is a key source of values and opinions for the democratic process, as shown by the heavy reliance on polls and surveys in the media and among policymakers. However, the public has generally not been given the status of a stakeholder group in the field of evaluation. Research demonstrating the strong impact of the public's attitudes on the shaping of policy (Page & Shapiro, 1992; Stimson, 1998; Fishkin, 1995; Monroe, 1998) highlights the inappropriateness of ignoring public opinion and values. Henry (1996b) has detailed three ways in which information from public opinion surveys can be useful for evaluation: framing the questions to be addressed in the evaluation, exposing myths or incorrect beliefs about a program, and assessing the level of public support or opposition for potential evaluation recommendations. In addition, information from public surveys may allow the evaluator to frame other evaluation findings in a manner consistent with extant public values.

Along with the surveys of the three stakeholder groups mentioned earlier, the ongoing longitudinal evaluation of the Georgia Prekindergarten Program used general population surveys of the public (Henry, 1999). These surveys of Georgia residents were conducted using random digit dialing techniques that do not require a list of residents to generate the sample. The technique reduces nonsampling errors, such as those that result when residents have recently moved or have unlisted numbers. Of course those without telephones cannot be surveyed, which will bias the results of this kind of survey, but less and less so as the telephone becomes more and more ubiquitous. General population surveys are usually conducted over the phone or on a face-to-face basis. Budgetary limits favor the telephone for surveys of the public in evaluation. In addition, many national and state-level survey organizations have established periodic surveys to which questions can sometimes be added for use in values inquiry.

Types of questions to be asked. Survey responses can be influenced to some extent by the way questions are asked and who asks the questions (Groves, 1989). The first distinction to consider in the type of questions to be asked involves a choice between open-ended and fixed-response formats. Open-ended questions allow respondents to provide answers with fewer cues, but they require more time for each response, for recording it, and for analyzing it. Fixed-response, or close-ended, questions, which ask respondents to chose one or more of the alternatives in a set of answers, can be administered more quickly and require less cognitive processing on the part of the respondent but guide the respondent to the appropriate range of responses. Both have a place in values inquiry. In general, open-ended items are more appropriately used when interviews are more personal, either face to face or, to a lesser extent, over the phone. Open-ended items on mailed surveys and self-administered surveys require the respondent to write an answer and may reduce the likelihood of a response, especially among groups with relatively low levels of literacy.

Sometimes open-ended questions calling for short responses are a useful compromise. For example, members of a stakeholder group might be asked the open-ended question, What do you think are important consequences of the publicly provided preschool program for four-year-olds? Or the same question might be asked as a fixed-response question, with respondents asked to rate each item from a list that is read to them, using a rating scale of one for unimportant and ten for very important. The list could include numerous items that respondents might feel are important but might not recall in response to an open-ended question. In any event, the design of fixed-response items should result at least in part from previous pilot testing that included open-ended questions designed to learn what kinds of items respondents think are important and from a review of relevant literature and program documents. Another compromise is to ask respondents to provide a "top of mind" response to a question and then to follow up with fixed-response list of answers for the same question to obtain a more comprehensive set of ratings.

In addition to questions that produce ratings or rankings (see Singer & Presser, 1989), forced-choice questions are often useful in developing a sense of people's priorities among different values. Questions that require respondents to choose from two responses the one that best represents their position are statistically reliable and may be used to see if the values asked about have a strict hierarchical structure. An example of forced-choice question is, Some people believe that improved scores on math and reading tests are the most important objective for Georgia's preschool program, others say improving classroom behavior in kindergarten and the first grade is most important. Which do you believe is more important?

In addition to asking about overall benefits for the program recipients, it is important to consider asking about benefits for each of the embedded levels of systems and to focus on the distributive consequences of the program. In the surveys for the evaluation of Georgia's Pre-K Program, potential outcomes were stratified into three levels: child related, family related, and state related. Ratings were taken on the valuation of possible outcomes at each level. Stakeholders were also asked to make choices about whether the program should help accelerate gifted students or concentrate on getting the least developed children ready for kindergarten. These ratings were used to discover both consensus and conflicts in outcome preferences and also preferences about the distribution of effects. The results have been incorporated in plans for measuring specific outcomes during the twelve-year evaluation and for reporting results to highlight those most relevant to each group.

Methods of survey administration. Some types of surveys tend to be aligned with specific methods of administration. For example, general population surveys are most often conducted by phone. But most surveys can be conducted in more than one way. Evaluators must choose between mail, telephone, face-to-face, and on-site self-administered surveys. Deciding which to use requires that evaluators consider feasibility, costs, and the desired accuracy of the data. Less structured interviews require human interaction, with face-to-face interviews usually being preferred and telephone interviews a possibility. More structured interviews can use any of the modes of administration, as long as good lists are available with names, addresses, and telephone numbers. But in surveys of the public, the general lack of accurate lists usually leads to telephone or face-to-face interviews that can be conducted with random digit dialing or area probability samples, respectively, instead of actual population lists (Kish, 1965; Hess, 1985). Mail and self-administered surveys require greater literacy from the study population and should be designed especially carefully if the population has members with low levels of literacy. Although response rates are somewhat lower for mail as compared to telephone surveys, with proper follow-up, including multiple mailings and reminders by phone, response rates can be increased. At the same time, responses rates for telephone surveys, especially random digit dialing surveys, have fallen.

Costs for conducting a survey have changed somewhat as mailing costs have gone up and long distance charges for phone surveys have declined. More and more survey researchers are considering the use of incentives, either for all respondents or for those who initially refuse to participate. Mail surveys have costs for letters, questionnaires, postage, handling receipts and follow-ups, and data entry. Telephone surveys have costs for phones, phone service, long distance calls, training interviewers, conducting the interviews (including selecting or confirming the eligibility of each respondent), and data entry (if computer-assisted telephone interviewing, CATI, is not used), and programming time (if CATI is used). For face-to-face interviews, evaluators must allot large amounts of the survey budget for travel and interviewer time. Some monitoring of the interviews must also be done. The use of self-administered computer surveys is likely to increase greatly as more of the population becomes comfortable with using computers and the cost of portable computers decrease.

The impact of the mode of administration on the accuracy of responses has been a topic of concern among survey researchers for some time. Some have examined the relationship between mode of administration and response bias (McClendon, 1991). For example, one set of response biases (such as primacy effects from choosing the first response in a printed list) may affect mailed surveys and another set of response biases (such as latency effects from choosing last item mentioned in a list) may influence telephone surveys (Dillman, Sangster, Tarnai, & Rockwood, 1996). Rapport with interviewers and social pressures resulting from the interview situation have also been related to bias in responses (Bradburn & Sudman, 1988).

In many cases, using mixed modes of administration is a reasonable strategy. For example, those who do not respond to mailed follow-ups for mail surveys can be called and asked to participate in a telephone survey. Or telephone surveys can be attempted for those who refuse face-to-face surveys. Of course mixed modes also can produce biases in responses that must be considered. But even with the need for such judgments, surveys can provide a far better picture of the existing values of stakeholders and the public than would exist in the absence of systematic values inquiry.

Group Interview Techniques. The survey methods just discussed provide evaluators and others with a snapshot of the values held by stakeholder groups and the general public. Such snapshots, however, have limitations and are unlikely to reveal the more subtle and nuanced views within complex values. One aspect of this complexity is that values are fundamentally contextual. In particular, they may be contingent on the social context involved. For example, Nida-Ruemelin, Schmidt, and Munk (1996) found that people's preferences are influenced by their understanding of the preferences of those around them, by the *interpersonal interdependence of values*. If this is so, then the typical survey approach of questioning individuals in isolation from others may produce results somewhat at odds with the values that would be revealed in a more social context. Though the natural processes of most social contexts are not directly accessible, stakeholder groups can be organized by evaluators to provide opinions about values in a way that may capture the contextual complexity of the interpersonal interdependence of values.

One method of doing this to conduct group interviews, in which six to eight people are interviewed together. Group discussions have a long tradition in European social inquiry (Flick, 1998); many people in the United States are acquainted with such methods under the label *focus groups*. Focus groups were developed for market research. Potential customers were brought together to talk about their needs and their thoughts on various ways to satisfy those needs (Ward, Bertrand, & Brown, 1991). Somewhat different practices may carried out under the banner of the focus group. In at least some cases, focus group methods may be accurately described as group interviews rather than as more interactive and deliberative group discussions. Group interviews offer the efficiency of conducting multiple interviews at the same time. They also offer a form of quality control, in that other members of the group can help filter out irrelevant or unrepresentative value stances. And they allow the assessment of values in a social context, which may be useful given the interpersonal dependency of values.

For an example of the use of focus groups for values inquiry, consider the effort of Peirson, Prilleltensky, Nelson, and Gould (1997), who wanted to understand stakeholder values as they related to mental health services for youths. In addition to conducting a survey, they also convened focus groups for each of the major stakeholder groups. By conducting twelve focus groups for clients, parents, and program staff, they were able to identify areas of agreement on values (parents and program staff agreed that the mental health center should be accessible and welcoming to clients, for instance) as well as areas of disagreement (the youths and their parents tended to disagree on what the real problems were that needed to be addressed). These stakeholder values were used, though not in some mechanical way, to suggest changes in the organization of the mental health center. Campbell (1997) described a similar use of consumer focus groups in conjunction with multi-stakeholder assessment teams to understand value positions relevant for mental health reform.

Among the important issues for group interview methods are the stakeholder (or public) groups to be included, the representativeness of the individuals chosen to participate, and the makeup of the interview groups (heterogeneous versus homogeneous). Many important stakeholder groups are easy to identify, but others require considerable insider knowledge. For example, in an evaluation of a major change in a school calendar, teachers, students, and parents are fairly obvious stakeholder groups. The janitors' union and summer employers may not be so apparent. In addition, the selection of the specific individuals for participation is a crucial decision for the evaluation and the acceptance of the findings. It is not easy to decide who speaks for teachers or who represents welfare recipients. Nonetheless, decisions about which groups and which representatives to include can be improved if evaluators "consciously explore the rationale for stakeholder par_icipation during the planning phase of an evaluation" (Mark & Shotland, 1985, p. 619).

Beyond this decision about whom to include in focus groups is the issue of the composition of particular focus groups. Should they be homogeneous, including only members of one stakeholder group, or should they be heterogeneous, with representative members of all groups? Deliberate heterogeneity can be useful for better understanding discordant opinions. Preexisting power relationships, however, can silence some groups. Homogeneous groups may have increased participation during the interview sessions but may also result in more extreme opinions, biased in the direction of group norms. One factor in choosing between homogeneous and heterogeneous groups ties back to the idea of the interpersonal dependency of values. If there is reason to believe that interpersonal influences are mostly within stakeholder groups (for example, teachers influence teachers but not administrators or vice versa), then homogeneous interview groups would better match the real-world context. Conversely, if interpersonal influences are mostly across groups, then heterogeneous interview groups would be better. Researchers may also hold some sessions of each type, to see how much difference the interaction of heterogeneous groups makes.

Another concern is how evaluators should use focus groups results. In the past, focus groups were often used in conjunction with other methods such as surveys, but increasingly, evaluators are employing them as a stand-alone method, raising the issue of the comparability of focus group and survey results. Ward, Bertrand, and Brown (1991) showed that for their cases, survey data and focus group results were quite similar, with the focus groups generally providing greater depth of inquiry. The similarity of responses may depend on the degree to which the issues being investigated have crystallized for the individuals participating in the focus groups and surveys. The degree of similarity in results across methods is also likely to depend on such things as how representative of the survey population the focus group participants are and how similar the questions are that are asked with each method. Nevertheless, the combination of group interviews and survey techniques, when feasible, is often the desirable option for representing stakeholder and public values.

In addition, some focus group approaches and other related techniques can do more than represent extant values. They can simulate the deliberations that are central to democratic processes.

Simulation of Deliberative Processes

Some methods of values inquiry are designed to go beyond getting a picture of the current values positions of stakeholder groups and the public. They are designed to go beyond triggering some contextual influence on values, such as the expressed values of others. These methods are used to simulate, or at least approximate, the natural valuation processes of democratic deliberation, which include debate and negotiation. House and Howe (1999) have recently advocated strongly for inclusive, dialogical, and deliberative processes in evaluation to more systematically and responsibly deal with sorting out issues of values, because "[e]valuation is as good or as bad as the value framework that constrains it, in the same way that it is as good or as bad as the research methodology it employs"

(p. 137). Deliberative involvement of an inclusive list of potential stakeholder groups is their solution for making the cognitive function of evaluation more responsive to democratic principles.

There are several possible methods for simulating deliberative process, ranging from less formal to more formal in terms of the extent to which the group processes are explicitly set up to model a real-world deliberative body. On the informal side is the group discussion format, such as sometimes occurs under the banner of focus groups, wherein group members are charged with discussing set topics with each other. Blumer (1969) claimed that "[s]uch a group, discussing collectively their sphere of life and probing into it as they meet one another's disagreements, will do more to lift the veils covering the sphere of life than any other device that I know of" (p. 41). Because real democratic deliberations generally require interplay between different stakeholder groups, the composition of group discussion groups will usually be heterogeneous.

In the context of evaluation of public programs or policies, one goal of this group approach is to involve stakeholders and citizens in values inquiry that goes beyond what is typical in survey research. By convening groups to raise and clarify those values that participants seek in the implementation of a policy, evaluators are attempting to put natural valuation processes into fast forward. These group processes are often highly structured because of time constraints and because they bring together group members who are from different stakeholder groups and who may have different views. These individuals are asked to raise and weigh the importance of various outcomes and potential spin-offs, to address more and less satisfactory ways of pursing the realization of the desired outcomes, and to deliberate openly about them. The hope is that the group process will produce a more refined understanding of values positions and, in the ideal result, a more focused consensus about them.

In some cases, more formal methods may be used in the attempt to achieve these goals. Worthen, Sanders, and Fitzpatrick (1997, chap. 9) review the history of formal deliberative methods in evaluation under the label *adversary-oriented* evaluation approaches. The most common efforts of this type have used a judicial model, with rule-governed proceedings and advocates on opposing sides (one defending a program and another attacking it, for example). Truly adversarial approaches may have disadvantages. For instance, the defending evaluator may overstate the merits of a program but do so persuasively (Worthen, Sanders, & Fitzpatrick, 1997). Our sense is that deliberative processes that are not rigidly adversarial are preferable. In addition, these and other methods for simulating deliberation are probably far better suited to sorting out values issues (which things matter to the participants) than they are in determining issues on the representational side of sensemaking.

Simulated deliberations, especially of the less formal type, will often be one-shot activities for the participants. In some instances, however, an evaluation might be informed throughout by the discussions of group of stakeholders who might have some direct responsibilities for parts of the evaluation or who might be solicited to offer advice or make decisions about the evaluation. Stakeholder advisory groups are sometimes formed to serve this kind of ongoing consultative function. Our impression, however, is that such groups often do not have the sort of deliberative structure and do not receive the kind of information or support that can sustain high-quality deliberations over the long run.

Unlike surveys or interviews intended to take an overall snapshot of existing values, deliberative methods are premised on the idea that by participating in discussion and negotiation groups, individuals may get beyond their preexisting opinions. In some of the most well publicized attempts to simulate deliberative processes, such as the *deliberative polling* done in 1996, few opinions about policy issues were changed (Fishkin, 1995; Merkle, 1996). However, other approaches, such as more formal methods that explicitly charge participants with a task like prioritizing outcomes may prove more successful when evaluators gain more experience with them. Dewey ([1916] 1966) and Habermas (1996a) indicate that deliberative discussion in the context of a democratic society is an ideal.

There are no ideal methods available for simulating deliberative processes for values inquiry. Still, we believe these deliberative methods of values inquiry deserve more application in practice to test their usefulness as an aid to collective sensemaking in evaluation.

Critical Review to Identify Values

The methods for representing extant values and for simulating deliberative processes are decidedly empirical. Data are collected. Observations are made. The newly acquired information is used to draw conclusions. In contrast, some methods for values inquiry are analytical. Rather than relying on data collection, they involve the application of some philosophical or similar system to examine value assumptions. We use the term *critical review* to refer to such methods for examining the value assumptions hidden in or obstructed by social policies and programs, and for tracing out the implications of those assumptions. Methods of critical review are consistent with Popper's view of critical discussion and the fundamental role it plays in the problem-solving process. According to Popper (1994, p. 157), it is by critical discussion along with imagination and empirical investigation to uncover error that individuals expose their prejudices. Similarly, critical review can expose values that have been hidden in other discussions about a program or policy.

Several approaches to critical review exist that can be applied to policies and programs. Perhaps the most familiar approach to critical review in evaluation is the use of Rawls's *theory of justice* (1971) to probe the values that might guide evaluation. House (1976, 1993) has applied Rawlsian analysis to suggest that evaluation should attend especially to the impact of programs and policies on the least well off. Critical review may also apply neo-Marxist frameworks to policies and programs. Such an analysis might, for example, point out that a program putatively for the poor might actually reinforce the existing power structure (perhaps by pacifying the poor and co-opting their possible activism without actually giving them control of resources). Feminist theory could also be applied in critical reviews, resulting perhaps in an identification of sexist or gendered activities in a program.

We have described these approaches to critical review only cursorily here. Although critical review can be of importance for identifying values concerns that have escaped notice, it seems unlikely to suffice as an alternative to the empirical methods for values inquiry described earlier. One reason is the antiformalism that Putnam (1995) describes as part of the commonsense realist stance and that we discussed in Chapter Six. Critical review will usually be too single-mindedly focused on one values position to correspond to the complexity of natural valuation. In addition, critical review is probably the least likely of the values inquiry methods to model the deliberative democratic processes through which social problems are defined and their solutions sought. Critical methods can, however, inform these deliberations about values issues that might otherwise be ignored.

Infusion of Values into Other Findings

In a sense this final set of methods provides a bridge between the results of values inquiry and other evaluation modes. When values inquiry yields a list of valued effects to be addressed in future evaluation inquiries, those effects may be directly incorporated as performance measures or as effects in causal analyses. But some values inquiries may raise concerns that require special techniques or methods in order to infuse these concerns into evaluation. An important and commonplace example of these methods is the examination of the distribution of program or policy effects.

Methods for Probing Distributional Consequences. There are several reasons to expect that the overall value people assign to a program will usually be influenced by its distributional consequences. Attention to distributional consequences of program and policies might arise because of people's interest in equality, their concern for the least well off, or their recognition that social betterment requires attention to the gaps in well-being and not just to the averages. If, as we suspect it commonly does, subsequent values inquiry indicates that distributional consequences are of concern, then it is important to have methods to assess and report these consequences. The *Sesame Street* example, described earlier, illustrates the importance of going beyond aggregate impacts in testing for program effects: programs may be helpful on the average but increase the gap between the best and the least well off (Cook et al., 1975).

Analysis of moderated relationships for equality of opportunities and of outcomes can be conducted with qualitative, quantitative, or mixed methods. Qualitative analyses can proceed in a number of ways, one being a multiple case study design in which two dimensions are used to differentiate four cases (Yin, 1994). For example, a researcher might be interested in two curricula for teaching mathematics, one that makes substantial use of computer technology to illustrate concepts and the other a skill-building approach that depends on traditional math exercises. Sensitivity to the distribution of the effects might lead an evaluator to examine both curricula in two types of settings, a wealthy community with computers available in most homes and a poorer community with few home computers available. Imagine that the four cases revealed that the technology-rich curriculum is somewhat more effective overall, but this overall positive effect occurs because the technology-rich curriculum is much more effective in the wealthy community but somewhat less effective than the traditional curriculum in the poorer community. This outcome would indicate an interaction between curricula and community type, such that the merit of a particular curriculum depends on community characteristics. In this light it might not seem fair to impose the high-technology curriculum on poorer communities despite its advantage on average over the traditional curriculum.

Note that for this type of distributional analysis to be effective, several things need to happen. First, to discover the interaction, enough must be known in advance to choose the cases that can reveal it. If the impact of the math curricula in the previous example were dependent not on the community characteristics of wealth but on a classroom characteristic such as the student-teacher ratio, this differential impact might be missed. In some instances, evaluators might use the methods of principled discovery, discussed in Chapter Nine, to explore for important, unexpected moderators. In addition, this case study approach works best when the cases being studied are, beyond the contrast hypothesized to be important, similar. If the communities receiving the two opposing math curricula were different in many ways, it would be difficult to conclude which dimension was critical; again, extensive qualitative inquiry, using the pattern matching logic described in the previous chapter, might then be required to identify the real causal agent.

More quantitative approaches to the study of moderated relationships can also take many forms. A traditionally important method involves the use of interaction terms in regression analysis to assess whether some groups benefit from the program more than others. Evaluators can also use ANOVA (analysis of variance), ANCOVA (analysis of covariance), or many multivariate procedures in a similar manner. The logic of this approach is the same as the logic of its qualitative variant in that the impact of a program or policy is examined to see if it varies across groups. In regression analyses, interaction terms are created by multiplying one variable by another and treating the product as a separate variable. For example, an evaluation of child-care facilities included an interaction term based on multiplying the quality of the program environment by the income level of the children's families (Peisner-Feinberg & Burchinal, 1997). The research found that although the quality of the services is important for all children, it is especially important for children from poor families.

If values inquiry reveals concern about the distributional consequences of a policy or program, moderated multiple regression or similar methods can be a useful way to infuse important values into evaluation in order to support natural valuation. These methods are not, however, without complications and potential shortcomings. Jaccard, Turrisi, and Wan (1990) and Aiken and West (1991) describe a variety of issues in the proper use and interpretation of interaction terms in regression analysis. One issue that is important for a commonsense interpretation of results is *centering,* in which values on variables are transformed by subtracting the mean values from all scores (they are centered in the sense that a value of 0.0 represents the mean of that variable). In addition, as McClelland and Judd (1993) have discussed, interaction terms may be relatively small in field settings for several reasons that are especially likely to arise in the absence of highly controlled experimental designs. In short, numerous technical issues need to be addressed in studying interaction effects.

One less technical complication usually takes the form of an argument against analyzing moderated relationships, defended by reference to Cronbach (1975). The argument is that there are many potential moderated relationships to study (including higher-order interactions, whereby one's interaction actually depends on some other contextual factor) and no fundamental reason to study some over others. The example of the *Sesame Street* findings, however, illustrates the sensemaking claim that consideration of context need not result in an infinite regress through ever more subtle contextual influences. Cook et al. (1975) did not look to see whether program impacts were moderated by such contextual factors as the size of the family television set or the number of hours of sunlight a day. Each of these and many other contextual factors could in principle have influenced program effectiveness, but they were not examined because it seemed plausible that their moderating effect on program effectiveness is likely to be small relative to the moderated effect associated with socioeconomic background and because contextual effects not related to differential socioeconomic advantages are of less concern for the valuation component of sensemaking. A view of evaluation as assisted sensemaking, therefore, directs evaluators to look for contextual influences but to do so within what are seen as realistic limits and with regard to the influences' relevance to valuation.

More General Methods for Translating Values to Other Evaluation Modes. Analyses of well-selected case studies or of interaction terms in regression can probe distributional consequences and produce important results for natural and assisted sensemaking. But evaluators will also find other tools important for translating values inquiry findings into the design of methods from other inquiry modes. In Chapter Five we identified a number of sequences across inquiry modes and recommended that values inquiry often precede and guide other inquiry modes. But how does one incorporate the results of values inquiry into an activity such as the selection of measures for a performance measurement system or a causal analysis or the selection of comparison groups or other standards?

This has been one of the stumbling blocks for earlier approaches to values inquiry, such as stakeholder analyses. After learning which possible outcomes each stakeholder group thinks are most important, what do you do? It is easy to proceed when there is widespread agreement on a value or set of values. But what if there is not? One possible response calls for more values inquiry rather than less. That is, a sequence of values inquiry activities might aid in translating values into other evaluation methods. For example, evaluators might begin with a survey or with group discussions to represent extant stakeholder values. This step might be accompanied by a critical review conducted by an appropriately qualified member of the evaluation team or a consultant. Then a deliberative simulation could be carried out. Participants representing different stakeholder groups and the public could be presented with the results from the previous values inquiry, a set of decisions that have to be made, and the apparent options. For instance, they might be told all the possible outcomes and their estimated measurement costs and asked to prioritize within the constraints of the budget.

Consensus might not occur in all cases. But a sequence such as this should at least some of the time provide a justification for the important decisions of an evaluation. Significantly, this justification will comport well with the very rationale for doing evaluation: to assist the sensemaking of those participating in the deliberative processes that seek to define and achieve social betterment. Moreover, when consensus cannot be achieved, the evaluator then knows that he or she has the burden of justifying the necessary decision about evaluation design and communicating both that justification and the limits of the evaluation findings relative to some stakeholder groups' values. Too often, the values that are represented in an evaluation are those implicit in the evaluator's training or those of a sponsor or those reflected in whatever measure happens to be handy. The kind of sequence of values inquiry we have just described has the potential to increase the infusion of stakeholder and public values in evaluation, so it can better address the actual values of those it serves.

Other Techniques for Studying Values

Many other methods can be used in conjunction with the methods just reviewed to probe existing values. For example, the methods of classification can reveal whether there are distinctive groups of people with different attitudes. Henry (1999), for instance, used confirmatory factor analysis to determine whether the stakeholder groups examined in the Georgia prekindergarten study and the general public had the same underlying structure in their values. Indeed, although the overall variables were similarly related across the groups, the analysis showed that the public divided the possible outcomes into less distinct groups than teachers or parents did. Also, as we suggested earlier, methods of causal analysis can be applied to values inquiry. For instance, one could carry out an experiment to examine how peoples' values change after they learn the results of a study assessing a program's outcomes. Do program advocates perhaps say some value is less important to them once they learn that the program does not help clients achieve that value?

These and many other ways of studying values are interesting and may contribute to knowledge development. However we expect the most important types of values inquiry for evaluation are those that assess the stakeholder and public values that can in turn guide the use of other evaluation inquiry modes.

Conclusion

Values inquiry requires methods that reflect the complexity of the domain being studied. Because natural valuation is complex, we have not attempted a formal theory of the values that should drive evaluation. We do not claim equity, equality, empowerment, efficiency, or some other value as *the* value for evaluation. Instead, we agree with Putnam (1990) that "the way *not* to solve an ethical problem is to find a nice sweeping principle that 'proves too much,' and to accuse those who refuse to 'buy' one's absolute principle of immorality" (p. 181). Staunch commitment to a single value leads almost inevitably to excess and violations of common sense. Nonetheless, a systematic approach to values inquiry is needed if evaluation is to achieve its potential in assisting sensemaking in the democratic processes that when properly informed are capable of contributing to social betterment. Methods for the representation of existing stakeholder and public values (such as surveys and group interview methods), methods for the simulation of deliberation (such as focus groups and discussion groups), methods for critical review (such as Rawlsian or feminist analysis), and methods for infusing values inquiry into other evaluation modes (such as moderated regression or multiple case studies to examine distributional consequences) are all imperfect relative to the complexities of natural valuation and democratic institutions. Yet each of these tools can assist evaluators to take account of the relevant values perspectives in the conduct of an evaluation. Each can improve assisted sensemaking, by clarifying what others value or by highlighting values issues previously ignored. And this is more than any alternative formal guidepost to values can do. Although no single method provides *the* perspective on values, each provides an additional perspective. Thus the methods of values inquiry, especially when combined and carried out in a thoughtful sequence, can contribute greatly to the planning of evaluation and to the valuation of its findings.

CONCLUSION

Meeting the Challenges of Evaluation

In many ways the field of evaluation is late in its adolescence, moving toward yet another rite of passage. Some youthful ways and excesses are mostly things of the past. No longer are evaluators blindly experimenting in an effort to determine the limit of their reach. The excessive mood swings between unrealistic optimism and utter despair, between positivism and radical constructivism, are waning. Having passed through the infancy of the field, evaluators have for the most part learned, albeit sometimes painfully, the limits of evaluation's ability to alleviate social problems. No longer is there an adrenaline rush of excitement and hubris from one more clever but untested idea, one more approach to be added to the litany of approaches that have been announced, tried, and discarded. Collectively, evaluators have some experience with what works. They have a sense about the kinds of activities that are both useful and in demand and about how to do them. They have a better sense of their role in the rough and tumble world of politics and policymaking. And they can apply reasoning and experience to the task of assisting democratic institutions in their pursuit of making the world a better place. But at this still youthful moment, the field of evaluation has yet to embrace an integrated framework for understanding the practice of evaluation and for guiding that practice.

The theory of evaluation laid out in the previous chapters is an effort to create the framework that is currently missing. We have attempted to consolidate some of the field's accumulated experiences, our best ideas for obtaining warranted conclusions, and a reasoned and reasonable view of the role of evaluation in informing democratic societies. We have defined evaluation in terms of the application of assisted sensemaking techniques to provide information for selecting, overseeing, improving, and making sense of social policies and programs. The importance of these potential contributions of assisted sensemaking is demonstrated by the fact that the evaluation function is recreated time and time again, even when those who request the information about a program and policy (or more tellingly, those who produce the information) may never have heard of the field of evaluation. It is comforting that the need for assisted sensemaking is spontaneously recognized over and over, but discomforting that learning about evaluation processes starts anew each time. We hope this volume captures some important past lessons and organizes them in a form useful for practitioners and others. At the least, we hope to stimulate productive debate toward the goal of achieving a common understanding of evaluation, its purpose, its role, and its conduct.

In Chapter One we set out two overarching and interlinked challenges for ourselves and others concerned with evaluation theory. The first challenge was to better understand the nature of the evaluation of policies and programs and its role in society. The second challenge was to establish a framework rooted in this understanding that could guide practice and enhance the contribution that evaluation can make to individuals, groups, and society. The following summary of key aspects of our responses to these challenges is intended not only as a recapitulation of the framework we have drawn and the evaluation purposes, inquiry modes, and methods that inhabit that framework but also as a new challenge, this time for all evaluators, to help fill the gaps that remain and move the field of evaluation further toward its ultimate goal.

The ultimate purpose of evaluation is to contribute to social betterment by informing actions taken and decisions made in democratically established institutions.

Evaluation is the primary means through which democratic institutions can take advantage of assisted sensemaking techniques for reducing bias in beliefs about public programs. Evaluation should assist those who have responsibilities in democratic institutions to better select, oversee, improve, and make sense of social programs and policies. Utilization of results is often considered a sign of evaluation success; however, a focus on utilization may draw evaluators into advocating specific changes or stretching findings further than they can reasonably go in order to support direct utilization. The more appropriate measure of evaluation success is not direct utilization of results but whether the results provide useful information that can be used—in conjunction with other considerations—in democratic deliberations.

Moreover, in light of the ultimate purpose of evaluation, evaluators should be shameless in broadly spreading their findings about public policies and programs. Legislators elected to select and oversee programs, program staff, current and prospective clients, and the members of the public all need to be informed about social policies and programs. In addition to traditional evaluation reports and briefings, Web sites, the media, and scholarly articles have roles in disseminating findings. More generally, evaluators need to take their proper place in the *policy community* (Kingdon, 1995). They should become principals in the debates that define social betterment and in the identification of policies and programs that stand the greatest chance of achieving it. They should bring the results of their assisted sensemaking to bear on the issues of the day for the purpose of improving social conditions.

Evaluation contributes to social betterment through assisted sensemaking that can reduce the biases and extend the scope of people's natural sensemaking about policies and programs.

People naturally form representations of the policies and programs that concern them. Parents may conclude, for example, that a drug abuse resistance program reduces the use of drugs among children. People also naturally reach valuations of policies and programs. The same parents may conclude that the antidrug program is a good thing. But such natural sensemaking may not suffice for judgments about social policies and programs. People who have some stake in a policy may be biased to believe that it works, whereas others may be biased to believe it will not. In addition, the evidence base people have available for natural sensemaking about any policy or program may be highly limited relative to that policy's or program's wide reach. Evaluation has access to a wide array of systematic assisted sensemaking techniques for enhancing natural sensemaking. Recognition of the link between natural and assisted sensemaking can guide evaluators in attending to such needs as addressing both the representational and the valuative side of sensemaking in their efforts to contribute to social betterment.

> *Although social betterment is the ultimate goal of evaluation, shorter term purposes should be selected for a specific evaluation. Among these purposes, there is a unique and hallowed place for the assessment of merit and worth, which examines a program or policy in terms of its stated objectives, unintended consequences, equity, and issues of human rights and liberties. However, evaluation can and must start doing more to serve other essential purposes as well. The choice of purpose or purposes to pursue in a given evaluation should be based on considerations related to social betterment.*

A focus on merit and worth is evaluation's birthright, and warranted information about merit and worth is evaluation's unique and most important contribution to social betterment. When people reinvent the idea of evaluation, the question that singularly defines their need is, Does the policy work? Or more elaborately,

Does the policy improve social conditions in the way we hope it will, without doing things that compromise other goals or social values? When evaluators apply the techniques of assisted sense-making to the question of merit and worth, they provide important information for making reasoned judgments about a program. They provide evidence that respects the possibility of both hopes and fears about a policy's consequences, using methods open to both possibilities. Evaluation is not worthy of its name if it does not include a vaunted place for the assessment of merit and worth.

However, the assessment of merit and worth serves social betterment best in those relatively rare instances when the policy environment is competitive and the question of adopting one policy or another is pressing. In the long stretches between these proverbial forks in the road, other purposes for evaluation produce more useful information. In particular, the attention evaluators should give to the evaluation purpose of program and organizational improvement increases substantially. This purpose approaches social betterment through discerning ways of doing business that are more likely to lead to desirable outcomes and avoid negative ones. That is, the evaluation issue should not simply be providing information for building a better client intake process, for example. Instead, the issue should be providing information for building a client intake process that better brings about the desired improvements in the welfare of those who need services.

Similarly, knowledge development and oversight and compliance can be important purposes for evaluation. Although these purposes are not as common as the assessment of merit and worth or program and organizational improvement, they both have a meaningful place in an integrated framework for evaluation. Oversight and compliance supports democratic officials who have responsibility for ensuring that programs are operating in ways that comply with enabling legislation and regulations. It also provides essential information about program compliance with more general requirements, such as nondiscriminatory hiring practices. Moreover, by increasing compliance in well-designed programs, oversight and compliance efforts can support improved program functioning and thus contribute to betterment. Conversely, when a program is not functioning as expected, an oversight and compliance evaluation that provides solid evidence that program design was accurately implemented may contribute momentum for policy change and open up a more competitive policy environment.

Knowledge development resulting from evaluation may suggest flaws in the conventional wisdom that underlies current policy. It may also lead people to insights that will help them create more effective interventions for the future. For example, an effort at knowledge development through the study of underlying mechanisms can often be a low-cost adjunct to an evaluation that primarily serves another purpose. In addition, when evaluation programs (using a series of evaluations rather than a single-shot evaluation) are implemented, more space can be carved out for knowledge development work. Agencies, foundations, and other organizations with long-term interests in specific social problems are most likely to have ongoing knowledge development activities. If evaluators can increase the role of knowledge development in evaluation, the process of scaling up interventions from the lab to field trials and on to full-blown implementation should proceed with greater certainty. Knowledge development, like the other evaluation purpose, has a role to play in social betterment.

The challenge for evaluators, as our framework recognizes, is to choose the right purpose or mix of purposes for the circumstances and then to choose inquiry methods that serve the purpose well.

> Methods should be selected according to the immediate purpose or purposes of the evaluation, in light of the sensemaking function that each inquiry mode serves and in light of the decision-making requirements of the situation.

Many different evaluation methods can be brought to bear in supporting the sensemaking needs of democratic institutions. Even when one evaluation purpose predominates, a plethora of methods are available to the evaluator. Consider the assessment of merit and worth. For confident assessment of the merit of a program, it is usually important to have a strong causal analysis in order to demonstrate what effects the program has. In addition, although many advocates of causal analysis have not yet recognized it, evaluators frequently should use descriptive methods in an adjunct capacity, especially when concerns exist about rights and liberties. Yet causal analysis is not always required for the assessment of merit and worth. Description alone can satisfactorily provide the needed information in some cases. Descriptive methods, especially in the form of ongoing performance measurement systems, can indicate whether conditions are improving after some policy or program has been implemented. To take a concrete example, states are taking a more definitive stance in selecting criteria and setting standards for judging the performance of schools. Using these standards to assess school performance may provide an indication of the merit of schools that is sufficient for the decisions that must be made. Now, a school's outcomes may be the result of factors other than the quality of teaching and learning (for example, they may result from the attributes of incoming students). Nevertheless, if the use of standards can direct the attention of school officials and state boards of education to schools that are clearly falling below acceptable performance levels, that may stimulate actions that result in students' being better off, even though the forces causing low levels of student learning have not been positively identified. This illustrates that evaluators must weigh the strengths and weaknesses of their assisted sensemaking techniques in producing information that can result in social betterment. Choosing methods is not simply a matter of choosing the techniques that allow the most confident causal attribution.

> *Evaluation practice can be enhanced by taking greater care*
> *and requiring more rigor in systematically probing values,*
> *including the values of those directly affected by the*
> *program and of those who have roles in democratic*

*societies, including the public. The results of values inquiry
should be incorporated in the planning of evaluations and
in the interpreting of their results.*

Values are as much a part of natural sensemaking as are representations of experiences. The same is true in assisted sensemaking. All Western democracies have ongoing open conflicts about which values are most important. For example, one enduring question is whether some restriction on individual liberties is justified by other societal benefits. Thus restrictions on drunk driving have been justified by U.S. society as a whole because of the benefit of increased public safety and specifically the reduction of traffic accidents and fatalities. However, in the United States, most restrictions on gun ownership have not yet been justified by society as a whole in terms of their potential to reduce deaths from gunshots. Values of society generally, values of those directly affected by the programs, and values of those elected to represent citizens in public decision making all should bear on how evaluations are conducted. The systematic study of the values surrounding a particular program can be sequenced with other evaluation activities. The findings generated in values inquiries can then be used in planning evaluations that will produce the appropriate and useful information. Values findings are especially critical for making choices about the outcomes to study, and are also often important in choices about the level(s) of aggregation to emphasize, the level(s) of molecularity to seek in explanatory accounts, and the mix of qualitative and quantitative methods that will best serve the information needs at hand. The results of values inquiry, which indicate what outcomes are most valued by whom, should also used in interpreting the findings from other inquiry modes.

Values inquiry is an alternative to other guides, such as program goals or individual needs, that might be used to direct evaluation planning and interpretation. Evaluations are improved when evaluators are sensitive to the interplay of values that surrounds every public program and to the choices in an evaluation that privilege some values over others. Bias in the selection of values will be reduced over the long haul as evaluators alter their conception of the processes that can illuminate values. Rather than focusing only on stakeholder processes or on procedures to develop logic models, evaluators should consider the full range of methods for exploring and confirming value positions, thereby increasing their awareness of the need for rigor and their ability to achieve it in order to reduce bias in conclusions about values.

> *Even in a single inquiry, evaluation should mirror natural sensemaking, with a dynamic interplay between evidence and explanations, between discovery and confirmation. And evaluation is best done when not restricted to a single inquiry.*

The benefits of sequencing values inquiry and other evaluation methods is one illustration of the benefits of combining methods from different inquiry modes. Many other examples exist, such as the use of classification to identify subgroups of clients that can then be examined in causal analysis. At the level of evaluation purposes, different purposes predominate at different stages in the life cycle of a policy or program, and evaluation activities should generally be tailored to the sensemaking needs of the day (or of the foreseeable future). In addition, funding agencies—including foundations—commonly should support a portfolio of evaluation projects to address the multiple information needs of different parties in a democracy at a given point in time as well as the different information needs expected for the future.

Even in a single evaluation, evaluators must be skilled both in testing explanatory accounts that have been proffered and in developing new explanations. Both are integral to the progress of knowledge and to the use of knowledge for social betterment. And both are part of the ongoing sensemaking process of developing possible explanations for events or experiences and then checking to see whether the explanations are consistent with patterns in the data.

This *retroduction* process involves moving from explanations to evidence and then using evidence to generate more precise explanations. Evaluators maximize the effectiveness of evaluations when they explicitly attend to underlying mechanisms and possible mediating and moderating effects. Evaluators studying these mechanisms need to be familiar with the array of methods that can be used to implement the pattern matching approaches of competitive elaboration and principled discovery.

> *Evaluation theory should be grounded in relevant philosophy of science as well as in evaluation theory and practice. Commonsense realism offers valuable support to an assisted sensemaking approach to evaluation.*

From the beginning of this book we have paid homage to our realist roots. Realism has appeal as both a social philosophy and a philosophy of science. American realists, such as Hilary Putnam, can help evaluators understand how needs and values are important in the context of developing sensemaking support for social betterment. Continental realists can contribute to an understanding of the complexities of the world and a clearer view of the process by which people can bring their understanding of the world into closer alignment with the way the world actually works. Both sets of contemporary realists strip away illusory goals of a singular, absolute truth. Together they provide a commonsense warrant for claims derived from systematic evaluation inquiry, a warrant that supports the justification provided by the successes of past practice.

Evaluators who strive to make sense out of the world and to contribute to social betterment should feel comfortable with a philosophy that recognizes that there are real, mind-independent conditions out there in the world that make a difference in the lives of people. Paraphrasing Bhaskar, one must be a realist about things to believe in the possibility of making things better. And commonsense realism has an extremely important additional benefit—it removes the necessity to take sides in the civil strife that has drained so much of evaluators' energy away from the real goal of social betterment, the paradigm wars.

> *Neither quantitative nor qualitative methods are superior in all evaluation situations. Each inquiry mode corresponds to a functional aspect of sensemaking and each can be addressed through both qualitative and quantitative methods. More generally, commonsense realism, integrated with sensemaking, offers a potent grounding for a lasting peace following the paradigm wars.*

A vocal minority of evaluators has too long dwelt on their preference for either quantitative or qualitative methods and on their concomitant ideological distinctions as the core of their professional identity. Too much time and intellectual capital have been spent in the paradigm wars. Although the qualitative and quantitative traditions each developed in association with somewhat different practice traditions, these distinctions no longer appear necessary. The very concept of sensemaking suggests a marriage of qualitative and quantitative methods, a union sanctioned by realism. Admittedly, certain methods may be preferable for certain functions in at least some contexts. With the wealth of tools at their disposal, professional evaluators need to be experts in establishing what it is that needs to be done and what methods it should be done with. Decisions about methods should revolve around the type of information that is most likely to lead to an adequate answer to an important issue for social betterment, whether the methods belong to the inquiry mode of description, causal analysis, classification, or values inquiry. The practice of evaluation will benefit, we are convinced, when the focus of discussion in the field about methods changes from qualitative versus quantitative to how best to combine and sequence purposes and inquiry modes.

We have offered some specific suggestions for bridging the gap between the quantitative and qualitative camps. For example, some quantitative proponents seem resistant to the study of values, whereas many qualitative proponents focus largely on values issues. Perhaps some quantitative evaluators will become more interested in values inquiry when they see that values are also amenable to investigation with methods they are comfortable with, such as surveys. Some qualitative proponents seem to dislike quantitative methods because traditional quantitative methods are usually preordained and thus less open to the emergence of new questions during the course of the investigation. Perhaps familiarity with quantitative methods of principled discovery will allow them to reconsider their views. We ourselves, perhaps because our training is not as deep in qualitative methods as in quantitative ones, have given somewhat more emphasis to quantitative than qualitative methods and examples in our discussions of description, classification, causal analysis, and values inquiry. If our fourfold categorization of methods is accepted and used by others, we expect that they will expand upon those discussions and examples.

> *The integrated framework and terminology of betterment, purpose, and inquiry modes should offer evaluators from different traditions and camps an opportunity to discuss how evaluations can be improved to achieve social betterment.*

It is not enough for all of us in evaluation to put aside our methodological issues under the banner of assisted sensemaking and realism. It is not enough to recognize that the means for assisting our natural sensemaking abilities have been developed through the years for very good reasons. We also need terms with shared meanings to facilitate our communication about what can be expected from an evaluation, the ways in which the evaluation intention may be realized, and how the evaluation will be conducted. Evaluation sponsors need to be able to speak a common language with evaluators. Evaluators and program personnel must be able to communicate directly and clearly. We need a language that provides sufficient detail for professionals and that conforms sufficiently with commonsense usage to enable conversations across these roles. Evaluation purposes—assessment of merit and worth, program and organizational improvement, oversight and compliance, and knowledge development—form the first layer of the needed vocabulary. Inquiry modes—description, classification, causal analysis, and values inquiry—form a second layer. With this framework, evaluators, evaluation sponsors, and others can talk with specificity during the planning, design, and critique of evaluation. By expanding our vocabulary in these ways, and by avoiding the hot button terms that distract evaluators and their potential audiences from the mission of social betterment, we may improve our collective ability to make sense of social programs and policies in the ongoing struggle toward social betterment.

References

Aaron, H. J., Mann, T. E., & Taylor, T. (Eds.). (1994). *Values and public policy*. Washington, DC: Brookings Institution.

Affholter, D. P. (1994). Outcome monitoring. In J. S. Wholey, H. P. Hatry, & K. E. Newcomer (Eds.), *Handbook of practical program evaluation* (pp. 96–118). San Francisco: Jossey-Bass.

Aiken, L. S., & West, S. G. (1991). *Multiple regression: Testing and interpreting interactions*. Thousand Oaks, CA: Sage.

Aitken, M., & Rubin, D. B. (1985). Estimation and hypothesis testing in finite mixture models. *Journal of the Royal Statistical Society, Ser. B(47)*, 67–75.

Altschuld, J. W. (1999). The certification of evaluators: Highlights from a report submitted to the Board of Directors of the American Evaluation Association. *American Journal of Evaluation, 20*(3), 481–493.

Alwin, D. F., & Krosnick, J. A. (1991). Aging, cohorts, and the stability of sociopolitical orientations over the life span. *American Journal of Sociology, 97*, 169–195.

Aronson, J. L., Harré, R., & Way, E. C. (1995). *Realism rescued*. Chicago: Open Court.

Arrow, K. J. (1963). *Social choice and individual values* (2nd ed.). New Haven, CT: Yale University Press.

Austin, J., Jones, M., & Boylard, M. (1993). The growing use of jail boot camps: The current state of the art. *A National Institute of Justice Research in Brief* (NCJ 143708). Washington, DC: National Institute of Justice.

Bailey, K. D. (1994). *Typologies and taxonomies: An introduction to classification techniques* (Sage University Paper Series on Quantitative Applications in the Social Sciences). Thousand Oaks, CA: Sage.

Bamberger, M. (2000). The evaluation of international development programs: A view from the front. *American Journal of Evaluation, 21*(1), 95–102.

Barnett, W. S. (1995). Long-term effects of early childhood programs on cognitive and school outcomes. *The Future of Children, 5*(3), 25–49.

Baron, R. M., & Kenny, D. A. (1986). The moderator-mediator variable distinction in social psychological research: Conceptual, strategic, and statistical considerations. *Journal of Personality and Social Psychology, 51*, 1173–1182.

Bartlett, F. C. (1932/1995). *Remembering: A study in experimental and social psychology.* New York: Cambridge University Press.

Behl-Chadha, G. (1996). Basic-level and superordinate-like categorical representations in early infancy. *Cognition, 60*, 105–141.

Behn, R. D. (1997). Linking measurement and motivation: A challenge for education. *Advances in Educational Administration, 5*, 15–58.

Behrens, J. T. (1997). Does the White Racial Identity Attitude Scale measure racial identity? *Journal of Counseling Psychology, 44*, 3–12.

Bentler, P. M. (1992). *EQS structural equations program manual.* Los Angeles, CA: BMDP Statistical Software.

Bentler, P. M., & Bonnet, D. G. (1990). Significance tests and goodness of fit in the analysis of covariance structures. *Psychological Bulletin, 88*, 588–606.

Berg, B. L. (1998). *Qualitative research methods for the social sciences* (3rd ed.). Needham Heights, MA: Allyn & Bacon.

Berlin, I. (1990). *The crooked timber of humanity: Chapters in the history of ideas* (H. Hardy, Ed.). Princeton, NJ: Princeton University Press.

Berlin, I. (1998). My intellectual path. *New York Review, 45*(8), 53–60.

Bezruki, D., Mueller, J., & McKim, K. (1999). Legislative utilization of evaluations. In R. K. Jonas (Ed.), *Legislative program evaluation: Utilization-driven research for decision makers* (New Directions for Evaluation, No. 81, pp. 11–22). San Francisco: Jossey-Bass.

Bhaskar, R. A. (1975). *A realist theory of science.* Leeds, UK: Leeds Books.

Bhaskar, R. A. (1978). *A realist theory of science.* Atlantic Highlands, NJ: Humanities Press.

Bhaskar, R. A. (1979). *The possibility of naturalism: A philosophical critique of the contemporary human sciences*. Hemel Hempstead, UK: Harvester Press.

Bhaskar, R. A. (1989). *Reclaiming reality*. New York: Verso.

Bickman, L. (1985). Improving established statewide programs: A component theory of evaluation. *Evaluation Review, 9*, 189–208.

Bickman, L. (Ed.). (1987). *Using program theory in evaluation* (New Directions for Program Evaluation, No. 33). San Francisco: Jossey-Bass.

Bickman, L. (Ed.). (1990). *Advances in program theory* (New Directions for Program Evaluation, No. 47). San Francisco: Jossey-Bass.

Bickman, L., & Peterson, K. A. (1990). Using program theory to describe and measure program quality. In L. Bickman (Ed.), *Advances in program theory* (New Directions for Program Evaluation, No. 47, pp. 62–72). San Francisco: Jossey-Bass.

Bishop, G. F., Tuchfarber, A. J., & Oldendick, R. W. (1986). Opinions on fictitious issues: The pressure to answer survey questions. *Public Opinion Quarterly, 50*(2), 240–250.

Blashfield, R. K., & Aldenderfer, M. S. (1988). The methods and problems of cluster analysis. In J. R. Nesselroade & R. B. Cattell (Eds.), *Handbook of multivariate experimental psychology* (2nd ed.), pp. 447–473. New York: Plenum.

Blumer, H. (1969). *Symbolic interactionism: Perspective and method*. Berkeley: University of California Press.

Bohman, J., & Rehg, W. (Eds.). (1997). *Deliberative democracy: Essays on reason and politics*. Cambridge, MA: MIT Press.

Boruch, R. F. (1997). *Randomized experiments for planning and evaluation: A practical guide*. Thousand Oaks, CA: Sage.

Boruch, R. F., & Cordray, D. S. (1980). *An appraisal of educational program evaluations: Federal, state, and local agencies*. Final Report of U.S. Department of Education Contract No. 300-79-0467.

Boruch, R. F., & Rindskopf, D. M. (1984). Data analysis. In L. Rutman (Ed.), *Evaluation research methods: A basic guide* (pp. 121–157). Thousand Oaks, CA: Sage.

Boruch, R. F., & Wothke, W. (Eds.). (1985). *Randomization and field experimentation*. San Francisco: Jossey-Bass.

Box, G.F.P., Jenkins, G. M., & Reinsel, G. C. (1994). *Time series analysis: Forecasting and control*. Upper Saddle River, NJ: Prentice Hall.

Boyd, R. (1990). Realism, conventionality and "realism about." In G. Boolos (Ed.), *Festschrift for Hilary Putnam*. Cambridge: Cambridge University Press.

Boyd, R. (1991). On the current status of scientific realism. In R. Boyd, P. Gasper, & J. D. Trout (Eds.), *The philosophy of science* (pp. 195–222). Cambridge, MA: MIT Press.

Bradburn, N. M., & Sudman, S. (1988). *Polls and surveys: Understanding what they tell us*. San Francisco: Jossey-Bass.

Braucht, G. N., & Reichardt, C. S. (1993). A computerized approach to trickle-process, random assignment. *Evaluation Review, 17*(1), 79–90.

Bredekamp, S. (1986). The reliability and validity of the Early Childhood Classroom Observation Scale for accrediting early childhood programs. *Early Childhood Research Quarterly, 1*(2), 103–108.

Bredekamp, S., & Copple, C. (1997). *Developmentally appropriate practice in early childhood programs*. Washington, DC: National Association for the Education of Young Children.

Brett, B. (1996). Using a template for a summarizing assessment of the Teachers Academy for Mathematics and Science. In M. A. Scheirer (Ed.), *A user's guide to program templates: A new tool for evaluating program content* (New Directions for Evaluation, No. 72, pp. 49–60). San Francisco: Jossey-Bass.

Bryk, A. S. (Ed.). (1983). *Stakeholder-based evaluation* (New Directions for Program Evaluation, No. 17). San Francisco: Jossey-Bass.

Bryk, A. S., & Raudenbush, S. W. (1992). *Hierarchical linear models: Applications and data analysis methods*. Thousand Oaks, CA: Sage.

Buckner, J. C. (1991). Pathways into homelessness: An epidemiological analysis. In D. J. Rog (Ed.), *Evaluating programs for the homeless* (New Directions for Evaluation, No. 52, pp. 17–30). San Francisco: Jossey-Bass.

Bugler, D. T., & Henry, G. T. (1998). Evaluation of Georgia's HOPE Scholarship Program: Impact on college attendance and performance. Council for School Performance, Georgia State University.

Bunge, M. (1997). Mechanism and explanation. *Philosophy of Social Sciences, 27*, 410–465.

Burchinal, M. R., Campbell, F. A., Bryant, D. M., Wasik, B. H., & Ramey, C. T. (1997). Early intervention and mediating processes in cognitive performance of children of low-income African American families. *Child Development, 68*(5), 935–954.

Byron, K., & Henry, G. T. (1998). *Quality of Georgia's Prekindergarten Program: 1997–98 school year.* Atlanta: Georgia State University, Applied Research Center.

Campbell, D. T. (1957). Factors relevant to the validity of experiments in social settings. *Psychological Bulletin, 54,* 456–453.

Campbell, D. T. (1966). Pattern matching as an essential in distal knowing. In K. R. Hammond (Ed.), *The psychology of Egon Brunswik* (pp. 81–106). Austin, TX: Holt, Rinehart, and Winston.

Campbell, D. T. (1969a). A phenomonology of the other one: Corrigible, hypothetical, and critical. In T. Mischel (Ed.), *Human action: Conceptual and empirical issues* (pp. 41–69). Orlando: Academic Press.

Campbell, D. T. (1969b). Reforms as experiments. *American Psychologist, 24,* 409–429.

Campbell, D. T. (1974a). Downward causation in hierarchically organized biological systems. In F. J. Ayala & T. Dobzhansky (Eds.), *Studies in the philosophy of biology* (pp. 179–186). London: Macmillan.

Campbell, D. T. (1974b). Evolutionary epistemology. In P. A. Schilpp (Ed.), *The philosophy of Karl Popper* (pp. 413–463). La Salle, IL: Open Court.

Campbell, D. T. (1974c). *Qualitative knowing in action research.* Kurt Lewin Address presented at the annual meeting of the American Psychological Association, New Orleans.

Campbell, D. T. (1975a). Assessing the impact of planned social change. In G. M. Lyons (Ed.), *Social research and public policies* (pp. 3–45). Hanover, NH: Dartmouth College, Public Affairs Center.

Campbell, D. T. (1975b). Degrees of freedom and the case study. *Comparative Political Studies, 8,* 178–193.

Campbell, D. T. (1977). *Descriptive epistemology: Psychological, sociological, and evolutionary* (William James Lectures, Harvard University).

Campbell, D. T. (1984). Can we be scientific in applied social science? In R. F. Connor, D. G. Altman, & C. Jackson (Eds.), *Evaluation studies review annual* (No. 9, pp. 26–48). Thousand Oaks, CA: Sage.

Campbell, D. T. (1988). *Methodology and epistemology for social science: Selected papers* (E. S. Overman, Ed.). Chicago: University of Chicago Press.

Campbell, D. T. (1990). Levels of organization, downward causation, and the selection-theory approach to evolutionary epistemology. In E. Tobach & G. Greenberg (Eds.), *Scientific methodology in the study of mind: Evolutionary epistemology* (pp. 1–17). Hillsdale, NJ: Erlbaum.

Campbell, D. T. (1991). Coherentist empiricism, hermeneutics, and the commensurability of paradigms. *International Journal of Educational Research, 15,* 587–597.

Campbell, D. T., & Fiske, D. W. (1959). Convergent and discriminant validation by the multitrait-multimethod matrix. *Psychological Bulletin, 56,* 81–105.

Campbell, D. T., & Stanley, J. C. (1966). *Experimental and quasi-experimental designs for research.* Skokie, IL: Rand McNally.

Campbell, J. (1997). How consumers/survivors are evaluating the quality of psychiatric care. *Evaluation Review, 21,* 357–363.

Caracelli, V. J., & Greene, J. C. (1997). Crafting mixed-method evaluation designs. In J. C. Greene & V. J. Caracelli (Eds.), *Advances in mixed-method evaluation: The challenges and benefits of integrating diverse paradigms* (New Directions for Evaluation, No. 74, pp. 19–32). San Francisco: Jossey-Bass.

Carmines, E. G., & Stimson, J. A. (1986). On the structure and sequence of issue evolution, *American Political Science Review, 80*(3), 901–920.

Cattell, R. B. (1952). *Factor analysis: An introduction and manual for the psychologist and social scientist.* New York: HarperCollins.

Chelimsky, E. (1991). On the social science contribution to governmental decision-making. *Science, 254,* 226–231.

Chelimsky, E. (1997). The coming transformations in evaluation. In E. Chelimsky & W. R. Shadish (Eds.), *Evaluation for the 21st Century: A handbook* (pp. 1–26). Thousand Oaks, CA: Sage.

Chen, H-t. (1990). *Theory-driven evaluations.* Thousand Oaks, CA: Sage.

Chen, H-t, & Rossi, P. H. (1983). Evaluating with sense: The theory-driven approach. *Evaluation Review, 7*(3), 283–302.

Chubb, J. E., & Moe, T. M. (1990). *Politics, markets, and America's schools.* Washington, DC: Brookings Institution.

Clogg, C. C., & Shockey, J. W. (1988). Multivariate analysis of discrete data. In J. R. Nesselroade & R. B. Cattel (Eds.), *Handbook of multivariate experimental psychology* (2nd ed., pp. 337–365). New York: Plenum.

Cochran, W. G. (1965). The planning of observational studies of human populations. *Journal of the Royal Statistical Society, 182*, 234–255.

Coffey, A., & Atkinson, P. (1996). *Making sense of qualitative data: Complementary research strategies*. Thousand Oaks, CA: Sage.

Cohen, D. K. (1983). Evaluation and reform. In A. S. Bryk (Ed.), *Stakeholder-based evaluation* (pp. 73–82). San Francisco: Jossey-Bass.

Cohen, J. (1988). *Statistical power analysis for the behavioral sciences*. Hillsdale, NJ: Erlbaum.

Cohen, J. (1997). Deliberation and democratic legitimacy. In J. Bohman & W. Rehg (Eds.), *Deliberative democracy: Essays on reason and politics* (pp. 67–92). Cambridge, MA: MIT Press.

Conner, R. F. (1977). Selecting a control group: An analysis of the randomization process in twelve social reform programs. *Evaluation Quarterly, 1*(2), 195–244.

Conrad, K. J., & Buelow, J. R. (1990). Developing and testing program classification and function theories. In L. Bickman (Ed.), *Advances in program theory* (New Directions for Program Evaluation, No. 47, pp. 73–88). San Francisco: Jossey-Bass.

Consortium for Longitudinal Studies. (1983). *As the twig is bent: Lasting effects of preschool programs*. Hillsdale, NJ: Erlbaum.

Converse, P. E. (1964). The nature of belief systems in mass publics. In D. E. Apter (Ed.), *Ideology and discontent* (pp. 206–261). New York: Free Press.

Converse, P. E. (1971). Attitudes and non-attitudes: Continuation of a dialogue. *Public Opinion Quarterly, 35*, 168–189.

Cook, T. D. (1993). A quasi-sampling theory of the generalization of causal relationships. In L. B. Sechrest & A. G. Scott (Eds.), *Understanding causes and generalizing about them* (New Directions for Program Evaluation, No. 57, pp. 39–82). San Francisco: Jossey-Bass.

Cook, T. D. (1997). Lessons learned in evaluation over the last 25 years. In E. Chelimsky & W. R. Shadish (Eds.), *Evaluation for the 21st century: A handbook* (pp. 30–52). Thousand Oaks, CA: Sage.

Cook, T. D., Appleton, H., Conner, R., Schaffer, A., Tamkin, G., & Weber, S. J. (1975). *"Sesame Street" revisited: A case study in evaluation research*. New York: Russell Sage Foundation.

Cook, T. D., & Campbell, D. T. (1979). *Quasi-experimentation: Design and analysis issues for field settings*. Skokie, IL: Rand McNally.

Cook, T. D., Leviton, L. C., & Shadish, W. R. (1985). Program evaluation. In G. Lindzey & E. Aronson (Eds.), *Handbook of social psychology* (3rd ed.) (pp. 699–777). New York: Random House.

Cook, T. D., & Reichardt, C. S. (1979). *Qualitative and quantitative methods in evaluation research*. Thousand Oaks, CA: Sage.

Cook, T. D., & Shadish, W. R. (1986). Program evaluation: The worldly science. *Annual Review of Psychology, 37,* 193–232.

Covert, R. W. (1995). A twenty-year veteran's reflections on the guiding principles for evaluators. In W. R. Shadish, D. L. Newman, M. A. Scheirer, & C. Wye (Eds.), *Guiding principles for evaluators* (New Directions for Evaluation, No. 66, pp. 35–46). San Francisco: Jossey-Bass.

Cronbach, L. J. (1975). Beyond the two disciplines of scientific psychology. *American Psychologist, 30,* 116–127.

Cronbach, L. J. (1982). *Designing evaluations of educational and social programs*. San Francisco: Jossey-Bass.

Cronbach, L. J. (1989). Construct validation after thirty years. In R. L. Linn (Ed.), *Intelligence: Measurement, theory, and public policy: Proceedings of a symposium in honor of Lloyd G. Humphreys* (pp. 147–171). Champaign, IL: University of Illinois Press.

Cronbach, L. J., & Meehl, P. E. (1955). Construct validity in psychological tests. *Psychological Bulletin, 52,* 281–302.

Dahl, R. A. (1956/1973). *A preface to democratic theory*. Chicago: University of Chicago Press.

Datta, L-e. (1994a). *A matter of consensus*. Washington, DC: U.S. Government Printing Office.

Datta, L-e. (1994b). Paradigm wars: A basis for peaceful coexistence and beyond. In C. S. Reichardt & S. F. Rallis, (Eds.), *The quantitative-qualitative debate: New perspectives* (New Directions for Program Evaluation 61, pp. 53–70). San Francisco: Jossey-Bass.

Datta, L-e. (2000). Crafting a non-partisan evaluation in a partisan world. *American Journal of Evaluation, 21,* 1–14.

Dembo, R., Turner, G., Schmeidler, J., Camille-Chin, S., Borden, P., & Manning, D. (1996). Development and evaluation of a classification of high risk youths entering a juvenile assessment center. *Substance Use and Misuse, 31,* 301–322.

Denzin, N. K., & Lincoln, Y. S. (1994). Introduction: Entering the field of qualitative research. In N. K. Denzin & Y. S. Lincoln (Eds.), *Handbook of qualitative research,* (pp. 1–18). Thousand Oaks, CA: Sage.

Dewey, J. (1966). *Democracy and education: An introduction of the philosophy of education.* New York: Free Press.

Diaconis, P. (1985). Theories of data analysis: From magical thinking through classical statistics. In D. C. Hoagland, F. Mosteller, & J. W. Tukey (Eds.), *Exploring data tables, trends, and shapes* (pp. 1–36). New York: Wiley.

Dillman, D. A., Sangster, R. L., Tarnai, J., & Rockwood, T. H. (1996). Understanding differences in people's answers to telephone and mail surveys. In M. T. Braverman & J. K. Slater (Eds.), *Advances in survey research* (New Directions for Evaluation, No. 70, pp. 45–61). San Francisco: Jossey-Bass.

Dillon, W. R., & Goldstein, M. (1984). *Multivariate analysis: Methods and applications.* New York: Wiley.

Divorski, S. (1996). Differences in the approaches of auditors and evaluators to the examination of government policies and programs. In C. Wisler (Ed.), *Evaluation and auditing: Prospects for convergence* (New Directions for Evaluation, No. 71, pp. 7–14). San Francisco: Jossey-Bass.

Edelman, M. (1964). *Symbolic uses of politics.* Urbana, IL: University of Illinois Press.

Elster, J. (1997). The market and the forum: Three varieties of political theory. In J. Bohman & W. Rehg (Eds.), *Deliberative democracy: Essays on reason and politics* (pp. 3–33). Cambridge, MA: MIT Press.

Entwhisle, D. R. (1995). The role of schools in sustaining early childhood program benefits. *The Future of Children, 5*(3), 122–144.

Erickson, E. P. & Entwhisle, D. R. (1994). Subcultural diversity in American families. In L. L'Abate (Ed.), *Handbook of developmental family psychology and psychopathology* (Wiley Series on Personality Processes, pp. 132–456). New York: Wiley.

Erickson, F. E. (1986). Qualitative methods in research on teaching. In M. Wittrock (Ed.), *Handbook of research on teaching* (3rd ed.) (pp. 119–161). Old Tappan, NJ: Macmillan.

Estlund, D. (1997). Beyond fairness and deliberation: The epistemic dimension of democratic authority. In J. Bohman & W. Rehg (Eds.), *Deliberative democracy: Essays on reason and politics* (pp. 173–203). Cambridge, MA: MIT Press.

Etzioni, A. (1995). *Rights and the common good: The communitarian perspective.* New York: St. Martin's Press.

Evans, J. W. (1977). Head Start: Comments on the criticisms. In F. G. Caro (Ed.), *Readings in evaluation research* (2nd ed., pp. 348–354). New York: Russell Sage Foundation.

Everitt, B. S. (1993). *Cluster analysis* (3rd ed.). New York: Halsted Press.

Festinger, L. (1957). *A theory of cognitive dissonance*. New York: Harper-Collins.

Fetterman, D., Kaftarian, S. J., & Wandersman, A. (1996). *Empowerment evaluation: Knowledge and tools for self-assessment and accountability*. Thousand Oaks, CA: Sage.

Fishkin, J. S. (1995). *The voice of the people: Public opinion and democracy*. New Haven, CT: Yale University Press.

Fiske, S. T., Kenny, D. A., & Taylor, S. E. (1982). Structural models for the mediation of salience effects on attribution. *Journal of Experimental Social Psychology, 18*, 105–127.

Fiske, S. T., & Taylor, S. E. (1991). *Social cognition* (2nd ed.). New York: McGraw-Hill.

Flew, A. (1990). Parapsychology: Science or pseudoscience? In P. Grim (Ed.), *Philosophy of science and the occult* (pp. 214–231). New York: State University of New York Press.

Flick, U. (1998). *An introduction to qualitative research*. Thousand Oaks, CA: Sage.

Fournier, D. M. (Ed.). (1995). *Reasoning in evaluation: Inferential links and leaps* (New Directions for Evaluation, No. 68). San Francisco: Jossey-Bass.

Frede, E., & Barnett, W. S. (1992). Developmentally appropriate public school preschool: A study of implementation of the High/Scope curriculum and its effects on disadvantaged children's skills at first grade. *Early Childhood Research Quarterly, 7*, 483–499.

Free, L. A., & Cantril, H. (1967). *The political beliefs of Americans: A study of public opinion*. New Brunswick, NJ: Rutgers University Press.

Friedlander, D., & Robins, P. K. (1997). The distributional impacts of social programs. *Evaluation Review, 21*, 531–553.

Gilbert, D. T. (1998). Ordinary psychology. In D. T. Gilbert & S. T. Fiske (Eds.), *The handbook of social psychology*, Vol. 2 (4th ed.) (pp. 89–150). New York: McGraw-Hill.

Gilbert, D. T., & Osborne, R. E. (1989). Thinking backward: Some curable and incurable consequences of cognitive busyness. *Journal of Personality and Social Psychology, 57*, 940–949.

Ginsberg, M. (1973). Progress in the modern era. In P. P. Weiner (Ed.), *Dictionary of the history of ideas* (pp. 633–650). New York: Scribner.

Glaser, B., & Strauss, A. L. (1967). *The discovery of grounded theory: Strategies for qualitative research.* Hawthorne, NY: Aldine de Gruyter.

Glazer, N. (1994). How social problems are born. *The Public Interest, 115,* 31–44.

Gore, A. (1993). *Creating a government that works better and costs less: The Report of the National Performance Review.* New York: Plume Books.

Gorman, D. M. (1998). The irrelevance of evidence in the development of school-based drug prevention policy, 1986–1996. *Evaluation Review, 22,* 118–146.

Gorsuch, R. L. (1983). *Factor analysis.* Hillsdale, NJ: Erlbaum.

Glymph, A., & Henry, G. T. (1997). How well did schools perform? Simpson's paradox and analyzing outcomes. In G. T. Henry (Ed.), *Creating effective graphs: Solutions for representing evaluation data* (New Directions for Evaluation, No. 73, pp. 33–42). San Francisco: Jossey-Bass.

Gramlich, E. M. (1990). *Benefit-cost analysis for government programs* (2nd ed.). New York: McGraw-Hill.

Greco-Vigorito, C. (1996). Categorization based on attribute versus relational similarity in 4- to 10-month-old infants. *Perceptual and Motor Skills, 82*(3, Pt. 1), 915–927.

Green, D. P. (1992). The price elasticity of mass preferences. *American Political Science Review, 86*(1), 128–148.

Greene, J. G. (1988). Stakeholder participation and utilization in program evaluation. *Evaluation Review, 12*(2), 91–116.

Greene, J. G., & Caracelli, V. J. (1997). Defining and describing the paradigm issue in mixed-method evaluation. In J. C. Greene & V. J. Caracelli (Eds.), *Advances in mixed-method evaluation: The challenges and benefits of integrating diverse paradigms* (New Directions for Evaluation, No. 74, pp. 5–17). San Francisco: Jossey-Bass.

Greenwald, A. G., Pratkanis, A. R., Leippe, M. R., & Baumgardner, M. H. (1986). Under what conditions does theory obstruct research progress? *Psychological Bulletin, 93,* 216–229.

Groves, R. M. (1989). *Survey errors and survey costs.* New York: Wiley.

Guba, E. G. (1990). The alternative paradigm dialog. In E. C. Guba (Ed.), *The paradigm dialog* (pp. 17–27). Thousand Oaks, CA: Sage.

Guba, E. G., & Lincoln, Y. S. (1989). *Fourth generation evaluation.* Thousand Oaks, CA: Sage.

Gueron, J. M. (1997). Learning about welfare reform: Lessons from state-based evaluations. In D. Fournier & D. J. Rog (Eds.), *Progress and future directions in evaluation: Perspectives on theory, practice, and methods* (New Directions for Evaluation, No. 76, pp. 79–94). San Francisco: Jossey-Bass.

Habermas, J. (1975). *Legitimation crisis.* Boston: Beacon Press.

Habermas, J. (1996a). *Between facts and norms: Contributions to a discourse theory of law and democracy.* Cambridge, MA: MIT Press.

Habermas, J. (1996b). Three normative models of democracy. In S. Benhabib (Ed.), *Democracy and difference: Contesting the boundaries of the political* (pp. 21–30). Princeton, NJ: Princeton University Press.

Habermas, J. (1997). Popular sovereign as procedure. In J. Bohman & W. Rehg (Eds.), *Deliberative democracy: Essays on reason and politics* (pp. 35–66). Cambridge, MA: MIT Press.

Hacking, I. (1991). Experimentation and scientific realism. In R. Boyd, P. Gasper, & J. D. Trout (Eds.), *The philosophy of science* (pp. 247–260). Cambridge, MA: MIT Press.

Harkreader, S. A., & Henry, G. T. (in press). Using performance measurement systems for assessing the merit and worth of reforms. *American Journal of Evaluation, 21*(2).

Harkreader, S. A., & Weathersby, J. (1998). Staff development and student achievement: Making the connection in Georgia schools. Atlanta Council for School Performance. Atlanta: Georgia State University.

Harms, T., & Clifford, R. M. (1980). *Early Childhood Environment Rating Scale.* New York: Teachers College Press.

Harré, R. (1986). *Varieties of realism.* Oxford, UK: Blackwell.

Hartigan, J. A. (1975). *Clustering algorithms.* New York: Wiley.

Hatry, H. P. (1997). Where the rubber meets the road: Performance measurement for state and local public agencies. In K. Newcomer (Ed.), *Using performance measurement to improve public and nonprofit programs* (New Directions for Evaluation, No. 75, pp. 31–44). San Francisco: Jossey-Bass.

Heclo, H. (1978). Issue networks and the executive establishment. In A. King (Ed.), *The new American political system* (pp. 87–124). Washington, DC: American Enterprise Institute.

Heider, F. (1944). Social perception and phenomenal causality. *Psychological Review, 51,* 358–374.

Henderson, L., Basile, K., & Henry, G. (1999). *Pre-kindergarten longitudinal study, 1997–1998 school year: Annual report*. Atlanta: Georgia State University, Applied Research Center.

Henry, G. T. (1990). *Practical sampling*. Thousand Oaks, CA: Sage.

Henry, G. T. (1995). *Graphing data: Techniques for display and analysis*. Thousand Oaks, CA: Sage.

Henry, G. T. (19̊ ̊a). Community-based accountability: A theory of accountability and school improvement. *Phi Delta Kappan, 78*(1), 85–90.

Henry, G. T. (1996b). Does the public have a role in evaluation? Surveys and democratic discourse. In M. T. Braverman & J. K. Slater (Eds.), *Advances in survey research* (New Directions for Evaluation, No. 70, pp. 3–15). San Francisco: Jossey-Bass.

Henry, G. T. (Ed.). (1997). *Creating effective graphs: Solutions for representing evaluation data* (New Directions for Evaluation, No. 73). San Francisco: Jossey-Bass.

Henry, G. T. (1999, November). *What do we expect from preschool? A systematic inquiry into values conflicts and consensus*. Paper presented at the annual conference of the American Evaluation Association, Orlando.

Henry, G. T., & Brackett, M. H. (2000). Council for School Performance. *American Journal of Evaluation, 21*(1), 105–107.

Henry, G. T., & Bugler, D. T. (1998, November). Evaluating Georgia's HOPE scholarship program: Impacts on college level performances. Paper presented at the annual meeting of the American Educational Research Association, Chicago, IL.

Henry, G. T., & Dickey, K. C. (1993, May–June). Implementing performance monitoring: A research and development approach. *Public Administration Review, 53*(3), 203–212.

Henry, G. T., Dickey, K. C., & Areson, J. C. (1991). Stakeholder participation in educational performance monitoring. *Educational Evaluation and Policy Analysis, 13*(2), 177–188.

Henry, G. T., & Gordon, C. S. (2000, November 2–4). The impacts of voluntary efforts to reduce air pollution: The case of the Clean Air Act of 1992. Paper presented at the Association for Public Policy Analysis and Management Annual Meetings, Seattle, WA.

Henry, G. T., & Julnes, G. (1998). Values and realist evaluation. In G. T. Henry, G. Julnes, & M. M. Mark (Eds.), *Realist evaluation: An emerging theory in support of practice* (New Directions for Evaluation, No. 78, pp. 53–72). San Francisco: Jossey-Bass.

Henry, G. T., McTaggart, M. C., & McMillan, J. A. (1992). Establishing benchmarks for outcome indicators: A statistical approach to developing performance standards, *Evaluation Review, 16*(2), 131–150.

Hess, I. (1985). *Sampling for social research surveys: 1947–1980.* Ann Arbor: Survey Research Center, Institute for Social Research, University of Michigan.

Hilgartner, S., & Bosk, C. (1988). The rise and fall of social problems: A public arenas model. *American Journal of Sociology, 94*(1), 53–78.

Hoffman, D. D. (1998). *Visual intelligence: How we create what we see.* New York: Norton.

Holtgrave, D. R. (1998). The cost-effectiveness of the components of a comprehensive HIV prevention program: A road map of the literature. In D. R. Holtgrave (Ed.), *Handbook of economic evaluation of HIV prevention programs* (pp. 127–134). New York: Plenum Press.

House, E. R. (1980). *Evaluating with validity.* Thousand Oaks, CA: Sage.

House, E. R. (1991). Realism in research. *Educational Researcher, 20,* 2–9.

House, E. R. (1993). *Professional evaluation.* Thousand Oaks, CA: Sage.

House, E. R. (1994). The future perfect of evaluation. *Evaluation Practice, 15*(3), 239–247.

House, E. R. (1995). Putting things together coherently: Logic and justice. In D. Fournier (Ed.), *Reasoning in evaluation: Inferential links and leaps* (New Directions for Evaluation, No. 68, pp. 33–48). San Francisco: Jossey-Bass.

House, E. R., & Howe, K. R. (1999). *Values in evaluation and social research.* Thousands Oaks, CA: Sage.

Hudson, W. W. (1969). *Project Breakthrough: A responsive environment field experiment with preschool children from public assistance families.* Chicago: Cook County Department of Public Aid.

Hurley, S. (1989). *Natural reasons: Personality and polity.* New York: Oxford University Press.

Jaccard, J., Turrisi, R., & Wan, C. K. (1990). *Interaction effects in multiple regression.* Sage University Paper series on Quantitative Applications in the Social Sciences. Thousand Oaks, CA: Sage.

Jaccard, J., & Wan, C. K. (1995). Measurement error in the analysis of interaction effects between continuous predictors using multiple

Lathrop, R. G., & Williams, J. E. (1990). The validity of the inverse scree tests for cluster analysis. *Educational and Psychological Measurement*, 50, 325–330.

Lin, E. L., & Murphy, G. L. (1997). Effects of background knowledge on object categorization and part detection. *Journal of Experimental Psychology: Human Perception and Performance*, 23(4), 1153–1169.

Lincoln, Y. S. (1990). The making of a constructivist: A remembrance of transformations past. In E. G. Guba (Ed.), *The paradigm dialog* (pp. 67–87). Thousand Oaks, CA: Sage.

Lincoln, Y. S., & Guba, E. G. (1985). *Naturalistic inquiry*. Thousand Oaks, CA: Sage.

Lincoln, Y. S. & Guba, E.G. (1994). RSVP: We are pleased to accept your invitation. *Evaluation Practice*, 15(2), 179–192.

Lind, E. A., & Tyler, T. R. (1988). *The social psychology of procedural justice*. New York: Plenum Press.

Lindblom, C. E. (1968). *The policy-making process*. Upper Saddle River, NJ: Prentice Hall.

Lindblom, C. E., & Cohen, D. K. (1979). *Usable knowledge: Social science and social problem solving*. New Haven, CT: Yale University Press.

Lindsay, B. G., & Basak, P. (1993). Multivariate normal mixtures: A fast consistent method of moments. *Journal of the American Statistical Association*, 88, 468–476.

Lipsey, M. W. (1993). *Theory as method: Small theories of treatments*. In L. B. Sechrest & A. G. Scott (Eds.), *Understanding causes and generalizing about them* (New Directions for Program Evaluation, No. 57, pp. 5–38). San Francisco: Jossey-Bass.

Lipsey, M. W. (1997). What can you build with thousands of bricks? Musings on the cumulation of knowledge in program evaluation. In D. Fournier & D. J. Rog (Eds.), *Progress and future directions in evaluation: Perspectives on theory, practice, and methods* (New Directions for Evaluation, No. 76, pp. 231–259). San Francisco: Jossey-Bass.

Lipsey, M. W., & Wilson, D. B. (1993). The efficacy of psychological, educational, and behavioral treatment: Confirmation from meta-analysis. *American Psychologist*, 48, 1181–1209.

Lord, C. G., Ross, L., & Lepper, M. R. (1979). Biased assimilation and attitude polarization: The effects of prior theories on subsequently considered evidence. *Journal of Personality and Social Psychology, 37,* 2098–2109.

Loucks-Horsley, S. (1996). The design of templates as tools for formative evaluation. In M. A. Scheirer (Ed.), *A user's guide to program templates: A new tool for evaluating program content* (New Directions for Evaluation, No. 72, pp. 5–24). San Francisco: Jossey-Bass.

Mackie, J. L. (1965). Causes and conditions. *American Philosophical Quarterly, 2*(4), 245–255, 261–264.

Mackie, J. L. (1974). *The cement of the universe: A study of causation.* Oxford, UK: Clarendon.

Madison, J. (1953). *The complete Madison, his basic writings* (S. K. Padover, Ed.). New York: HarperCollins.

Mansbridge, J. (1994). Public spirit in political systems. In H. J. Aaron, T. E. Mann, & T. Taylor (Eds.), *Values and public policy* (pp. 146–172). Washington, DC: Brookings Institution.

Marcantonio, R. J., & Cook, T. D. (1994). Convincing quasi-experiments: The interrupted time series and regression-discontinuity designs. In J. S. Wholey, H. P. Hatry, & K. E. Newcomer (Eds.), *Handbook of practical program evaluation* (pp. 133–154). San Francisco: Jossey-Bass.

March, J. G., & Simon, H. A. (1958). *Organizations.* New York: Wiley.

Marcon, R. (1992). Differential effects of three preschool models on inner-city four-year-olds. *Early Childhood Research Quarterly, 7,* 517–530.

Marcon, R. (1994a). Doing the right thing for children: Linking research and policy reform in the District of Columbia public schools. *Young Children, 50*(1), 8–20.

Marcon, R. (1994b). *Early learning and early identification follow-up study: Transition from the early to the later childhood grades.* Washington, DC: District of Columbia Public Schools. (Eric Document Reproduction Service No. ED 263 984)

Marcon, R. A. (1999). Differential impact of preschool models on development and early learning of inner-city children: A three-cohort study. *Developmental Psychology, 35*(2), 358–375.

Mark, M. M. (1990). From program theory to tests of program theory. In L. Bickman (Ed.), *Advances in program theory* (New Directions for Program Evaluation, No. 47, pp. 37–51). San Francisco: Jossey-Bass.

Mark, M. M., Feller, I., & Button, S. B. (1997). Integrating qualitative methods in a predominantly quantitative evaluation: A case study and some reflections. In J. C. Greene & V. J. Caracelli (Eds.), *Advances in mixed-method evaluation: The challenges and benefits of integrating diverse paradigms* (New Directions for Evaluation, No. 74, pp. 47–59). San Francisco: Jossey-Bass.

Mark, M. M., & Henry, G. T. (1998). Social programming and policymaking: A realist perspective. In G. T. Henry, G. Julnes, & M. M. Mark (Eds.), *Realist evaluation: An emerging theory in support of practice* (New Directions for Evaluation, No. 78, pp. 73–88). San Francisco: Jossey-Bass.

Mark, M. M., Henry, G. T., & Julnes, G. (1998). A realist theory of evaluation practice. In G. T. Henry, G. Julnes, & M. M. Mark (Eds.), *Realist evaluation: An emerging theory in support of practice* (New Directions for Evaluation, No. 78, pp. 3–31). San Francisco: Jossey-Bass.

Mark, M. M., Henry, G. T., & Julnes, G. (1999). Toward an integrative framework for evaluation practice. *American Journal of Evaluation*, 20(2), 177–198.

Mark, M. M., Hofmann, D., & Reichardt, C. S. (1992). Testing theories in theory-driven evaluations: (Tests of) moderation in all things. In H-t Chen & P. H. Rossi (Eds.), *Using theory to improve program and policy evaluations* (pp. 71–84). Westport, CT: Greenwood Press.

Mark, M. M., Reichardt, L. S., & Sanna, L. J. (2000). Time series analysis. In H.E.A. Tinsley & S. R. Brown (Eds.), *Handbook of applied multivariate statistics and mathematical modeling* (pp. 353–389). Orlando: Academic Press.

Mark, M. M., Sanna, L. J., & Shotland, R. L. (1992). Time series methods in applied social research. In F. B. Bryant, J. Edwards, R. S. Tindale, E. J. Posavac, L. Heath, E. Henderson & Y. Suarez-Balcazar (Eds.), *Methodological issues in applied social research: Social psychological applications to social issues* (Vol. 2, pp. 111–133). New York: Plenum.

Mark, M. M. & Shotlad, R. L. (1985). Stakeholder-based evaluation and value judgments. *Evaluation Review*, 9, 605–626.

Martinez, I. M., & Shatz, M. (1996). Linguistic influences on categorization in pre-school children: A cross-linguistic study. *Journal of Child Language*, 23(3), 529–545.

Martinson, R. (1974). What works? Questions and answers about prison reform, *Public Interest, 35*, 22–45.

Mawhood, C. (1997). Performance measurement in the United Kingdom (1985–1995). In E. Chelimsky & W. R. Shadish (Eds.), *Evaluation for the 21st century: A handbook* (pp. 134–143). Thousand Oaks, CA: Sage.

Maxwell, J. (1996). *Qualitative research design: An interactive approach.* Thousand Oaks, CA: Sage.

McCain, L. J., & McCleary, R. (1979). The statistical analysis of simple interrupted time series quasi-experiments. In T. D. Cook & D. T. Campbell (Eds.), *Quasi-experimentation: Design and analysis issues for field settings* (pp. 233–293). Skokie, IL: Rand McNally.

McCleary, R., Hay, R. A., Meidinger, E. E., & McDowall, D. (1980). *Applied time series analysis for the social sciences.* Thousand Oaks, CA: Sage.

McClelland, G. H., & Judd, C. M. (1993). Statistical difficulties of detecting interactions and moderator effects. *Psychological Bulletin, 114*, 376–390.

McClendon, M. J. (1991). Acquiescence and recency response-order effects in interview surveys. *Sociological Methods & Research, 20*(1), 60–103.

McClintock, C. (1990). Administrators as applied theorists. In L. Bickman (Ed.), *Advances in program theory* (New Directions in Program Evaluation, No. 47, pp. 19–33). San Francisco: Jossey-Bass.

McCombs, M., & Zhu, J-H. (1995). Capacity, diversity, and volatility of the public agenda: Trends from 1954 to 1994. *Public Opinion Quarterly, 59*, 495–525.

McKey, R. H., Condelli, L., Ganson, H., Barrett, B. J., McConkey, C., & Plantz, M. C. (1985). *The impact of Head Start on children, families, and communities* (DHHS Publication No. OHDS 85–31193). Washington, DC: U.S. Government Printing Office.

McKillip, J. P. (1998). Need analysis: Process and techniques. In L. Bickman & D. J. Rog (Eds.), *Handbook of applied social research methods* (pp. 261–284). Thousand Oaks, CA: Sage.

McLaughlin, M. W. (1975). *Evaluation and reform: The Elementary and Secondary Education Act of 1965: Title I.* New York: Ballinger.

McLaughlin, M. W. (1985). Implementation realities and evaluation design. In R. L. Shotland & M. M. Mark (Eds.), *Social science and social policy* (pp. 96–120). Thousand Oaks, CA: Sage.

McSweeney, A. J. (1978). Effects of response cost on the behavior of a million persons: Charging for Directory Assistance in Cincinnati. *Journal of Applied Behavior Analysis, 11*, 47–51.

Medin, D. L., & Aguilar, C. M. (1999). Categorization. In R. A. Wilson & F. C. Keil (Eds.), *The MIT encyclopedia of the cognitive sciences* (pp. 104–106). Cambridge: MIT Press.

Medin, D. L., Lynch, E. B., Coley, J. D., & Atran, S. (1997). Categorization and reasoning among tree experts: Do all roads lead to Rome? *Cognitive Psychology, 32*(1), 49–96.

Medin, D. L., & Ortony, A. (1989). Psychological essentialism. In S. Vosniadou & A. Ortony (Eds.), *Similarity and analogical reasoning* (pp. 179–195). New York: Cambridge University Press.

Medin, D. L., & Shoben, E. J. (1988). Context and structure in conceptual combination. *Cognitive Psychology, 20*, 158–190.

Meehl, P. E. (1986). What social scientists don't understand. In R. A. Schweder & D. W. Fiske (Eds.), *Metatheory in social science: Pluralisms and subjectivities* (pp. 315–338). Chicago: University of Chicago Press.

Meehl, P. E. (1995). Bootstraps taxometrics: Solving the classification problem in psychopathology. *American Psychologist, 50*, 266–275.

Meehl, P. E., & Younce, L. J. (1994). Taxometric analysis: I. Detecting taxonicity using covariance of two quantitative indicators in successive intervals of a third indicator (MAXCOV procedure). *Psychological Reports, Monograph Supplement, J-V78*, 1091–1227.

Melkers, J., & Willoughby, K. (1998). The state of the states: Performance-based budgeting in 47 out of 50. *Public Administration Review, 58*(1), 66–73.

Merkle, D. M. (1996). Review: The National Issues Convention deliberative poll. *Public Opinion Quarterly, 60*(9), 588–619.

Miles, M. B., & Huberman, A. M. (1994). *Qualitative data analysis: An expanded sourcebook*. Thousand Oaks, CA: Sage.

Milligan, G. W. (1981). A review of Monte Carlo tests of cluster analysis. *Multivariate Behavioral Research, 16*, 379–407.

Mintrom, M. (1997). Policy entrepreneurs and the diffusion of innovation. *American Journal of Political Science, 41*(3), 738–770.

Mohr, L. B. (1995). *Impact analysis for program evaluation* (2nd ed.). Thousand Oaks, CA: Sage.

Molenaar, P. C., & von Eye, A. (1994). On the arbitrary nature of latent variables. In A. von Eye & C. C. Clogg (Eds.), *Latent variables analysis: Applications for developmental research* (pp. 226–242). Thousand Oaks, CA: Sage.

Monroe, A. (1998). Public opinion and public policy: 1980–1993. *Public Opinion Quarterly, 62*(1), 6–27.

Morrell, J. (2000). Internal evaluation: A synthesis of traditional methods and industrial engineering. *American Journal of Evaluation, 21*(1), 41–52.

Mowbray, C. T., & Bybee, D. (1998). The importance of context in understanding homelessness and mental illness: Lessons learned from a research demonstration project. *Research on Social Work Practice, 8*(2), 172–199.

Mulaik, S. A. (1972). *The foundations of factor analysis*. New York: McGraw-Hill.

Munro, D. (1992). Process use structure vs. levels of analysis in psychology: Towards integration rather than reduction of theories. *Theory and Psychology, 2,* 109–127.

Murray, C. (1984). *Losing ground: American social policy: 1950–1980*. New York: Basic Books.

Muthen, B. O., & Curran, P. J. (1997). General longitudinal modeling of individual differences in experimental designs: A latent variable framework for analysis and power estimation. *Psychological Methods, 2,* 371–402.

National Association of State Mental Health Program Directors Research Institute. (1996). Performance measures: A five state pilot study. Unpublished report. Alexandria, VA.

Nelson, B. J. (1984). *Making an issue of child abuse*. Chicago: University of Chicago Press.

Newcomer, K. E. (1997). Using performance measurement to improve programs. In K. E. Newcomer (Ed.), *Using performance measurement to improve public and non-profit programs* (New Directions for Evaluation, No. 76, pp. 5–14). San Francisco: Jossey-Bass.

Newman, O., & De Zoysa, R. (1997). Communitarianism: The new panacea? *Sociological Perspectives, 40*(4), 623–638.

Nida-Ruemelin, J., Schmidt, T., & Munk, A. (1996). Interpersonal dependency of preferences. *Theory and Decision, 41,* 257–280.

Niebuhr, R. (1952). *The irony of American history*. New York: Scribner.

Office for Civil Rights (1991). *Equal opportunity in intercollegiate athletics: Requirements under Title IX of the Education Amendments of 1972.* Washington, DC: U.S. Department of Education.

Okun, A. M. (1975). *Equality and efficiency: The big tradeoff.* Washington, DC: Brookings Institution.

Orwin, R. G. (1997). Twenty-one years old and counting: The interrupted time series comes of age. In E. Chelimsky & W. R. Shadish (Eds.), *Evaluation for the 21st Century: A handbook* (pp. 443–465). Thousand Oaks, CA: Sage.

Page, B. I., & Shapiro, R. Y. (1992). *The rational public: Fifty years of trends in Americans policy preferences.* Chicago: University of Chicago Press.

Patton, M. Q. (1987). *How to use qualitative methods in evaluation.* Thousand Oaks, CA: Sage.

Patton, M. Q. (1990). *Qualitative evaluation and research methods.* Thousand Oaks, CA: Sage.

Patton, M. Q. (1997). *Utilization-focused evaluation: The new century text.* Thousand Oaks, CA: Sage.

Patton, M. Q., Grimes, P. S., Guthrie, K. M., Brennan, N. J., French, B. D., & Blyth, D. A. (1997). In search of impact: An analysis of the utilization of federal health evaluation research. In C. H. Weiss (Ed.), *Using social research in public policy making.* Blue Ridge Summit, PA: Lexington Books.

Paulos, J. A. (1998). *Once upon a number: The hidden mathematical logic of stories.* New York: Basic Books.

Pawson, R., & Tilley, N. (1997). *Realistic evaluation.* Thousand Oaks, CA: Sage.

Peirson, L., Prilleltensky, I., Nelson, G., & Gould, J. (1997). Planning mental health services for children and youth. Part II: Findings of a value-based community consultation project. *Evaluation and Program Planning, 20,* 173–183.

Peisner-Feinberg, E. S., & Burchinal, M. R. (1997). Relations between preschool children's child care experiences and concurrent development: The cost, quality, and outcomes study. *Merrill-Palmer Quarterly, 43*(3), 451–477.

Pepper, S. C. (1942/1970). *World hypotheses: A study in evidence.* Berkeley: University of California Press.

Perrin, B. (1998). Effective use and misuse of performance measurement. *American Journal of Evaluation, 19,* 367–379.

Petty, R. E., & Cacioppo, J. T. (1986). *Communication and persuasion: Central and peripheral routes to attitude*. New York: Springer-Verlag.

Plantz, M. C., Greenway, M. T., & Hendricks, M. (1997). Outcome measurement: Showing results in the nonprofit sector. In K. E. Newcomer (Ed.), *Using performance measurement to improve public and nonprofit programs* (New Directions for Evaluation, No. 75, pp. 15–30). San Francisco: Jossey-Bass.

Platt, J. R. (1964). Strong inference. *Science, 146,* 347–353.

Popper, K. R. (1994). *In search of a better world*. New York: Routledge.

Powell, B., & Steelman, L. C. (1996). Bewitched, bothered and bewildering: The use and misuse of state SAT and ACT scores. *Harvard Educational Review, 66*(1), 27–59.

Putnam, H. (1975). *Mind, language, and reality: Philosophical papers, Vol. II*. Cambridge: Cambridge University Press.

Putnam, H. (1981). *Reason, truth, and history*. Cambridge: Cambridge University Press

Putnam, H. (1987). *The many faces of realism*. LaSalle, IL: Open Court.

Putnam, H. (1990). *Realism with a human face*. Cambridge, MA: Harvard University Press.

Putnam, H. (1995). *Pragmatism*. Oxford, UK: Blackwell.

Quine, W.V.O. (1969). *Ontological relativity and other essays*. New York: Columbia University Press.

Quine, W.V.O. (1991). Natural kinds. In R. Boyd, P. Gasper, & J. D. Trout (Eds.), *The philosophy of science* (pp. 159–170). Cambridge, MA: MIT Press.

Ramsey, M. (1992). *Human needs and the market*. Aldershot, UK: Avebury.

Rapkin, B. D., & Luke, D. A. (1993). Cluster analysis in community research: Epistemology and practice. *American Journal of Community Psychology, 21,* 247–277.

Raser, J. R. (1969). *Simulation and society: An exploration of scientific gaming*. Needham Heights, MA: Allyn & Bacon.

Rawls, J. (1971). *A theory of justice*. Cambridge, MA: Harvard University Press, Belknap Press.

Reichardt, C. S. (1979). The statistical analysis of data from nonequivalent group designs. In T. D. Cook & D. T. Campbell (Eds.), *Quasi-experimentation: Design and analysis issues for field settings* (pp. 147–205). Skokie, IL: Rand McNally.

Reichardt, C. S., & Mark, M. M. (1998). Quasi-experimentation. In L. Bickman & D. J. Rog (Eds.), *Handbook of applied social research methods* (pp. 193–208). Thousand Oaks, CA: Sage.

Reichardt, C. S., & Rallis, S. F. (Eds.). (1994). *The qualitative-quantitative debate: New perspectives* (New Directions for Program Evaluation, No. 61). San Francisco: Jossey-Bass.

Reynolds, A. J. (1998). Confirmatory program evaluation: A method for strengthening causal inference. *American Journal of Evaluation, 19*(2), 203–221.

Richardson, H. S. (1997). Democratic intentions. In J. Bohman & W. Rehg (Eds.), *Deliberative democracy: Essays on reason and politics* (pp. 349–381). Cambridge, MA: MIT Press.

Rindskopf, D. M. (1986). New developments in selection modeling for quasi-experimentation. In W.M.K. Trochim (Ed.), *Advances in quasi-experimental design and analysis* (New Directions for Program Evaluation, No. 31, pp. 79–89). San Francisco: Jossey-Bass.

Roberts, R. N., & Wasik, B. H. (1994). Initial evaluation of 1992 funded community integrated service systems projects, Maternal and Child Health Bureau (HRSA 93–410 and HRSA 93–506).

Rog, D. J. (1985). *A methodological analysis of evaluability assessment.* Unpublished doctoral dissertation, Vanderbilt University, Nashville, TN.

Rog, D. J. (1991). Editor's notes. In D. J. Rog (Ed.) *Evaluating programs for the homeless* (New Directions for Evaluation, No. 52, pp. 1–4). San Francisco: Jossey-Bass.

Rog, D. J. (1994). Constructing natural "experiments." In J. S. Wholey, H. P. Hatry, & K. E. Newcomer (Eds.), *Handbook of practical program evaluation*. San Francisco: Jossey-Bass.

Rog, D. J. (1999). The evaluation of the Homeless Families Program. *American Journal of Evaluation, 20,* 558–575.

Rosch, E., & Lloyd, B. B. (Eds.). (1978). *Cognition and categorization.* Hillsdale, NJ: Erlbaum.

Rosenbaum, P. R. (1984). From association to causation in observational studies: the role of tests of strongly ignorable treatment assignment. *Journal of the American Statistical Association, 79,* 40–48.

Rosenbaum, P. R. (1995). *Observational studies.* New York: Springer-Verlag.

Rosenbaum, P. R., & Rubin, D. B. (1983). The central role of the propensity score in observational studies for causal effects. *Biometrika, 70*(1), 41–55.

Rosenthal, R. (1994). Science and ethics in conducting, analyzing, and reporting psychological research. *Psychological Science, 5,* 127–134.

Ross, H. L., Campbell, D. T., & Glass, G. V. (1970). Determining the social effects of legal reform: The British "Breathalyser" crackdown of 1967. *American Behavioral Scientist, 13,* 493–509.

Rossi, P. H., & Freeman, H. E. (1993). *Evaluation: A systematic approach* (5th ed.). Thousand Oaks, CA: Sage.

Rossman, G., & Rallis, S. F. (1998). *Learning in the field: An introduction to qualitative research.* Thousand Oaks, CA: Sage.

Rubin, D. B. (1974). Estimating causal effects of treatments in randomized and nonrandomized studies. *Journal of Educational Psychology, 66,* 688–701.

Rule, J. B. (1978). *Insight and social betterment: A preface for applied social science.* New York: Oxford University Press.

Rutman, L. (1980). *Planning useful evaluations: Evaluability assessment.* Thousand Oaks, CA: Sage.

St. Pierre, T. L., & Kaltreider, D. L. (1997). Strategies for involving parents of high-risk youth in drug prevention: A three-year longitudinal study in Boys and Girls Clubs. *Journal of Community Psychology, 25*(5), 473–485.

St. Pierre, T. L., Kaltreider, D. L., Mark, M. M., & Aikin, K. J. (1992). Drug prevention in a community setting: A longitudinal study of the relative effectiveness of a three-year primary prevention program in Boys and Girls Clubs across the nation. *American Journal of Community Psychology, 20,* 673–706.

Sanders, J. R. (1999). An evaluation of "The effectiveness of comprehensive, case management interventions: Evidence from the national evaluation of the Comprehensive Child Development Program" (St. Pierre et al.). *American Journal of Evaluation, 20*(3), 577–582.

Scheirer, M. A. (1987). Program theory and implementation theory: Implications for evaluators. In L. Bickman (Ed.), *Using program theory in evaluation* (New Directions for Program Evaluation, No. 33, pp. 59–76). San Francisco: Jossey-Bass.

Scheirer, M. A. (1994). Designing and using process evaluation. In J. Wholey, H. P. Hatry, & K. E. Newcomer (Eds.), *Handbook of practical program evaluation* (pp. 40–48). San Francisco: Jossey-Bass.

Scheirer, M. A. (Ed.). (1996). A *user's guide to program templates: A new tool for evaluating program content* (New Directions for Evaluation, No. 72). San Francisco: Jossey-Bass.

Scheirer, M. A. (in press). Getting more "bang" from your performance measurement "buck". *American Journal of Evaluation, 21*(2).

Schnoes, C. J., Murphey-Berman, V., & Chambers, J. M. (2000). Empowerment evaluation applied: Experiences, analysis, and recommendations from a case study. *American Journal of Evaluation, 21*, 53–64.

Schwandt, T. A. (1997). The landscape of values in evaluation: Charted terrain and unexplored territory. In D. Fournier & D. J. Rog (Eds.), *Progress and future directions in evaluation: Perspectives on theory, practice, and methods* (New Directions for Evaluation, No. 76, pp. 25–40). San Francisco: Jossey-Bass.

Scriven, M. S. (1967). The methodology of evaluation. In R. W. Tyler, R. M. Gagne, & M. S. Scriven (Eds.), *Perspectives of curriculum evaluation* (AERA Monograph Series on Curriculum Evaluation, No. 1, pp. 39–83). Skokie, IL: Rand McNally.

Scriven, M. S. (1973). Goal-free evaluation. In E. R. House (Ed.), *School evaluation: The politics and process* (pp. 319–328). Berkeley, CA: McCutchan.

Scriven, M. S. (1980). *The logic of evaluation.* Inverness, CA: Edgepress.

Scriven, M. S. (1991). *The evaluation thesaurus* (4th ed.). Thousand Oaks, CA: Sage.

Scriven, M. S. (Ed.). (1993). *Hard-won lessons in program evaluation* (New Directions for Evaluation, No. 58). San Francisco: Jossey-Bass.

Scriven, M. S. (1994). The final synthesis. *Evaluation Practice, 15*(3), 367–382.

Scriven, M. S. (1997a). Minimalist theory: The least theory that practice requires. *American Journal of Evaluation, 19*(1), 57–70.

Scriven, M. S. (1997b). Truth and objectivity in evaluation. In E. Chelimsky & W. R. Shadish (Eds.), *Evaluation for the 21st century: A handbook* (pp. 477–500). Thousand Oaks, CA: Sage.

Scriven, M. S., & Roth, J. (Eds.). (1978). *Needs assessment: Concept and practice* (New Directions for Program Evaluation, No. 1). San Francisco: Jossey-Bass.

Sechrest, L. (1997). Review of the book *Empowerment evaluation: Knowledge and tools for self-assessment and accountability,* edited by D. M. Fetterman,

S. J. Kafterian, & A. Wanderman. *Environment and Behavior, 29*(3), 422–426.

Sellars, W. (1963). *Science, perception, and reality.* New York: Humanities Press.

Shadish, W. R., Cook, T. D., & Leviton, L. C. (1991). *Foundations of program evaluation: Theories of practice.* Thousand Oaks, CA: Sage.

Shadish, W. R., Newman, D. L., Scheirer, M. A., & Wye, C. (Eds.). (1995). *Guiding principles for evaluators* (New Directions for Program Evaluation, No. 66). San Francisco: Jossey-Bass.

Sherman, L. W., & Berk, R. A. (1984). The specific deterrent effects of arrest for domestic assault. *American Sociological Review, 49,* 261–272.

Sherman, L. W., Smith, D. A., Schmidt, J. D., & Rogan, D. P. (1992). Crime, punishment, and stake in conformity: Legal and informal control of domestic violence. *American Sociological Review, 57,* 680–690.

Shotland, R. L., & Mark, M. M. (Eds.). (1985). *Social science and social policy.* Thousand Oaks, CA: Sage.

Shulha, L. M., & Cousins, J. B. (1997). Evaluation use: Theory, research, and practice since 1986. *Evaluation Practice, 18*(3), 195–208.

Simon, H. A. (1957). *Administrative behavior: A study of decision-making processes in administrative organizations* (2nd ed.). New York: Free Press.

Singer, E., & Presser, S. (Eds.). (1989). *Survey research methods: A reader.* Chicago: University of Chicago Press.

Smith, E. R., Fazio, R. H., & Cejka, M. A. (1996). Accessible attitudes influence categorization of multiply categorizable objects. *Journal of Personality and Social Psychology, 71,* 888–898.

Smith, J. K., & Hanushius, L. (1986). Closing down the conversation: The end of the qualitative-quantitative debate among educational inquirers. *Educational Researcher, 13*(1), 4–12.

Smith, M. L. (1994). Qualitative plus/versus quantitative: The last word. In C. S. Reichardt & S. F. Rallis (Eds.), *The qualitative-quantitative debate: New perspectives* (New Directions for Program Evaluation, No. 61, pp. 37–44). San Francisco: Jossey-Bass.

Smith, M. L. (1997). Mixing and matching: Methods and models. In J. C. Greene & V. J. Caracelli (Eds.), *Advances in mixed-method evaluation: The challenges and benefits of integrating diverse paradigms* (New Directions for Evaluation, No. 74, pp. 73–85). San Francisco: Jossey-Bass.

Smith, N. L. (1992). Aspects of investigative inquiry in evaluation. In N. L. Smith (Ed.), *Varieties of Investigative Evaluation* (New Directions in Program Evaluation, No. 56, pp. 3–13). San Francisco: Jossey-Bass.

Sorokin, P. (1957). *Social and cultural dynamics*. Boston: Porter Sargent.

Spearman, C. (1904). "General intelligence," objectively determined and measured. *American Journal of Psychology, 15*(2), 201–293.

Stake, R. E. (1967). The countenance of educational evaluation. *Teachers College Record, 68,* 523–540.

Stake, R. E. (1997). Advocacy in evaluation: A necessary evil? In E. Chelimsky & W. R. Shadish (eds.), *Evaluation for the 21st century: A handbook* (pp. 470–476). Thousand Oaks, CA: Sage.

Stigler, S. M. (1987). Testing hypotheses or fitting models? Another look at mass extinctions. In M. H. Nitecki & A. Hoffman (eds.), *Neutral models in biology*, pp. 145–149. Oxford: Oxford University Press.

Stimson, J. A. (1998). *Public opinion in America: Moods, cycles, and swings* (2nd ed.). Boulder, CO: Westview Press.

Stufflebeam, D. L., Foley, W. J., Gephart, W. J., Guba, E. G., Hammond, R. L., Merriman, H. O., & Provus, M. M. (1971). *Educational evaluation and decision making*. Itasca, IL: Peacock.

Stufflebeam, D. L., & Shinkfield, A. J. (1985). *Systematic evaluation*. Boston: Kluwer-Nijhoff.

Suchman, E. A. (1967). *Evaluative research: Principles and practice in public service and social action programs*. New York: Russell Sage Foundation.

Sudman, S., Bradburn, N. M., & Schwarz, N. (1996). *Thinking about answers: The application of cognitive processes to survey methodology*. San Francisco: Jossey-Bass.

Telfair, J., & Leviton, L. C. (1999). The community as client: Improving the prospects for useful evaluation findings. In J. Telfair, L. C. Leviton, & J. S. Merchant (Eds.), *Evaluating health and human service programs in community settings* (New Directions for Evaluation, No. 83, pp. 5–15). San Francisco: Jossey-Bass.

Tharp, R. G. (1981). The meta-methodology of research and development. *Educational Perspectives, 20,* 42–48.

Thompson, M., Ellis, R., & Wildavsky, A. (1990). *Cultural theory*. Boulder, CO: Westview Press.

Thurstone, L. L. (1935). *The vectors of mind*. Chicago: University of Chicago Press.

Toal, S. B. (1998). *A summary report: Workshop to develop a framework for evaluation in public health practice*. Atlanta, GA: Centers for Disease Control and Prevention.

Tong, R. (1987). Ethics and the policy analyst: The problem of responsibility. In F. Fischer & J. Forester (Eds.), *Confronting values in policy analysis* (pp. 192–211). Thousand Oaks, CA: Sage.

Trochim, W.M.K. (1982). Methodologically based discrepancies in compensatory education evaluation. *Evaluation Review, 6*(4), 443–480.

Trochim, W.M.K. (1985). Pattern matching, validity, and conceptualization in program evaluation. *Evaluation Review, 9,* 575–604.

Tukey, J. W. (1977). *Exploratory data analysis*. Reading, MA: Addison-Wesley.

Tukey, J. W. (1980). Methodological comments focused on opportunities. In P. R. Monge & J. Cappella (Eds.), *Multivariate techniques in communication research* (pp. 489–528). New York: Academic Press.

Tukey, J. W. (1986). *The collected works of John W. Tukey: Vol. 4. Philosophy and principles of data analysis: 1965–1986*. Monterey, CA: Wadsworth.

Tyler, R. W. (1935). Evaluation: A challenge to progressive education. *Educational Research Bulletin, 14,* 9–16.

Tyler, T. R., & Lind, E. A. (1991). Procedural processes and legal institutions. In R. Vermunt & H. Steensma (Eds.), *Social justice in human relations: Vol. 2. Societal and psychological consequences of justice and injustice*. Critical issues in social justice, pp. 71–98. New York: Plenum Press.

U.S. General Accounting Office (1997). *Earned income credit: Claimants' credit participation and income patterns, tax years 1990 through 1994*. (GGD-97-69). Washington, DC: Author.

U.S. General Accounting Office (1998a). *District of Columbia: Extent to which schools receive available federal education grants*. (GAO/HEHS-99-1). Washington, DC: Author.

U.S. General Accounting Office (1998b). *Home improvement: Weaknesses in HUD's management and oversight of the Title I program*. (GAO/RCED-98-216). Washington, DC: Author.

U.S. General Accounting Office (1999). *Community development: Progress on economic development activities varies among the Empowerment Zones*. (RCED-99-29). Washington, DC: Author.

Waller, N. G., & Meehl, P. E. (1998). *Multivariate taxometric procedures: Distinguishing types from continua* (Advanced Quantitative Techniques in the Social Sciences, Vol. 9). Thousand Oaks, CA: Sage.

Waller, N. G., Putnam, F. W., & Carlson, E. (1996). Types of dissociation and dissociative types: A taxometric analysis of the dissociative experiences scale. *Psychological Methods, 3,* 300–321.

Ward, V. M., Bertrand, J. T., & Brown, L. F. (1991). The comparability of focus group and survey results: Three case studies. *Evaluation Review, 15*(2), 266–283.

Weick, K. E. (1979). *The social psychology of organizing.* New York: Random House.

Weick, K. E. (1995). *Sensemaking in organizations.* Thousand Oaks, CA: Sage.

Weiss, C. H. (1977a). Improving the linkage between social research and public policy. In L. E. Lynn (Ed.), *Knowledge and policy: The uncertain connection* (pp. 23–81). Washington, DC: National Academy of Sciences.

Weiss, C. H. (1977b). Research for policy's sake: The enlightenment function of social research. *Policy Analysis, 3,* 531–545.

Weiss, C. H. (1983). The stakeholder approach to evaluation: Origins and promise. In A. S. Bryk (Ed.), *Stakeholder-based evaluation* (New Directions for Program Evaluation, No. 17, pp. 3–14). San Francisco: Jossey-Bass.

Weiss, C. H. (1988a). Evaluation for decisions: Is anybody there? Does anybody care? *Evaluation Practice, 9*(1), 5–20.

Weiss, C. H. (1988b). If program decisions hinged only on information: A response to Patton. *Evaluation Practice, 9*(3), 15–28.

Weiss, C. H. (1997a, November). Do we know any more about evaluation use? Plenary address at the annual meeting of the American Evaluation Association, San Diego, CA.

Weiss, C. H. (1997b). Theory based evaluation: Why aren't we doing it. In D. Fournier & D. J. Rog (Eds.), *Progress and future directions in evaluation: Perspectives on theory, practice, and methods* (New Directions for Evaluation, No. 76, pp. 41–55). San Francisco: Jossey-Bass.

Weiss, C. H. (1998). *Evaluation: Methods for studying programs and policies.* Upper Saddle River, NJ: Prentice Hall.

Weiss, C. H., & Bucuvalas, M. J. (1980). *Social science research and decision-making.* New York: Columbia University Press.

Whitmore, B. (Ed.). (1998). *Understanding and practicing participatory evaluation* (New Directions for Evaluation, No. 80). San Francisco: Jossey-Bass.

Wholey, J. S. (1979). *Evaluation: Promise and performance.* Washington, DC: Urban Institute.

Wholey, J. S. (1983). *Evaluation and effective public management.* Boston: Little, Brown.

Wholey, J. S. (1987). *Organizational excellence: Stimulating quality and communicating value.* Blue Ridge Summit, PA: New Lexington Press.

Wholey, J. S. (1994). Assessing the feasibility and likely usefulness of evaluation. In J. S. Wholey, H. P. Hatry, & K. E. Newcomer (Eds.), *Handbook of practical program evaluation* (pp. 15–39). San Francisco: Jossey-Bass.

Wholey, J. S. (1997a). Clarifying goals, reporting results. In E. Chelimsky & W. R. Shadish (Eds.), *Evaluation for the 21st century: A handbook* (pp. 95–105). Thousand Oaks, CA: Sage.

Wholey, J. S. (1997b). Trends in performance measurement: Challenges for evaluators. In E. Chelimsky & W. R. Shadish (Eds.), *Evaluation for the 21st century: A handbook* (pp. 124–133). Thousand Oaks, CA: Sage.

Wholey, J. S., Scanlon, J. W., Duffy, H. G., Fukumoto, J. S., & Vogt, L. M. (1970). *Federal evaluation policy: Analyzing the effects of public programs.* Washington, DC: Urban Institute.

Wildavsky, A. (1991). Efficiency as a function of culture. In A. Wildavsky (Ed.), *Administration in social work* (pp. 147–153). Berkeley, CA: Hayworth Press.

Wisler, C. (Ed.). (1996). *Evaluation and auditing: Prospects for convergence* (New Directions for Evaluation, No. 71). San Francisco: Jossey-Bass.

Wohlstetter, P. (1991). Accountability mechanisms for state education reform: Some organizational alternatives. *Educational Evaluation and Policy Analysis, 13,* 31–48.

Wood, B. D., & Waterman, R. W. (1991). The dynamics of political control of the bureaucracy. *American Political Science Review, 85*(3), 801–828.

Wood, B. D., & Waterman, R. W. (1994). *Bureaucratic dynamics: The role of bureaucracy in a democracy* (Transforming American Politics, Vol. 16). Boulder, CO: Westview Press.

Worthen, B. R. (1999). Critical challenges confronting certification of evaluators. *American Journal of Evaluation, 20*(3), 533–555.

Worthen, B. R., Sanders, J. R., & Fitzpatrick, J. L. (1997). *Program evaluation: Alternative approaches and practical guidelines* (2nd ed.). White Plains, NY: Longman.

Wortman, P. M. (1983). Evaluation research: A methodological perspective. *Annual Review of Psychology, 34*, 223–260.

Wortman, P. M., Reichardt, C. S., & St. Pierre, R. S. (1978). The first year of educational voucher demonstration: A secondary analysis of student achievement test scores. *Evaluation Quarterly, 2*, 193–214.

Wright, J. D. (1987). Homelessness is not healthy for children and other living things. *Child and Youth Services, 14*, 65–88.

Wright, J. D. (1991). Methodological issues in evaluating the National Health Care for the Homeless program. In N. L. Smith (Ed.), *Varieties of investigative evaluation* (New Directions for Program Evaluation, No. 52, pp. 61–74). San Francisco: Jossey-Bass.

Wynn, K. (1992). Addition and subtraction by human infants. *Nature, 358*, 749–750.

Yankelovich, D. (1994). How changes in the economy are reshaping American values. In H. J. Aaron, T. E. Mann, & T. Taylor (Eds.), *Values and public policy* (pp. 16–53). Washington, DC: Brookings Institution.

Yin, R. K. (1993). *Applications of case study research*. Thousand Oaks, CA: Sage.

Yin, R. K. (1994). *Case study research: Design and methods* (2nd ed.). Thousand Oaks, CA: Sage.

Zigler, E. F., & Muenchow, S. (1992). *Head Start: The inside story of America's most successful educational experiment*. New York: Basic Books.

Name Index

Subject Index

K

K-means clustering methods, 223
Kaldor-Hicks criterion of program value, 295, 296
Knowledge development (evaluation purpose), 125–126; and causal analysis, 246, 251–254; characteristics of, 58; and classification, 216–217; definition, 13; and description, 179; focus of, 51; generalizable explanation theory of practice and, 61, 126, 264; as priority, with secondary purpose, 69, 118–119, 122–123; as pure purpose, 134, 136; quality of different inquiry modes for, 97, 99, 100; questions illustrating, 53; rationale for selection as evaluation purpose, 68–69, 70, 73, 329, 330; and relationships with other purposes, 13, 14, 71, 115–123; as secondary rather than primary purpose, 68–69, 110, 119, 125–126, 127, 128, 130, 133–134, 135, 136; social betterment function of, 68–69; traditions in, 122–123; and values inquiry, 302. See also Research, social science

L

Language and terminology, evaluation, 336–337
Latent factor models, 235
Latent growth curve modeling, 234
Legislation: evaluation mandated by, 50, 57, 59–60, 66–68; GPRA, 77, 95, 174–175, 196; and social problems, 27, 33–34. See also Oversight and compliance (evaluation purpose)
Levels of analysis: and classification schemes, 240–242; and performance indicators, 198–199; stratified, 154–156, 300. See also Underlying structures
Levels, embedded, 240–241, 300
Liberty: and equality, 297; social benefits and restriction on, 332
Literacy, study population, 307, 309
Logic modeling, 118
Logic and rational thought, 144
Logical positivism, 141, 146, 161, 252, 325; and the fact-value dichotomy, 158–159, 292–293

M

McDonald's fallacy, 192
Mailed surveys, 308–310
Majorities and minorities, 294
Malfunction-based definition of need, 36, 37
Managers, program. See Stakeholders
Mandated program evaluation. See Oversight and compliance (evaluation purpose)
Manipulable solution theory of practice, 59
Mass opinion, stability of, 304
Matrices: inquiry mode classification, 82n.1; of primary and secondary evaluation combinations, 118–119, 127, 130, 135
Maturation and internal validity, 267, 269, 275, 277, 284
Meaning, focus on, 164
Measurement. See Performance measurement; Quantitative methods
Mechanisms. See Underlying mechanisms
Media and methods, survey. See Surveys
Mediators (mediated relationships), 188, 189, 191, 195, 256; moderated, 263; the study of, 250, 278. See also Underlying mechanism
Mental health disorders, 224, 225, 226, 238
Mental health services, 128, 184, 203; and deinstitutionalization, 108; values affecting, 43, 111, 311
Mentally ill, homeless, 24, 26, 27
Merging databases, 186–187
Merit, definition of, 54
Merit and worth assessment. See Assessment of merit and worth (evaluation purpose)
Merit and worth evaluation, questions illustrating, 52
Meta-analysis, 61–62, 69, 71, 149
Method-driven approach to evaluation, 10–11
Minimal needs, 36–37
Minimal theory evaluation, 118, 124
Minorities: treatment of, 43; voice and consideration of, 294
Mixed methods: competitive elaboration and principled discovery, 263–265, 280; qualitative and quantitative and, 219–220, 280–281